LOGICAL ISSUES

BRITANNIA PRESS

LOGICAL ISSUES

LOGICAL ISSUES

M. F. H. Roe

Determinatio negatio est

THE BRITANNIA PRESS
LONDON

First published in Great Britain in 1996
by The Britannia Press
8 Caledonia Street
London N1 9DZ

ISBN 1 872571 05 0
Typeset in 10pt Baskerville by Three Rivers Design
Printed in Great Britain

Logical Issues

TABLE OF CONTENTS

Preface

Anyone who is so presumptuous as to question the reach of rationalism must face immense resistance, primarily as an underminer of discipline, which, such is the convention, can only have one form, formal logic. His thought is regarded, if not with contempt, certainly with indifference, as unworthy of serious consideration, when it is not condemned as showing a failure to understand or appreciate the recent refinements of formal logic, or simply scorned as the perpetration of an absurd and worthless doctrine.

Yet there are certain points that cannot be brushed aside as void of substance, unless we are so blinded by prejudice as to regard them as inoperative. Two of these relate to recent discoveries in science. The first is that some 90% of our responses to stimuli emanating eternally are mediated subconsciously and that of the remaining 10% only a fraction involves clear consciousness, which interprets what it receives through a filtering process, objectifica-tion, which cannot but involve a measure of distortion.

The second is that, whether this is acceptable or not, we are now obliged to accede, as a presupposition, to a holistic ontology – the idea that externality is a dynamic, indivisible, interrelative complex – such that induction, presumed to be one of the planks of a rationalistic approach, can no longer be regarded as a satisfactory means of procedure. And if it continues to be adopted in science, that is not because its limits are not recognized but because no adequate alternative to it has as yet been discovered or devised.

Apart from these highly significant points, a loose use of terms is characteristic of modern logic, which not only fails to distinguish two meanings of truth, but harbours the belief that rationalism and reasoning have the same meaning and function, when in fact they serve quite different purposes. Everyone reasons, by virtue of the fact that he or she is human. No one, except formal logicians conversing with their colleagues (for in private life they also use reason) makes use of formal logic, since it is powerless to engage actualities or the contingent, the subtleties of language as it is employed in normal communication. Finally, there seems to be a failure to recognize that the ideal world and the real world, the world in which we live and have our being, are entirely different and represent wholly different fields of enquiry, realms of discourse. This means that the presuppositions adopted to serve either one must themselves be divergent and cannot but be so, as related to static or staticized and dynamic worlds respectively. That the real world is made up of particulars and that absolute truth refers externally – though that is blurred when truth as absolute is assumed to have the same meaning as truth when that is referred to practicalities and is rather to be regarded as 'reliable knowledge' – are never seriously questioned because it is so convenient to disregard them as placing limits on the reach of formal logic.

All this is very brief and in that sense superficial, so that it is necessary to develop the implications of these findings in greater depth. That is then the theme of this book which, as the third of a series turning on them, deals with the problem of how to discipline discourse (which might be distinguished as extra-cognitive or evaluative) when formal logic is seen to have such grave limitations. For if discourse is concerned with other than cognitive interests, which, as evaluative, necessarily refer to deeper response to the complex of reality, itself beyond the reach of propositional logic as it itself in some sense recognizes in its attempts to develop deviant logics – then, since those retaining rigour fail to meet requirements, another approach must be considered; and that is the concern of this book. Anyone, then, who thinks it worthwhile to read it, has been warned that it goes against the current of conventional thinking, the direction of which it has the affrontery to challenge.

It is normal in a preface to express one's thanks to those who have by reading the text and making critical comment on it aided the writer in his task; and that is a very proper procedure. Alas, I cannot in this case make mention of the leading thinkers in this country from whom, with one notable exception, Professor Sprigge of Edinburgh University, I have not received much encouragement or grasp of the issue really at stake. However, I should certainly mention others: Dr. Lunn, whose comments were very penetrating, Dr. Rose, Dr. Jackson, Mr. Smithson and, Dr. Meizoso y Gonzales, with whom I have discussed this thought at length. I also owe much to Professor Nicolau of Bucharest, who has shown great interest in it. Only one of these men is a philosopher in a strict sense, which tends to show that the questioning of conventional attitudes is external. Hence this thinking is projected in a somewhat ambiguous atmosphere, since it is outsiders, concerned not with verbal but with vital problems, who recognize that this thought may serve some purpose, even to give philosophy a meaningful direction.

London, 1995 M. F. H. Roe

Introduction

Much thought has been given to the title of this book, which, though finally accepted for want anything better, still leaves something to be desired. For 'logical' as an adjective is not wholly satisfactory in view of its present associations, which will in this text have in part to be challenged. For different reasons, however, like reservations apply to any alternatives to it, since they also have meanings which might lead to misunderstandings. There is no adjectival term which is wholly free, it seems, from a measure of ambiguity and which could be used with confidence to engage the problem at issue without some question about its appropriateness in the present context. Let us then consider other possible terms, procedural, methological, disciplinary, each in turn, to elicit reasons why, though feasible as terms to qualify the noun, they all present certain difficulties. For that will aid understanding of the theme to be developed.

Leaving 'logical' itself for later consideration as the term that will have to be used, of the others the last is suitably taken first. 'Disciplinary' may then be taken to have two meanings, which, though closely allied, are not quite the same. For one is clearly linked to its basic form 'disciple', *disciplinus* or *discipulus,* giving *disciplina* for 'discipline', in the original Latin, with roots in the verb *discere,* meaning 'to learn' or 'to take in knowledge'. These words refer respectively to one who receives instruction and to the means of providing it. Hence, a disciple is one who attends to or follows a master, a religious, philosophical or professional teacher, for the purpose of learning about or in admiration of what he has to convey. It also seems to have meant, even in classical times, one who undergoes a process of training or drill, in military form in the main, or submits to some kind of systematic direction, a discipline that is, in which sense it is used in the academic world to mean pursuing a course of study, though the modern term is student rather than disciple. The second meaning of this term is of special interest in context because it implies a form of checking, a refusal, that is, to accept what is inappropriate, sometimes with coercion, which may even lead to punishment. And it is in these especially that discipline is used in military and custodial spheres, when it gives a rather false picture, too harsh, albeit it may be just, for what is here intended. Thus, despite a liberal element present in its use, it cannot be accepted as an unambiguous term without question about its fitness on the present occasion. For in the sense that is now envisaged, checking does not involve any coercive action, but rather the need to check oneself and to think a little more deeply, so that whoever is under such a softer restraint is a relatively free agent, or freer at least than those who are subjected to a discipline in a stronger form. In order to avoid such an association as that, to which the adjective 'disciplinary' is normally applied, the term has had to be abandoned, if with some reluctance, as failing to meet requirement.

Turning to 'methodological', that is rather a formidable term, which, for all its scholarly bearing, as signifying a study of appropriate procedures, does not wholly meet the need at present in mind, in part because it does not *decisively* carry the notion of checking. 'Method', as its Greek form *méthodos*, from *méta-ódos*, suggests, means 'a way of doing things', of 'arriving at an end', a meaning it still carries. Thus, it could mean a way of doing things with words, a relatively recent usage of somewhat limited application. But its usual employment in modern times generally relates to scientific procedures, as in those of formal logic when it claims to be a science.[1] That the last in its present form is to be questioned as limited in the following pages raises issues in as far as, if it is regarded as the only acceptable method in philosophical discourse, its use as a term would suggest that that is the concern of this book, which would then be but a further text in formal logic. Though procedures in formal logic are certainly methodical, or systematic if that term is to be preferred, the methods it adopts clearly limit its reach, since properly it can only deal with symbols or with words and has but a dubious relation to ultimate realities, to encounter which its procedures were not really devised.[2] Those in mathematics, are designated 'algorisms' and refer to the methods that mathematicians adopt. And though there is no generic term that applies in formal logic, in which several refer to various aspects of its procedures – unless 'ratiocination' may be taken to afford one – they all relate to its limited ends, to strictly verbal abstractions. When, then, the need is to deal with realities bearing on life, such limited ends as those cannot be accepted. If a method, in fine, is to be devised by means of which directed discourse may be disciplined, it cannot be that adopted in traditional formal logic, to which philosophy has latterly been confined. Methodological is a suitable word with which to qualify or describe any disciplinary procedure, but in so far as it has this narrow reference in that specific field, it is not an unambiguous term and that might lead to confusion through association. Hence, it was not considered fitting in this context.

This leaves the term 'procedural' as a possible alternative, and it is not to be denied that it has a certain virtue. For what is envisaged is undoubtedly a procedure albeit a rather unusual one, since its aim is to limit or reduce rather than to arrive at some positive achievement, which is quite a significant difference. 'To proceed', reflecting *procedere* its Latin root, imports 'to go forward', 'to make progress'; and 'procedure', its derivative, refers to a means of achieving a positive end, in which negation plays but a subsidiary part, to indicate the need for modification or improvement. This is shown in the procedure designated 'trial-and-error', in which the primary interest is the trial aimed at successful testing or proof, error involving no more than the need with failure to try again. So with falsification in formal logic, which is simply a check on the way to eliciting truth. As negation will be urged as the crucial means in the discipline now to be discussed, procedure in its normal sense is not really the fitting term for what is then envisaged, and so it has to be relinquished, even though what is intended might well be regarded as a form or type of procedure. Since that, however, is usually taken to be a positive mode of doing things, aimed at a positive achievement, an explanation for example, it was decided not to use it in a qualifying form as 'procedural' in the present context.

*

'Logical' may be held to have effectively the same weaknesses, in this sense also to be ambiguous, since, as referring to 'formal logic', its aim is very plainly positive, to elicit irrefragable truth. That that is its only meaning is not, however, the case; and, as other meanings are legitimate, as will be shown in the body of the book, it has been chosen as the most appropriate word with which to cover the needs of the occasion. This is not the time to elaborate on that point or to contend that a prejudice which is deeply entrenched has limited it to a certain acceptance excluding other readings. For at once it is enough to remark that it is indeed a prejudice that has so restricted its meaning and application. For there is not, as will be seen, but one acceptable form of logic, since in fact there are several, which have either been forgotten or unheeded under the demand for a positive achievement, as though any other were void of meaning and so had no standing. Logic is generally agreed to be an *organon,* that is to say, an instrument for disciplining thinking, which should not be confined to rationalistic thinking but should properly encompass all thought whatsoever. Indeed, its forms should be adopted, as are those of knives – scalpels, butter knives, fish knives, carving knives, paper knives, and so on – in accordance with the task that has to be performed. To confine it to a single task is as though a surgeon were obliged to use a butter knife for cutting sinews or a reader a carving knife for slitting pages. For that is what that limitation implies, the dismissal of all but one function.

There are clearly many problems which formal logic is powerless to engage, tensing discounted, which it can only handle with clumsy circumlocutions. And these are matters of no small importance in that they relate to action and need in living in its complex and varied forms. In so far, indeed, as they relate to actualities involving adaptation to the process of becoming, they are beyond the reach of formal logic, since they cannot in their complexity be objectified, analysed or particularized without a measure of distortion. Absolute truths are of their very nature timeless, *sub specie aeternitas* as is said. Thus there is good reason to think that a broader approach to such problems is required, which, and that is undeniable, has to be no less disciplined, subjected to appropriate critique. That there is no disciplined alternative to formal logic – though experimental testing against external reality is the procedure adopted by science – is rather a defensive or prejudiced contention than a thoughtful approach of the nature of involvement. If that view, indeed, is allowed to pass unchallenged, then any matter which cannot be so disciplined can only be dealt inadequately, or otherwise said improperly. Questions of value, for example, cannot be answered by cognitive means, if only for the reason that value, or value at least in a general sense, accrues from response to the dynamic of becoming and is not to be defined in objective or 'factual' terms. Rationalists commonly assume that they are equipped to deal with *all* problems, but that is certainly not the case. For the methods they adopt are clumsy and insensitive means of procedure, as is instanced in social engineering, which may well be the cause of a certain unrest, since people are not 'objects' to be manipulated objectively but sentient beings with subtle needs which cannot be made explicit because many of them are subconscious and others involve but 'dim perception'.

There are many problems beyond the reach of explanatory or strict rational enquiry and the methods it applies, since they are other than material and are not submissive to measurement. How then to deal with such matters as these in a sufficiently disciplined manner is a very pertinent question. And although the approach required may be difficult to devise, the more so with the resistance it is likely to evoke as challenging rationalistic prejudices, that is not a reason for dismissing thought about it. That which is now to be projected does not pretend to afford a final answer, for it is no more than a tentative proposal. But it is not so much the answer that is given, which is open to revision and refinement, as the issue raised for discussion that is now significant. For that issue is a real one, and one that should surely concern philosophy as a distinctive discipline giving thought to that which is beyond the scope of science, the values by which men most sensibly live as they confront reality and through that relate to each other. Nor is this a concern with 'necessary truth', which, apart from involving its seekers in arcane technical problems affording no final answers, is as a form of enquiry so recondite and abtruse that no layman understands it;[3] it is very much other. Nor is it epistemic, if that differs from searching for truth, since, though not so arcane, epistemology deals with problems restricted to cognitive enquiry, so that others of greater importance, if that is the only approach, receive but scant attention, as if they were subsidiary. It is, however, ontic in the sense that the manner in which the world, the external world that is, is viewed determines how we approach it, how we understand valid relations to it as conditioning all that we do, life in all its aspects. Essentially, then, though the immediate concern is with apt procedures, thought ultimately bears on axiological problems, as those which have the greatest significance. For in the final analysis it is the enhancement of life in some form or another that justifies all thinking, and that must surely include its spiritual dimensions no less than those that are material and in such sense largely cognizable, whereas the first are too opaque, fluid, subtle and complex to submit to any such treatment. The manner in which enquiry can be conducted properly to meet such interests as these has then first to be considered once it is grasped that the methods hitherto adopted are not correctly fitted to deal with what they involve, and tend without modification to engender misunderstanding, or worse misrepresentation of these vital interests. Hence, even if the proposals now to be presented are far themselves from adequate and accordingly fittingly criticized, the issue raised is beyond serious question meaningful; and that, if nothing else, must justify the attention now to be given to this issue.

'Logical' then defines a discipline with which loose or improper statement may be subjected to proper check, and that includes all statements that are publicly expressed. So, if logic is an organon, as is generally agreed, it constitutes an instrument which should be used to discipline any assertion whatever which aims to exert an influence. That logic in a formal mode 'disciplines all thought' is not only over-ambitious but also highly restrictive, since it can only discipline propositional statement, as if that were all that logic could do. Nor is this merely restrictive, it is even grossly delimiting. For the latent power of logic, viewed in broader terms and applying its checks to statements rather than to thoughts – which need not be expressed – is obscured by such a claim. That itself is readily falsified and is accordingly *not* true. It represents a statement that is subject to critique within the sphere of formal logic. Thus, the fuller meaning of logic as an instrument intended to place limits on what is said on matters of importance is narrowed by such circumscription. In so far, then, as discourse is strictly propositional, the logic it involves is justly defined as 'formal', a qualification confining it to a restricted task, of value within its limits, no doubt, but only as those are clearly recognized. Its concern is then with form rather than with content, although it claims to deal with the latter by referring to verbal conventions, when its content relates to meaning only in one sense. For, if meaning is properly *influence*, flowing from whatever source it emanates to exert it,[4] it, despite dictionary definitions, is verbal only when interest is confined to what is said. It follows, if vital interest has a wider range and as words themselves are regarded as no more than a means to an end, which end is usually more than verbal, that this acceptance stands. Of course, words have to be used in any form of discussion, but what discussion is about is not essentially verbal, unless that is the interest studied. It refers to interests which are other then linguistic. And those, as they relate to need in the actual process of living, constitute the interest of directed, meaningful discourse. It is not, then, when real problems come up for consideration, that form, veridical formulation, comprises what is needed; it is an assurance that what is said justly applies to realities, which seldom allow of exact, positive definition. As statement referred externally is usually precarious, so complex are events and relations in actuality, the need, to be met by extending the powers implicit in the critical aspect of enquiry, is to subject what is said to sufficient discipline, to ensure that it is not misplaced or mistaken. Thus, the term 'logic', or 'logical' to give it its adjectival form, is properly used in a wider, a more extended sense, as an instrument with the potential to serve a broader function than it can have when confined to propositional statement, aimed at positing absolute truth. The problem is then to determine the form that it might have, which is precisely the issue to be discussed in this book.

Chapter One

The Origins of the Term 'Logic'

The decision to use the term 'logical' in this wider sense raises the issue of the warrant for so doing, since it has not been used in that fuller way for two thousand years or so. And since the Greek word *lógos,* with its Latin form *logica,* had a chequered history in classical antiquity, it is to the point to consider how it finally came to have its present meaning. For that is not only of interest in a scholarly sense, in that this matter has not as yet been studied by philosophers, such that it is in general assumed that it has always had the meaning that is now attached to it, but also because that gives warrant for its wider usage. In its formal aspect, as that qualification indicates, the term emerged from a complex involvement with other meanings from which it only freed itself to acquire that special meaning in later classical times. Moreover, its etymological roots have some bearing on the way that thought is now developing, when, admittedly under another name, one of the meanings of *lógos* becomes increasingly germane. Its long lost ontic import is in process of being recovered, and that has no small influence on how we interpret the meaning of reality today. In relation to that, the legacy we have received from the thought of classical antiquity has tended to be seen in a rather partial manner, in part because of a paucity of documentation referring to one aspect of it, and in part because of a bias in later Western thinking, which stems from Imperial times. Without enlarging on this at once, it now suffices to note that that has not only restricted ontological thinking, but also the procedures adopted in the service of what was thus presupposed: that the terminus of enquiry claiming to be serious was irrefragable truth as distinct from deeper human need. Ontology and logic are linked in such a way that the first conditions the second, both with respect to its role and to the means it deploys to serve it. Hence, ideas in the field of ontology effectively determine the character of logic, such that, if those are limited, they restrict the scope of logic as a disciplining instrument, which thus restricts ideas about what really counts in life. Finally, which is undoubtedly more significant, a fitting approach towards the fundamental problem – man's relation to the world in which he is enmeshed – is not properly adopted, with the consequence that many grave mistakes have been made, and still are being made, with regard to that salient issue.

This is not for want of serious attempts on the part of logicians to discern the principles implicit in clear thinking, which has distinguished Western development with its almost unique idea of what constitutes the purpose of philosophic enquiry. It is because the notion of what is confronted is taken – all thought of a supersensuous world immediately discounted – to be the phenomenal world, which is potentially knowable, rather than the deeper world that lies behind it, which is that with which we are really involved and with which, if we are to live more sanely, we have to come to terms, difficult though that may be when the intellect is worshipped, as if all else were inferior. In saying which it is well to bear in mind as operative that this has undoubtedly had an effect upon approaches, to generate a preference for what is more accessible, cognizable or rational. It is further to the point that intellectual satisfaction, obtainable by such means, is effectively the interest of comparatively few, whereas relation to reality, which is other than intellectual, is something that bears on everyone and alone is truly general. For these reasons we have tended to deal essentially with appearances, which the intellect can grasp, as if underlying reality were the interest alone of a group called 'metaphysicians', believing that in some way that could also be rationalized, to generate much confusion and as a consequence a withdrawal into ratiocination.[1] In fine, philosophy is now in something of a quandary. For, if it does that, there comes a growing realization that a strict rationalistic approach has very great limitations and that with it certain problems have been seriously neglected. For, with the determination to know, to explicate or explain what is in fact beyond the reach of cognitive explanation, nothing of real meaning is ultimately attained, and the effects of this endeavour on the lives of men at large, if it touches them at all, are evidently remote. The theses then projected are scarcely understood – assuming that they are known at all outside a narrow circle – in a way that allows of some insight into what is actually confronted. Thus, any influence which is slight or, if it is present in any effective form, rather tends to confuse than to illuminate understanding of what is really significant. The fact is that there are no final answers to questions which relate to deeper problems, and that the attempt to find them in the form of truths is misplaced, because both the presuppositions made and thence the procedures adopted disallow of such answers except on a strictly rational plane which does not touch real issues. Were we less ambitious, perhaps, something further might be achieved; and the key to that might well be a deeper understanding of the ancient meanings of *lógos,* more particularly that with ontological bearing.

That word is regarded as the nounal form, with a change of vowel sound, as with the English word 'sight,' of the verbal *légein* and undoubtedly it is so. But matters are not quite so simple as that, since *légein* has more than one meaning, which is reflected in *lógos.* Hence Hellenists are doubtful whether it had one root and was not, like the English word 'cleave', a word with more than one origin. For that would account for the three quite distinctive meanings it carried, which, despite the efforts of Heidegger to bring them into relation, cannot with conviction be taken to coincide. But it is indeed their diversity rather than any connectedness that is now significant. *Lógos,* whatever its roots, is a word of very deep origin, as are *tao* and *vác,* with not dissimilar meanings[2] in languages other than Greek, and it certainly predated any commitment to writing. Three different meanings of *légein* are to be found in Homer, and these are reflected in *lógos.* They may then be listed as follows: 1) to nod or to put to sleep, used by Homer in the sense of to lie in ambush; 2) to accord or bring together, with later derivations, to count, to compute or to calculate; and 3) to say or to speak, with many later variants, to extol, to sing, to name, to recount, and later still to think and from that to reason carefully. So different are these three meanings that a common root is doubtful; and if in later times there was some coalescence of the second and the third, that should not blind us to the point that *lógos,* the noun, had initially also three different meanings: nodding, assembling or ordering, and speech as in conversation.

The first may be disregarded since it is without interest philosophically and so has no significance in context. Meanwhile, the second and the third call for closer study, especially because of a later tendency to assimilate these meanings and to confuse them with each other. Logic, for example, despite its verbal character, involves a measure of computation, as is seen in such expressions as 'propositional calculus' or 'the algebra of classes'. It is the more important, then, that this plain distinction in their pristine meanings is properly sustained, since the immediate interest lies in the manner in which Heraclitus interpreted the second, which has nothing to with do with relations established ideally, that is, with conversation, which might refer to the many, as characterizing discourse, rather than to the one, which characterizes "all things" to bring them into harmony. Nor is such a notion entirely lost today, as discourse and what is referred to in thought about reality are seen to be different realms. For among the meanings given to *lógos* in modern dictionaries, reflecting modern usage, one is 'rapport', which may be rare but indicates none the less that the meaning Heraclitus gave to *lógos* still survives in some sense. 'Putting together', 'assembling', 'arranging' or 'composing', 'harmonizing' especially, although they may be human acts, as in composition, may also fairly be said to be acts performed by impersonal nature, as it orders movements of all sorts to bring them into harmony[3] or better dynamic equipoise, in a never-ending process. This might also have some relation to *kósmos* as used by Homer to refer to the mustering of armies in battle order. But that appears to be a rather more static concept, replaced today by the idea of order in the cosmos, which involves persistent movement of broadly regular form in mathematical terms. But this should not be taken as the meaning of *lógos,* since it is too rigid. Again, although we now regard the pressures at work as physical, physical to exclusion, forgetting that this is but one form of exerted energy, Heraclitus, together with the Taoists and certain others, held to a rather more subtle view, reasonable enough when we take vitality into account. Indeed, it is said that he opposed the materialistic attitudes of his Ionian precursors, who, like their successors today, were reluctant to accept that an extra-material influence, *natura naturans* or *l'élan vital,* may enter the equation. The evocation of fire, as opposed to more steady and concrete elements, was plainly to use a metaphor for a continually changing structure, for something which was immeasurable, volatile and fluid, even in some sense spiritual. For nature is not merely physical, though cognitivists like to think so, nor is it superstitious to hold that something more informs it.

Without enlarging on this, which is almost heretical in the cognitively-oriented, logocentric civilization, which is dominant today, so misunderstood has his doctrine become that his insight has largely been lost. One, entrapped in the idea that science provides the criterion by which everything is to be judged, even went so far as to say, apparently with conviction: "Heraclitus thus foreshadowed the modern conception of the uniformity of nature"[4] as if uniformity were the same as interrelativity, implicit in acceptance of a holistic ontology. Though plainly a monist, that thinker scarcely harboured so simple a notion, since he had no use for hylic explanation and rather declared for becoming, for a structure that could not be stilled, arrested for inspection, made to conform to rational laws, such as those which cognitivists conceive to be constant and unvarying. But resistance to his position has a very much longer history. For, even in his lifetime, Parmenides protested against what it represented, advocating in contrast an idealistic truth and declaring that a homogeneous and unchanging Being was the only reality. That this as an alternative had profound effects on later Western thinking is one of the facts of history, though it was not until much later that it came to be dominant, as if the other conception were an idea that had to be discarded. History, however, does not stand still and by a change of circumstance, which has produced a deeper understanding, matters bid fair to be reversed and becoming has now to be seen as a more penetrant doctrine than that of a static being.

Fully to grasp what *lógos* meant for Heraclitus it is necessary to recognize that the idea he projected constituted an insight and *not* an explanation. To which it might be added that when reference is to reality, regarded as indivisible, an interrelative complex, it is, as sceptics have throughout the ages contended, something quite beyond the reach of rational explanation, as, to bring the point nearer home, is human desire and conduct in its immense variety. At the time when Aristotle was devising a procedure intended to produce irrefragable answers to all matters raised for enquiry – though properly in respect of phenomenal presentations and not, to do him justice, of external reality – Hui Shih in China put forward another doctrine. This goes by the name of *ming-shih* and has had as great an influence on Chinese thought thereafter as has that of Aristotle's *analytiké* in the West. *Ming* means concept or its expression, *shih* external reality, as opposed to phenomenal being, and the thesis is simply this: that there is no power by means of which *ming* can comprehend *shih*. If this is condemned as defeatist or a mystical conception, as if that put it out of court, that is nothing more than an idealistic prejudice, which involves a refusal to see reality as it is, as if it were through perception cognizable, all sceptical doubts disregarded.[5] Nor is such an idea archaic or outmoded, of mere historic interest as it is sometimes taken to be, since it now becomes increasingly germane with an obligation to accept a holistic ontology. This may not be pleasing to rationalists, but it represents, as rationalism cannot, a view of the world that must now ground all serious thinking, specifically that referred to man's relation to reality, to nature, which cannot be merely cognitive and clearly includes much more.

Reference to *tao* has some point in context, since unlike what *lógos* meant in its now forgotten meaning, what it imports has never been lost or suffered to pass unnoticed as an influence on thought, as on artistry, in China, to render that realistic in a sense that that of the West, as idealistic, was not. Indeed, in such forms as *bushido, chado* and *tao-i-hsin* more especially it relates to attitudes to life which are highly refined and involve the cultivation of attunement to nature's rhythms. Though usually translated 'the way', the way of conducting life in responsive terms,[6] *tao* in its ontic meaning refers to the way or pulse of nature, regarded as a hidden or underlying power acting to influence everything, a force with which the sensitive man aspires to be in rapport. How far the *lógos* doctrine reflects this is an open question. For Heraclitus did not, it seems, concern himself with behaviour, unless to be contemptuous of attitudes blindly adopted, and in that sense whatever guidance in living was given was addressed to the individual, as was broadly the case with the Cynic and Epicurean doctrines, "medicine for the soul", as the last was described. Hence, as counsels with social bearing *lógos* and *tao* diverge. But it is said that the sceptics questioned rationalistic pretensions not merely to be perverse but because the approach adopted to serve them inhibited understanding of what ethics really involved. Even so, unless as Sophists, these critics never themselves produced an ethic of any sufficiency, as contrasted with the moralities propounded by their opponents.[7] If this is doubtful, however, one thing is tolerably certain: that both doctrines were concerned with an ontic issue, that is, with the characteristic of underlying reality, with that which conditions everything and constitutes the ground on which a deeper understanding of man's relation to nature in a social sense must rest. Thus, inasmuch as *tao* is alien to our culture, as *lógos* so seen is not, we must recognize that in this, its Heraclitan sense, it has great significance ontologically. That that thinker and his followers failed, in as far as we know, to develop its implications, is not a reason for us to do so. It is our obligation, now that holism as a grounding has to be accepted, to study these more deeply; and that study can only begin with the recognition of the evident limits of a logocentric approach and with it the cult of truth, which is meaningless in this connection.

*

Whether from the fragments, which are all that remain, this, and the consequences drawn, fairly represent the doctrine of Heraclitus may well be open to question. But certain recorded statements of his seem to confirm the reading that is here presented, as in Fr. XXXVI. For that is surely misread in such a rendition as this: "It is wise, listening not to me but to the report, to agree that all things are one".[8] For the expression 'the report', a later meaning of *lógos* linked to its import as 'speaking', does no more than reiterate 'listening to me', when what it almost certainly meant was listening to the *lógos,* the rhythm or pulse of nature, in other words, to understand the process of becoming, There is surely little doubt, for on this there is general agreement, that Heraclitus was projecting an ontology of becoming, of the interplay of forces, which is translated as 'strife' – *eris* in the Greek

– and seems to mean the counteraction of forces which was needed to ensure that new balances were engendered. Eccentric movement was required for growth and for decay, for a continually changing equipoise. Strife and contention, in other words, interrelative action, is necessary to ensure that movement and change take place, for inertness and immobility are the characteristics of death. And indeed, the living body is in a constant state of adjustment to the pressures playing on it, triumphant in health but defeated as disease takes a hold upon it and cannot with ease be thrown off. Though the notion *tao* seems softer,[9] stressing natural harmony rather than how it is achieved, even harshly at times, the meaning of *lógos* is effectively the same: that what we confront is a state of becoming to which we wisely learn to adapt.

Unlike *tao,* however, the meaning of *lógos* underwent several permutations in the course of Western development. As that had decisive effects on approaches adopted in respect of nature as a creative force its history must be given closer and deeper attention. Though never entirely lost to view as an influence on thinking, *lógos* as becoming, which now takes on greater and greater importance, was largely forgotten, overlaid by other ideas in the West, as its modes of thinking became increasingly idealistic and as a consequence personalized. Whether this was the outcome of Parmenides' stress on being and its correlative emphasis on truth as the end of philosophy is by no means certain, since rationalism did not emerge in full until the time of Plato, in this manner diverging from Socrates, although he retained his name to support very different approaches.[10] But the antithesis between these two earlier thinkers, Heraclitus and Parmenides, is an accepted feature of philosophical history, to show that different ontologies and intellectual attitudes were sustained in the classical age and indeed continued throughout it. That this dualism ended in the triumph of the second, the ontology of being and the terminus of truth, is also a fact of history, stressed as such by Russell.[11] However, that triumph was far from complete, a simple advance to maturity seen in rationalistic terms, and was in fact continually challenged. Cratylus is known to have adopted the *lógos* doctrine, and the later Sceptics plainly resisted the idea that rational truth was available in respect of external reality, echoing Sophist thinking. This may be the hidden reason for Plato's condemnation of the Sophists, since asking fees for instruction, the accepted procedure today, is scarcely a grievous fault, and we have no more than his word for it that their teaching was wrongly directed. Indeed, some of the Sophists seem to have promoted the soundest ideas, as witness Gorgias' 'probability' and his balanced social views, Lycophron's 'social contract', Protagoras on the value of proper education, Prodicus on courage and Hippias, echoing the implicit sceptical strain in the Heraclitan *lógos,* on the unknowable laws of nature. And that Socrates was a negativist need scarcely now be stressed. What Plato really deplored, it seems, was the denial that absolute truth was an attainable end, and that man, uniquely gifted with intellectual powers, could through them attain an insight into perfection, by reaching into realms wholly transcendent of nature. But, like later fashions in thought, interest tended to turn on what was rationalizable, which plainly cannot refer to forms of underlying reality, to the world beyond perception, though it could, as he showed, be taken into the realms of abstraction. Further, if he doubted, as Aristotle did not, that phenomenal being was knowable, partially at least, that did not really authorize an escape into transcendence, since lives are not lived in 'caves' but in the open environment. Though the world may be deceptive at times it has yet to be confronted, as he himself admitted when he turned his attention to political issues, which he sought to idealize in an even vicious manner.

Meanwhile, what took place in thought, as it were below the surface and accordingly lost to us or accessible only in fragments, may have been more than can now be seen. But it is tolerably certain that the doctrine of becoming did not wholly disappear with the advent of the Academy, since it rose again a century or so later, as is evident from the Stoics' use of a certain expression. *Lógos spermatikós* clearly referred, at least when first evoked, to real forces and not to words, not to Ideas for that matter, so that it was being used in a Heraclitan sense, when showed that that still played some part in the thinking of the time. Nor is it without significance that in the previous generation the Sceptics had made their appearance, apparently reflecting attitudes of the Sophists. Little is known of others than the schools that stemmed from Plato, though it is recognized that two of these, the Cynics and Cyrenaics, were by no means rationalistic, for Antisthenes regarded himself as the spiritual heir of Socrates, and Aristippus was sceptical of rationalistic procedures.[12] Further, our views of the first, from whom the Stoics are said to descend, are warped by the reported antics of Diogenes, who may not have been quite so eccentric, since he is also held to have urged the doctrine they later adopted, of disciplined self-control when confronted with disturbance. This idea seems to have passed from him, with a Megarian mixture, to Zeno, who studied various systems, although there is no evidence of a Heraclitan influence, which may yet have been present, even if not recorded. For in fact there were many schools of thought in Athens at that time, including almost certainly thinkers of that persuasion. After Cratylus, however, who died some eighty years before Zeno was born in Cyprus, leaving no known disciples, nothing is known of the further fate of the *lógos* doctrine. Even so, it re-emerged, if in a modified form, with the arrival of the Stoics; and that suggests, if nothing more, that it had in some sense persisted.

The early Stoics clearly believed that all things were related and that everything existing was in a state of continuing change. Hence, it is fairly conjectured that the doctrine of becoming exerted a continual influence, though little evidence is available to substantiate it.[13] With the further idea that strict knowledge was, despite some interest in logic, unattainable in respect of external reality, the doctrine of Carneades, showed that the scepticism implicit in the principle of becoming was active in antiquity no less than Attic rationalism. He was doubtless influenced by the later Sceptics, of whom again we know little, and more particularly by Archesilaus, who, though an Academic, was sceptical of the powers of attaining to truth, which curiously had now become the interest of the Stoics in a kind of transmutation of principles. But changes in Stoic thinking, with its later personalized character, make it difficult to determine what its attitudes were towards the doctrine of becoming, since with subjectivity it became more idealistic, to be challenged by the Platonists, who themselves became more sceptical. A further influence at that time was the cult of *ataráxia,* which, even if supported by a materialistic thesis – intended only to counter superstitious tendencies – in Epicurean philosophy, is now of interest because it relates to 'listening to the logos' as a form of attunement to nature, the key to acquiring tranquillity. Finally, though a Stoic, possibly influenced by it, Posidonius projected a doctrine of vital force, which, though said to stem from the *Timaeus,* is perhaps more suitably held to reflect the doctrine of becoming, which the theory of ebb and flood certainly seems to echo. So much for the history of *lógos* in its second sense in classical antiquity, rescued so to say from relative obscurity, and so to some real purpose. For in that sense it bears evident relation to the holistic ideas of today. So far from being obsolete, then, 'decadent' as has been said, though it fell into desuetude, it must now be given attention.[14]

*

Before passing to the time when its original meaning, in philosophy at least, had effectively been forgotten, or rather overlaid and confused with another meaning of *lógos,* interest is suitably turned to the Latin word *ratio.* This is taken to be equivalent to *lógos* and to encompass the same idea, though that leaves some room for question. Lexicons are not helpful in this, for the meanings they distinguish all appear to relate to speech or to thought in some form or another, argument included. But whether that suffices may quite reasonably be doubted, for certain meanings given, 'rapport' and 'proportion' for instance, may have wider import and relate to the *lógos* discussed. *Ratio,* like *lógos,* developed several meanings, some of which in derivative forms are found in modern languages. As a noun which was formed on *ratus,* the past participle of *reor,* its meanings should be related to what that verb referred to. But *reor* carries only what are clearly subjective meanings, 'to think', 'to believe', 'to suppose', 'to imagine' or 'to judge', with various later derivatives, 'to rationalize' and so on. *Res,* it may then be noted, has among its meanings ideas that are very different, such as 'things combining to form the actual or physical world', as in *summa rerum;* and among those attributed to 'ratio' itself, 'proportion' and 'relation' are given in scholarly dictionaries, as are 'ruling principle' and 'the characteristic behaviour of things in relation to one another'. Possibly, given that, whether it was or was not among its earlier basic meanings, it does have some affinity with the Heraclitan *lógos,* though, in view of the fate that overtook the last, this is said a little hesitantly. But, taking an accepted modern reading of 'ratio' reflecting that used by Vitruvius, it signifies 'proportion', 'relation between parts', normally understood in a quantitative sense. That is not always the case, however, for balance, which implicitly resides in nervous response to form – as that word is used in artistry – is plainly rather qualitative.

The question that then arises is this: What are these relations and where do they have their being? Are they relations in nature, considered as external, are they relations sensed in the act of response, or are they relations detected in the phenomenal world, when they are potentially rationalizable? Rationalists naturally adopt the last of these three meanings; but that does not imply that that is the only meaning, with which artists and sensitive persons would certainly not agree. If the first is further considered, that aligns the meaning of *ratio* with the Heraclitan *lógos,* as referring to the forces that generate balance in nature, that is, the dynamic equipoise in the complex of reality. If the second, it refers to direct response to its pulse, relation in the form of psychosomatic reaction. As for the third, that reading refers to another meaning of *lógos,* not merely conversation but intellectual ordering or ratiocination. Thus, when thinkers speak of 'ratio in nature', as rationalists they speak of conceptions formed about it, based on what is ostensively assumed to be wholly detached, 'objective', observation. And that, in contrast to such insights as *lógos* or as *tao,* is most improperly held to comprehend reality. Rationalists, indeed, impose their conceptualizations on that which both those doctrines held to be beyond a rational, cognitive grasp. *Lógos,* as reflecting *tao* and *ratio* in one sense, refers to the dynamic, interrelative manifold which is nature itself, to which one is advised to 'listen', to 'sense' as might be said, without pretence, which would be presumptuous, to know or to define it. Just, then, as it is possible to entertain an insight[15] about ratio in nature between its multifarious modes, about the creative thrust which brings them into harmony, so is it possible, even easy, employing rational powers, to think of ratio as simply quantitative proportion in phenomenal presentations or abstract formulations. The mistake, and it is a grave mistake, which a long tradition neither justifies nor hallows, is to equate or identify these two distinctive meanings. For that is simply to confuse the real with the ideal, and in that way to inhibit a capacity to see nature, in which man is enmeshed and cannot stand apart from, as it is in itself.

In classical times this tendency, essentially idealistic, was continually subject to sceptical attack; and, if it is not so today, that is most unfortunate, for a price has to be paid. But this error is deeply entrenched. With the advent of various faiths, particularly Christianity, in the later days of the Empire, scepticism was disallowed, and the idea of truth as absolute, only heretically questioned, dominated thought, saved from logical narrowness by the acceptance of an ultimate mystery, transcendent or supernal. Nor, despite Urban,[16] is that threatened by sceptical thinking directed specifically against rationalistic pretensions, since experience now shows that those are more of a threat than is doubt in such a form, which, and this is pertinent, gives opening to sensitivity, allows the numinous some meaning. But even that is discarded, reduced to sentimentality, with the rise of secular thinking, with the implicit idea that man himself is divine, master of all he surveys and potentially omniscient. That attitude culminated in an approach that was wholly materialistic, as cognitive involvement necessarily is, however much it is glorified as "piercing the veil of truth."[17] And that, though a change is now imminent, is the present form of our attitude in the face of nature, seen as something to be controlled, and so through objectification. 'To what does *ratio* refer?' is then a pertinent question.

With this the role of ontology, as basic to all thinking and the methods it adopts, which depend on presuppositions about the nature of what is confronted, is seen in relation to logic, plainly a method itself, and so to the dual meanings of the classical *lógos*. For how reality is conceived determines how we relate to it, at least in conscious states. What then does it comprise, or rather, what is its form? Is it the world we aspire to explain in strict rational terms, or is it that which cannot in any strict sense be known, because it is defiant of any objectification? Modern science in projecting, almost accidentally, an all-embracing holistic ontology, the idea in effect that everything is influenced, directly or indirectly, by every thing else in the universe, that nothing exists alone or is in any real sense self-sufficient, has brought about a change. And if its implications are accepted with reluctance, since induction as a means is clearly shown to be limited, that is a transient phase, linked to the patent difficulty of arranging accepted approaches in a fundamental way. But once it has been accepted no alternative really has standing; and, even if the methodological problems it presents are to appearance formidable, they cannot be disregarded. It is interesting then to note that when Bacon and others recognized the limits of traditional deduction, they developed induction as a more fruitful method, and thus gave scope to the great advance of science in modern times. And in effect this was because they subscribed to a new ontology, referred to the physical world, then accepted as ultimate, as it is today by empiricists, as opposed to the transcendent, supernal world of theology, which up to that time had been the only acceptable reading. The last to accede to this change will be the logocentric philosophers, since it constitutes a threat to all that they hold dear: the idea of truth as absolute and timeless. But scientists themselves, or the more astute among them, have recognized the problem with which they are now confronted, even if an alternative to induction as a procedure is not at once apparent. Yet, in so far as philosophy claims to give, or at least to have given, its procedures to science, it would seem that it should now take that as one of its tasks; indeed, that epistemology, which rose out of the needs of science, might well extend its studies to consider this new need, which is rather more than cognitive in a traditional sense. And, as *epistémé* in its pristine meaning seems to have meant the power of 'sensing' situations, as when riding a horse – for it only later came to have the meaning of strict knowledge – there is some justification for extending its present reach.[18]

However, that is not now to the point, which rather has this form: that there is some relation between logic understood as a means of disciplining discourse and the *lógos* of Heraclitus, in that discourse referred to relations in actuality must take account of what that involves in respect of the means that have to be adopted in order to engage it properly. For, if externals are seen as aspects or modes of becoming, whatever the ontology projecting that is called, *lógos* or a holistic manifold or complex, then the procedures employed to achieve some understanding of it must have a form appropriate to what is being studied. In other words, logic is not, or sensibly should not be, formal to exclusion, since that confines it to what alone can be given strict rational form. For, in whatever sense it is taken, it constitutes a discipline, a means of checking statements or the expression of ideas. Seen improperly as an organon that claims to discipline all thought – since thought itself is private – it should surely let nothing pass without the application of its critical powers. Indeed, if it cannot adapt itself to serve this further purpose, to answer this need in effect, quite apart from the consequence that discourse referred in that way will not be properly held to account, it is confined to abstractions, to what alone can be rationalized, can correctly be defined in propositional terms. This carries no suggestion, of course, that the creative *lógos* is projected as the root of 'logic' as that term is commonly used, which it is certainly not; and the time has come to consider that point, often misunderstood, and the manner in which it came to have the meaning now attached to it.

*

Reverting, then, to the history of *lógos* as a term with two significant meanings, let the third now the second of them be more closely considered. That, as is known, meant 'speech', or the 'Word' in familiar translations; and, like the other *lógos,* was later extended to cover many variants of it. Its pristine meaning, however, was what we now call 'talking', ordinary conversation with its *nuances* and suggestiveness. And so it seems to have been used, as it is in modern Greek, to refer to exchange in the market-place and in social intercourse generally. Plato used it in that sense, as did Aristotle, who did *not* employ it to describe what we now call his 'logic', to which he gave the more precise title, *analytiké.* Throughout the classical age it was normally used in this sense, rather than rationalistically, by the Fathers of the Church, and doubtless also by others. But perhaps it was used in two senses, quite apart from special derivatives, 'parole', 'rumour', 'recital', and so on. For, by the time of Cicero it had acquired a scholarly meaning, with his known translation of *logiké téchne* as *ars logicae,* 'the art of logic or reasoning', to indicate that it took on the meaning of argumentation late in Republican times and presumably also in Greece. Hence, there is little doubt, though evidence is lacking, that it played part in education, particularly that of lawyers. But it was not until the time of Martianus that this usage is confirmed, by his inclusion of *logica* in the *trivium* he devised. Its passage, however, unless in this pedagogic sense, was by no means straightforward or simple during the four hundred years or so prior to that event.

The key to this confusion is to be discovered in the thought of Philo Judaeus, a Jew brought up on the Bible who was attracted by Greek philosophy, which he aspired to reconcile with his own tradition where he believed the the truth to lie But the salient point is that, citing the first verse of *Genesis* – "God *said,* let there be light ..." – he brought the two meanings *lógos,* as the creative act or pulse and as talk or saying, together. Thus speech and creativity were made to coincide. Without commenting on his reasons, which were essentially moral, to elevate Greek thought to Hebraic standards by introducing the idea of divine intervention on the part of a single Godhead, it is enough to say that his influence was profound. For, with the Roman conquests, the ancient titulary gods, which had an intimate appeal, lost their erstwhile authority as they fell before or were conquered by a distant Roman Mars, too remote to have the same meaning and representing a warlike power to which they had to submit. The consequence was a felt need to seek a more personal form of security – a process, incidentally, which had been gathering strength since the Alexandrian conquests had undermined the city state – and people tended to turn on themselves since a social sense had weakened. It was thus that the idea of a transcendent Godhead, promising salvation, exercized an appeal, and the gradual introduction of oriental religions gave scope to this felt need. Nor was this need confined to simple unlettered people, for it was as much a concern of the thinking classes. The trend of thought, especially in the early days of the Empire, stimulated in part by the breakdown of moral standards that then distinguished the leading classes, who, abandoning their ancient self-control with the growth of wealth and luxury, became increasingly God-centred, as with Seneca, Plutarch, Epictetus, Marcus Aurelius and the Neo-Platonists, well before the ultimate triumph of Christianity. For the upsurge of religions with personal, moral appeal became a feature of the period, so that philosophic detachment almost ceased to exist.[19]

Let us return, however, to this identification of the two meanings of *lógos.* Not long after the death of Philo this received confirmation in the Gospel of Saint John, where Logos is rather unhappily translated as 'The Word'. That this signifies a vocable is questionable indeed, notwithstanding the idea of creation by dictate. It is better understood as Divine Power, Truth or Reason, which was far from presuming rational powers in men as reflecting those of the Deity, was nonetheless dubiously interpreted as the Principle of Reason in a secular sense.[20] Indeed, this reading of *lógos* was not unrelated to creativity as a continuing process, so ordered by Divine Reason. This idea of a transcendent *lógos,* though at times it was held to be immanent, by Clement for example, in the sense that reasoning power in men was regarded as divine, dominated thinking for the next three hundred years. But so, however, with persistent dispute as to what it comprised or where it resided as a power which descended on men uniquely as that which raised him above brute beasts. Nor was such thinking as this confined to Christian theologians, for both Plutarch, who regarded it as the divine soul of the world, which formed a link between God and men, and Aristocles, who held not dissimilar views, not to mention others, notably the Platonists, were much concerned with the questions of the nature of the divine and the relation of man to God. And this interest in various forms persisted with the idea that reasoning powers in men, linked to moral attitudes, were an almost Godlike quality. For Christian thinkers, however, influenced by the *Lógos* of the Johannine Gospel and conscious of the gulf between men and the God they worshipped, matters were rather more complex, since the idea of a Redeemer, in some sense distinguished from the Creator, the only God of the Pagans, enters into the equation. The question then was whether the *Lógos* should be referred to the Father or the Son, "the Second God begotten of the First", as Albinus put it. This permitted Origen, refining on Iranaeus, to distinguish two *Logói,* the Father alone the true God, *Aléthinos Théos,* and the Son, the *Christos,* Who, though associated with Him in a filial relation, was the link between Him and men. It further allowed him to contend that through the Son and the Spirit transcended all *logikói,* men with the powers of reason, They Themselves were yet transcended by the Father, albeit that *logikói* were co-eternal with the *Lógos.* The Gnostics even held the view that only those *logikói* who understood the mystic significance of the *Lógos* could attain to salvation. And so these arcane debates continued, together with other disturbing disagreements which characterized the early Church, attempting to reconcile classical detachment with adherence to the mysteries of the faith.

The need to establish some agreement on the tenets of the faith then became incumbent; and that involved devising a *credo* to which general assent could be accorded. For, apart from disputes about the *Lógos* and in some sense related to them, many heresies were rife, which recognition did not still, but even, with freedom from persecution, increased. Of the many creeds composed by the Fathers of the Church three were regarded as of especial importance: the Apostles' creed, the Nicean Creed and that of Saint Athenasius, the last of which is of particular interest in context. Without assuming to delve into the subtleties of the homoousian dispute, which turned on the status of the Persons of the Trinity, it suffices to say that it was divisive and that it was such divisions that Athenasius sought to allay, by insisting that the Three in One constituted a mystery, which did not lend itself to differences of opinion, still less to acrimonious dispute. In sum, there was but one God Whose aspects were three, which it was heresy to doubt. But all that is of moment in the present context, which is in no sense theological, is that disputes about the *Lógos* were, as an outcome of this attempt to unify belief, eventually under the influence of Saints Ambrose and Augustine declared anathema at the Synod of Sirmium (451 AD). Thereafter, apart from the reading of it implicit in the Gospel of Saint John, as Divine Power or Truth, distinct from any human capacity, even to know or to understand it, *Lógos* ceased to be the subject of theological disputation. This permitted its rational, that is secular meaning, embodied in *logica* and the verbal import of *lógos,* to free itself from the confusing association with which it had been encumbered for so many years. Its meaning now became verbal to exclusion, and so its links with cognitive enquiry were quite firmly re-established and the Aristotelian legacy once more received attention.

*

The subsequent history of logic is by no means, however, that of an uninterrupted advance to unquestionable authority. It certainly persisted as a pedagogic instrument, a system of disciplined training, throughout the following ages; but, apart from that, its career was far from straightforward and its status was often challenged even by those who were reared on its tenets in the schools. Well before its clear emergence as a disciplinary process, its credentials had been subjected to continuing challenge from thinkers as diverse as Sextus and Tertullian; and that attitude persisted into later times, notably with the mystics. It is difficult to determine what took place in the period that followed the fall of Rome, rightly called the Dark Ages, though logic was plainly studied as the only form of strict thinking in the emerging monastic schools, and its use in that capacity is recorded both in the Christian and the Mohammedan worlds. Indeed, it had attained considerable importance in both by the end of the millennium and continued to be studied with increasing application as the support of active discussion. As is invariably a consequence when it is too demanding, scepticism rose against its claims to total authority in the Eleventh Century with Manegold in the West and Al-Ghazali in the East, defending revelation against rationalistic pretensions. And that approach continued to be active throughout the Middle Ages, both on the part of the mystics, as with Hugh and Richard of the Abbey of St. Victor and such broad-minded thinkers as d'Autrecourt, Gerson, Cusanus. Although not much in evidence at the time of the Reformation, religious disputes gave an impetus to forms of sceptical thinking, to stimulate the growth of approaches of that type in the later part of the Sixteenth Century. Montaigne was such a thinker, as was Bruno, a near contemporary, who, influenced by Cusanus, propounded a doctrine resembling that of Heraclitus, admittedly evoking God rather than his *lógos* as the creative power, since the last was at that time scarcely known and was in any case unacceptable in the sense that the Godhead was personalized and not otherwise conceivable.

Logic continued to be taught In the universities; but, as an instrument for dealing with the matters that now comprised the essential concern, human interrelationships, it was seen to be largely inappropriate and was indeed regarded as a remnant of scholasticism which had by that time generally ceased to exert an influence. Except, then, for its cultivation by the Port Royal School and those who were influenced by it, Malebranche for example – for Pascal was later inclined to be sceptical and Leibniz's interest in it weakened with maturity[21] – interest in it fell effectively into desuetude, except as a pedagogic instrument. Throughout the Eighteenth Century logic as such was not called into play, for what was under discussion, the nature of response, the form of nature itself and of man's relation to it as a religious and social being, scarcely called for its application, since it was unsuited for dealing with such questions. The single exception to this, if it ranks as an exception, was the logic of Hegel, which bore little relation to formal logic as such and amounted to an attempt, which was even realistic – though seldom employed by him in practice – to devise a procedure for dealing with changing actualities, states of affairs as they actually occurred. Interest in this proposal resides in its use of negation in other than a propositional sense. For, although it may be true that every thesis brings to being an antithesis from which a synthesis emerges as a further thesis, and so on *ad infinitum,* this is scarcely a truth in logic, since it cannot be held to be absolute when it is plainly recurrent.

After two hundred years of neglect, interest in formal logic revived towards the middle of the Nineteenth Century. Reasons for this are not easy to determine, for thinking at the time was little inclined towards it; but in the 1840's a series of texts, mainly German and English, were published almost simultaneously. The influence of these was such that from that time forward, if with reservation, formal logic has increasingly been taken as the essential gift of philosophy, as that which gives it its distinction and authority. Philosophy of mind, referring to how we think, and epistemology, concerned with what we know, survive as closely related to it, whilst metaphysics and ethics, despite a recent revival of interest in the latter, have tended to be neglected, if not positively dismissed curiously, as 'unphilosophical'. In vain have various thinkers, sceptical of its reach, protested against its unwarranted dominance, its blighting effects on both science and philosophy. But, since it is fashionable in the schools because it is easy to teach and seems to provide a vicarious sense of primacy together with an apparent power to discredit what its proponents regard as loose or subjective thinking, it continues more or less unchallenged notwithstanding its limitations. Those who subscribe to it professionally cannot but be aware of its obvious inadequacies, which they try to overcome by refining its procedures, as if that gave them justification. But that is not to be achieved for as long as they cling to its ideal of rigour and its end of eliciting indisputable truth. Harbouring a blind belief that formal logic can now be rendered more flexible, as it doubtless can within it's given limits, though scarcely in the sense that it can be applied in its inelastic forms to thought directed towards real problems, involved with the complexity of changing actualities, has had the effect of crippling that when its claims that it comprehends it. The various forms of 'extended' or what are called 'deviant' logics are not sensibly taken up by those who deal with practical problems, if indeed they are aware of their existence. In fact the forms of formal logic remain, as Gomperz so acidly said: "... a curiosity preserved by the history of science but never put to practical use by science itself".[22] For as long as logic is formal, then, it is as an instrument restricted, for it cannot even solve such basic problems as tensing unless by means of clumsy circumlocutions, which cannot begin to compete with the powers of ordinary languages deploying natural logic, which is something very different. In other words, the precision on which it so prides itself as a contribution to the process of thinking is obtained at no small cost, for nobody actually uses it in its rigorous forms, except as a weapon with which to debate or to discomfit other philosophers.

This may not be wholly just, for the critical powers that it develops are used, if less meticulously, in other spheres of discourse, in which rhetoric or loose statement is properly subjected to criticism and check. In so far, however, as suggestion based on experience has to be employed in directed discourse by practical professionals – "a nod is as good as a wink" – recourse to formal logic is simply not a requirement. Finally, if the problems of life as it is actually lived are at all the concern of philosophy as an evaluative discipline, their intricacy is such that thought about them has to be more flexible. Formal logic then falls into the place that it should occupy, as a pedagogic means of sharpening critical powers in preparation for thinking on more complicated issues, on solutions rather than words, which function simply as means to ends. For it is otherwise parasitic on directed discourse applied to real concerns. In the external world, that which is actually confronted, irrefutable answers are seldom to be found. Nor does that mean that answers must then be loose or erroneous. It merely means, with critical powers as the check to be applied, that to be valid they must be apt, fitted to meet what is then of concern, disciplined less by formal logic than by the needs of the occasion. Protection is given, so to say, by sufficient awareness of what the requirement comprises and of what its meeting involves. Formal logic has its uses but its limits must be recognized, particularly as they impose restrictions on thinking about real issues, which in the general interest must always have priority. Purity is one thing, vital need is quite another. Accordingly, to claim that formal logic in strict sense is essential to philosophy is to make what amounts to an unwarranted claim.

So far from being frivolous, then, a mere rejection of logic, this on the contrary presents a challenge to logicians as they are ready to exploit the powers that are latent in an organon of which the end is to discipline approaches, all approaches whatsoever, not merely those aspiring to truth. With this in mind logicians either pick up the gauntlet, that is to say, develop more flexible means of control – when 'flexible' implies rather more than attempts to formalize 'fuzziness' – or shrink into their shell, justifying that act on the score that rigorous procedures must at all costs be sustained lest a modification of them results in an undermining of discipline. If, then, this challenge is taken up, a *real* problem is confronted and the narrowness of persisting in an outmoded idealist tradition is recognized for what it is, an unwillingness to move forward. And difficult though it may be to abandon an ideal aim, the search for absolute truth, for a kind of Holy Grail, so sublime is this search considered – though such truth is only available in abstract or verbal forms – logicians must give thought to another, more meaningful terminus, not that of an unattainable truth but of a deeper understanding. For the ultimate purpose of thinking in a philosophical sense is to grapple with those problems which are vital to society. And such thought must be realistic, referred to real conditions which allow of no simple answers. No absolute truth can be found unless it is either narrow or obvious, though ideas that are less pretentious are sometimes granted that status in that they cannot readily be faulted.[23] Nor is knowledge in strict sense true; it is often contingent, which does not mean that it must then be unreliable, fail to serve the purpose that warranted its projection, but merely that its reach and strength may with further findings be modified or improved. But error, correctly failure to fit, may certainly be detected, as Spinoza's *determinatio negatio est* – in which determination should not be taken as truth but as a measure of finality related to the occasion – effectively confirms. And it is that to which logic is fittingly addressed when it is applied to referential statement. This is not the time to discuss what this involves in depth, since the matter is far from simple when its implications are studied in full and the problems then presented are seen for what they are. Sufficient for the moment that those comprise the concern of this book, turning on the powers that are latent in negation, which have yet to be given the attention they merit. For once it is accepted that logic has a purpose related to real issues, the meeting of that purpose calls for long and persistent study – the possible forms of which is but suggested here – not by one but by many minds conscious of the problem raised with this acceptance. Aristotle devised what has now to be seen as a somewhat limited system, which he supposed to be adequate for the largely empiric enquiries that he was undertaking, since his ethics scarcely observes it, unless in the sense that value consists in theoretical enquiry and the contemplation of truth – surely a view that confines a satisfying life to a rather limited class. It must now be recognized that the modern problem, as that is other than cognitive simply, is of quite a different character, and that a holistic ontology of dynamic interrelationships demands more than conclusive answers, which do not relate to externals unless in an indirect sense. How adequately to relate to those or, more to the point at once, to discipline statements about them, constitutes the problems that has now to be confronted. And that clearly cannot be met by traditional procedures, which are essentially ideal and even subjective despite the claims that they are objective or neutral.

*

A few further thoughts on the two essential meanings of *lógos* may not be inappropriate to round out what has been said. These meanings in modern terms, as holism and formal logic, could scarcely be further apart, as a result of which any relation between them is difficult to detect. For the first is as it is and cannot but be accepted, though it cannot even be engaged by the second as propositional. If any progress is to be made it must then be in procedures which alone are modifiable. If logic can be widened, then, formed to extend its reach, some interrelation may conceivably be established, even if incompletely. And it is the problem that this presents that has in some way to be met, in as far as it may be. Nor does this presume a final resolution of the perennial problem, that of bridging the gulf between the ideal and the real; for, if the first as intellectual affects to be detached, that as an aim can never in the nature of the case be more than partial. Of course, we have no alternative than to use the powers of reason whenever we give thought to what is at last confronted. But reason is not intellection, rationalism that is, despite a long tradition which presumes them interchangeable terms, a reading that is, to say the least, insensitive. For this tendency to equate rationalism and reasoning, or to suppose that the second is subsumable under the first, is quite improper when the case, if they differ, is just the reverse, That means that ratiocination is a member only of the class of reasoning – of which another member is, for instance, intuition[24] – and a rather special form of it. Furthermore, this questionable acceptance may well be one of the reasons why, in philosophy at least, the second has not been given any serious study. Consider, for example, a characteristic of reasoning – a power, it is noted in passing, with which everyone is endowed – which may be put in this way. That in order to gather truth or scientific knowledge, the intellect must objectify by picking out particulars, which it relates subjectively in the ideal forms of logical universals or intellectual constructs, neither of which can be said to be real. Reason, conversely, takes in relationships as they are, and acts upon them accordingly as events that hold together. All response, of course, is liable to error, though at this lower level it is generally more precise, and must be because a mistake might bring about disaster. The jumping cat, for instance, cannot afford to be clumsy, nor can human beings in certain situations. Hence, as we leave the realm of rational involvement, we enter another sphere with different characteristics, in that what is then engaged is directly related to living, living in a complex which is properly indivisible.

The problem might then be said to be in some way to engage what is extra-phenomenal or, if in some sense phenomenal, relates to interrelationships which cannot be particularized without a loss of their meaning, the influence they bring to bear on life as it is lived. *Prima facie,* this might seem to be an impossible task, and it certainly is so for as long as we aspire to rationalize. But in the process of living we normally engage the interrelative manifold which we confront with ease. Nature indeed ensures that we are gifted with that capacity, as modern science shows the manner in we exercise certain innate powers, in that way revealing what takes place in nature below the level of consciousness to allow of ready relation to incessant changes in it. But a deep discussion of these pertinent discoveries is not now a requirement. Enough at once that it is now generally accepted that some 90% or so of our responses to stimulation are mediated subconsciously. Of the remainder the greater part are quasi-conscious and may, for want of a better expression fairly be defined as involving 'dim perception'. Only relatively few are fully conscious or conceptual, although, as in that form they allow of analytic investigation, concentration is turned upon them, effectively to exclusion, as if other forms of response were without meaning or influence. For the last is a less ambiguous term when meaning itself is invariably taken to be conscious. It is fitting then to distinguish between what is here called 'dim perception' and what in its turn may be entitled 'clear perception', which is of course required for the acquirement of strict knowledge. It is even required for response to events, as that demands clear knowledge as a means to an end, the end, that is, of living. But to exploit that similarity leads to misunderstanding of what is implicit in this distinction.

It is further fitting to note that logic, as natural logic spontaneously applied, is active on these lowly levels, which may itself afford a clue to what is under consideration. For the vital interest is not to explain, it is to thread a way through life, in which truth, if evoked at all, is used in quite a different way than it is in formal logic. For instance, truth in a moral sense, is not opposed to error, which is rectifiable, but to lying or deceit, which is more pernicious – a meaning which is reflected in law in which when one swears to tell the truth, the whole truth and nothing but the truth, all that one is swearing to, for that is all one can do, is not to embroider subjective impressions. But that is by the way. The concern is now with natural logic as a means of engaging reality. The two essential rules or principles implicitly applied in this form of logic are, first, a demand for consistency, since otherwise all is confused, and, second, the application of negation or denial, the correction or checking of what will not do or should not be allowed to pass. If these are reflected in the rules of formal logic, that is scarcely surprising, since that was built on natural logic, which it stiffened for precision. The point that has then to be borne in mind, to make the distinction between them sharper, is that, when natural logic is applied, it is applied to actualities, to the complex of interrelationships that comprises external reality. In other words, we are with its use involved in that and do not affect to be detached, which, if that state is really attainable, is so at best but partially, undetectable forces intervening. In sum, once we leave the simple sphere of rational, rationalistic enquiry – the endeavour to explain, even to explain the inexplicable, such as involvement in the social complex – we can apply the critical powers implicit in natural logic to what is improperly said about relations within it or in the natural world.

Returning to the two philosophically important meanings of *lógos* in Greece, they have either then to be seen in the first case as an influence that has to be accepted as the actual state of affairs that constitutes the reality that we must somehow engage if our thought is to be meaningful, *or,* in its later form of *logica,* as the instrument that must be developed as a means of disciplining what is said about the first. As has already been observed, the procedure required in some sense resembles the well-known Socratic Method, adopted prior to the invention of formal logic in its early form of *analytiké,* so that there is a measure of precedent for thought on such a procedure as this. Precisely how it should be applied, as *lógos* referred to *lógos* is, of course, a further question. For Socrates had no knowledge of what is known today, although he may have 'sensed' certain of its features, namely that the bulk of our responses are subconscious[25] and that the truly external world is a dynamic, indivisible complex – a notion to which he was doubtless heir through the Heraclitan tradition. We should now be fully aware of these latter-day discernments, which come to us through science, though rationalism resists them, and recognize that they influence all our thinking, especially as that is directed to man's relation to reality. And that demands that we find fitting means of applying disciplined thought to the problems which are then presented rather than confining it to readily treated issues, phenomenal presentations and linguistic or verbal abstractions. Finally, if we cannot know, find adequate explanations that cover the most important aspects of life, man's relation to nature and through that to his fellow men, we certainly have the power to detect what is unfitting or out of place, not simply in what is said, though that is the present concern, but also in what is done, which is the ultimate warrant for thought. As we are thinkers, then, under some obligation to express ideas on such matters, language has to be employed, and the immediate problem is to ensure that it is used correctly, less in the sense that it is rationally immaculate than in the sense that it is sufficiently sensitive to the nature of need and involvement.

Since scientists, seeking knowledge, have to engage phenomena, for that is all they can do even when with instruments they penetrate more deeply, it is essentially to philosophers, rather concerned with general evaluation, that these thoughts are addressed. Science may be, must be left to grapple with its own problems, which presumably it can tackle most fitly in its own terms, in full awareness of what those are. Philosophers, conversely, having at present no other test than that of a limited formal logic and no criterion except an elusive or abstract truth, are more confused about their purpose. And the reason for this is tolerably plain: that they are apparently tied to an idealistic tradition, which they are reluctant to slough. Idealism refers to the formulation of ideas on an intellectual plane, often of ideas only, which, as visionary or notional bear but little relation to living actualities. But ideas need not have that form, and indeed in early Greek *idéa* simply referred to a manner or mode of thinking without essential suggestion that thought had to be fully conscious or formed clearly and precisely. In fact, as we largely form ideas, or simply said, have thoughts throughout our waking lives, not to mention dreams in sleep, spontaneously, to insist that they should have strict propositional form is really little more than a rationalistic prejudice. Ideas may justly then be said to have two distinctive forms: precise ideas which relate specifically to particulars or relations formed by the intellect, *and* broader, generally vaguer ideas which rather refer to impressions received more or less immediately. Only the latter presume direct relations to reality; and those are what should now receive philosophic attention, since, when that is turned almost to exclusion to what formal logic engages, they and their implications have largely been neglected. It is quite proper, then, to distinguish between impressions with their continually changing forms, and concepts presumed, as true, to be constant and unchanging. For instance, more firmly to make this point, it is impression, nervous at base, that comprises the basic form of response to artistic presentations. That ceases to be rhythmic, sensuous or direct when it is intellectualized and rendered subjective, conceptual, in a later stage of reception, commonly called 'aesthetic' – a term introduced by a rationalist, not one employed by artists whose concern is with rhythmic form.[26] And if 'appreciation' refers to that latter stage and has then a self-conscious character, its urging is pernicious. For it is in effect a stance imposed on the ordinary sensuous man by those, in this sense insensitive, who think that knowledge is all. Hence that as an attitude stands in the way of a natural development of sensuous and direct response to rhythmic presentations, which is the key to culture, and so to general refinement. But leaving that point for the moment, important though it is, the interest is to refer, with the aim of refinement through checking, as in the Socratic Method, to forms of response which are general, immediate, spontaneous and common to humanity, and remain so despite attempts to degrade or override them by insensitive intellectuals. For, of course, they are basic to normal life, impoverished without them. It is then response to the *lógos* as the underlying reality – which the intellect cannot reach when its aim is rationalistic – to which interest has now to be turned. In sum, if logic is thought of as essentially an organon, a disciplinary instrument referred to whatever is said, as opposed to a means alone of substantiating truth claims, its critical potential may and should be further developed, in such a way as to engage real or vital problems, to relate to direct response.

Chapter Two

The Two Basic Forms of Logic

Addressing attention, then, to what the word 'logic' means when used without qualification – for the qualification 'formal' implies that there must be at least one other form of logic – let an alternative be considered. It is well-known to philosophers, if not to the general public, that formal logic has latterly diversified itself into several distinctive logics, which differ from traditional and later classical logic as extended variants of it. Modal, tensed or temporal, deontic, interrogative, quantum and fuzzy logics constitute some of the forms that they take, and this is but a selection.[1] Moreover, elaborations on classical logic itself, such as Propositional Calculus, Disjunctive and Categorical Syllogistics, Functional Calculus of the First Order, the Algebra of Classes, the Theory of Types and so on further demonstrate the extent to which logic has developed, primarily with the emergence of symbolic logic, 'logistics'. But inasmuch as all of these may be distinguished as 'formal', as concerned, that is, with abstract, strict analytic relations, it is not to them that attention will at once be turned when further thought is given to an alternative logic and the role it has to perform. For, using the term 'logic' in its broadest sense, as meaning an organon for disciplining what is said on any matter whatsoever, logic must be given a rather wider reference, to be inclusive of other forms which have tended to be neglected with this stress on strict formality, the search in effect for absolute truth, peremptory precision, effectively regardless of the nature of what is under consideration.

Any further form, of course, has also to be verbal, and accordingly sentential, since logic, as derived from *lógos* meaning 'speaking' is always related to language, the expression of ideas. But unlike formal logic, confined to formal relations, to propositional statements shown to be true or false,[2] others refer to real events, to relations in actuality, without pretence to total or absolute precision. Such events are those which *lógos* in its meaning of natural becoming, as "the only begetter" of movement and change as that affects the psyche in response to stimulation, as the underlying creative force which conditions everything, continually brings it to being. How far what influences man may be said to have this character must be considered later when the form of his acts in response to living actualities has been viewed in greater depth. For at once it is enough to note that formal logic is powerless to reach or to engage them, since it is at best confined to phenomenal presentations, delimited themselves, when seen as definable units, by the application of conscious objectification. This means that other approaches have to be considered, lest otherwise a power to place sufficient check on statements referred to real events cannot be developed or properly brought into play. That formal logicians do not take note of failure to apply discipline on this level or acknowledge limitations when they insist on rigour need not at once be stressed, although it is plainly a matter of moment. Sufficient that this matter constitutes a real problem, such that other forms of logic must be rescued from the neglect into which their study has fallen and be shown to operate on discourse, which is not simply subjective or loose because it is without the check that formal logic provides.[3]

The interest is then to distinguish what these further forms might be and how they could be employed to discipline what is said when enquiry is extra-cognitive, in order to ensure that that is adequate and pointed and does not confuse ideas when such issues as these are considered. To speak of other forms is at this stage premature, since the forms that they take are those within a primary division, which is here to be defined as *natural logic* contrasted with *formal logic* or complementary to it, granting that both are valid within their given spheres. But first it is requisite to stress, to avoid misunderstanding about it, that 'natural' in this context should not be taken to mean 'informal'. For, if 'informal' means 'without rules', unconstrained or irregular, a wholly false picture is given. Indeed, it would run counter to the accepted idea that there are laws of nature, which, if in part cognizable, though now shown to be more complex than was once supposed, must yet conform to rules of some sort or another, since the whole maintains its equipoise and does not collapse into disorder. And as man himself is a mode of it, he too sustains his equipoise if he does not go against it. In that sense nature gave him powers as a sentient being to face the conditions of life. The laws of natural logic are then laws with roots in nature, which, when seen in depth and in themselves so to say, conduce to interrelative harmony, the maintenance of equipoise in the complex of becoming. This may not at once be apparent when with his intellect man has power to override or disregard these laws and to develop his own, though always under penalty. It is, however, the normal case at more basic levels – a point of some bearing in context. Evolutionary processes have made man what he is, according to Aristotle 'a rational, reasoning animal'; and his reasoning powers were primarily developed to secure his survival in the complex conditions of living.

When man first came down from the trees and assumed an upright posture many problems faced him, for he was weak and vulnerable in relation to armed animals and could only survive with difficulty by finding further means, fire and weapons, for instance, to compensate for his weakness. How consciousness arose, to aid all mobile creatures to adjust to their environments, is and remains a mystery, and how self-consciousness came to being as a development on it, uniquely it seems to man, is certainly not less so.[4] Sufficient now that it did in the process of evolution, through which the brain developed to give man greater powers. In fine, the power to reason, dimly at first no doubt, gradually increased as the nervous system was formed to permit more delicate adaptation to the pressures bearing on man as a relatively weak creature, needing other means than talons or the powers of flight for survival. As part of this process he in various ways formed languages, primarily to cooperate with his fellow men, for there was safety in numbers, and to communicate in the service of their common interests, thereby to afford him further powers of ordering his life and adapting to his conditions. No thought has at once been given to the growth with a certain detachment of his intellectual powers, which could only develop with relative security. For the present point is to think about his basic power to reason, which is the ground of natural logic as a universal capacity related to balance in life.

It is not now necessary to discuss the manner in which from vestiges archaeologists have learnt about the ways men lived in the distant past, from the times when humankind emerged to what may be called 'humanity', when reasoning powers were what gave man that special character. For the present concern is simply how man's power to reason grew in time to maturity, probably long before remaining artefacts afford concrete evidence of it. Language which allows of better organization was, evidently a product of the development of the brain and other appropriate organs; and may itself be said to be a logical structure rooted in a requirement for mutual understanding. This presumes a grasp of consistency and negation, applied when the first is not sustained, and agreement, called definition, on the meanings that words carried, however vague initially these meanings may have been. But gradually, no doubt, a greater refinement developed and a fuller understanding of the principles needed to make meanings clear to others evolved in the process of time. And so natural logic as a means of ordering expression emerged to give a structure to language as related to vital needs. In so far as languages differed, in part perhaps in accordance with differing modes of life, as with hunters, nomads, seafaring and more settled peoples, dependent on tilling the soil, differing forms developed, stressing movement and change for instance,[5] although the basic principles of consistency and negation must have been everywhere observed As there are no people without a highly developed language, so natural logic is found as a factor in all of them, as a characteristic feature of thought in all human societies, however apparently primitive. It is a natural endowment of the human species with evolutionary origins, in which sense it became innate and was not an artificial acquirement, something consciously planned. It is hence picked up by children, organically equipped, in the process of maturation, slowly at first and then in its more intricate forms quite rapidly as its structure is grasped.

An interesting aspect of the growth of the power to reason is that formal logic, a very much later development, comprises an attempt to rationalize and bring into full consciousness what is innate in the human make-up[6], though it can only do so in part because reasoning in this basic sense is too subtle and resilient. This confirms that there is a form of meeting what is confronted in the face of reality which is essentially nervous at base and so properly called 'natural'. And if it is also called 'logical', that is surely in order in that it amounts to a structuring of expression. With its formalization other features are exposed, notably those that relate to arriving at firm decisions by means of reasonably clear definition, which is required to reduce or eliminate ambiguity – a development antecedent to the projection of formal logic. But the aim in natural logic is not to attain to irrefragable answers; it is rather to permit of appropriate mutual action with the recognition of limits, of that which will not do. It was, both in its origin and as it is used today, a practical instrument with which to deal with actualities; and therein lies its difference in a functional sense. For it is rather related to meanings than to words in themselves, which are essentially signals indicating interests, so that considerable scope is available in respect of selection linked to shades of meaning in sentential contexts. To this it might be added in thought of priorities of importance that in this functional sense natural logic has clear priority, since without its deployment in this flexible form life could scarcely be lived or normal relations sustained. Formal logic has uses, especially with respect to special types of enquiry, cognitive in character. It has doubtless been of value as the basis upon which mathematics and science in certain aspects rest. But that can be overstressed, as if knowledge in strict form – carried to the point, in recent years at least, of neglecting or misrepresenting other interests in an attempt to comprehend them in its narrow terms – was supreme as an interest in life. Hence, what vital interests involved in depth was not given proper attention, and so with some rather unhappy consequences.

*

To make this distinction clearer, it would be to the point to consider the character and the reach of both these forms of logic more fully, since that would bring out their difference, which has now to be seen as functional. What either can achieve as a means of meeting human needs establishes in effect their relative justification as instruments for controlling what is publicly said in respect of them. For in the meaning of speech logic plainly refers to statements publicly made and not to thought as such, which is private and much too fluid to be confined to rules and is only partially subject to external control. Indeed, thought is highly volatile, swayed, conditioned, affected in all sorts of subtle ways, which are not themselves in any strict sense definable and often have unexpected, adventitious sources, as in intuition and insight. Both of these are doubtless rooted in experience, though it would be a mistake to suppose that that was necessarily conscious, when it is in the main derived from pressures on the psyche in subconscious response to stimuli. All experience is empiric. But to use that term as empiricists do to serve their cognitive interests, to ground their rather narrow doctrine – for which it must, of course, be consciously received – is certainly a usage which limits its meaning unduly. For experience surely means all that we undergo, in *ex-per-i-entia,* in the act of going through in relation to externals. Thinking cannot be other than an internal process, as *man,* the etymon of mind, manifestly indicates; and its volatile nature is an aspect of its virtue, since without its free-ranging capacity inspired, creative ideas would never come to birth. It is well-known that thought can readily be concealed. For instance, dislike can be covered, though facial expression often gives it away. With age and increasing experience greater skill in hiding what is really thought from others is developed and refined, such that claims to know the content of other minds, unless those are simple and immature, are seldom very well founded. And that is as well since courtesy often involves concealment of one's real opinion. When interest turns on logic, then, it refers to what is overt, the spoken or written work; and, as that in some way exposes it, or part of the thought behind it, it is related to the statement and very little more. Logic can discipline only what is clearly expressed, perhaps to sharpen or modify further thought on the subject, but not to order thought as such, unless in this way indirectly. This said, it is clear what logic means when it is defined as a discipline justly applied to statements affecting to influence others, regardless of the forms they take, which have many varieties, descriptive, compulsive, persuasive, ironic, suggestive, sceptical, all of which should be subject to proper critical comment, that is, to some form of logic which "protects us against error".

Turning to formal logic, then, this is suitably said: that its limits lie precisely in its stress on rigour, its demand that statements shall be absolutely true, true in an indisputable sense, which in principle stand for all time. With this demand it is evident that many forms of expression, such as those that are suggestive, cannot come within its purview, though it would be absurd to hold that suggestive statements are devoid of serious content. And that they may exert an influence on those to whom they are addressed is even more significant, since that may be malign and so should surely be subjected to questioning. That a few such final truths as formal logic elicits exist is not, of course, to be doubted. Indeed, they are exemplified in the basic laws of logic, or in two of them at least, since the third, the excluded middle, when held to be universal, scarcely has a similar status, it is altogether too simple. Truths of that type, as that two things cannot be in the same place at the same time for instance, though doubtless true beyond question are scarcely very enlightening, since they seem to be little more than 'glimpses of the obvious', as are many findings of indisputable form, truism, tautologies. In fairness, however, it has to be said, that some such findings as these have been discovered and represent something rather more that 'that which goes without saying', even if few are positive. For positive truths, that 'man is mortal' for example, are at base empiric, *a posteriori,* derived from observation and in effect confirmed as deductive by induction. That everyone will die, for no man is immortal, or has yet been shown to be so, is a finding derived from observation of the deaths of those who were once alive, either in recent times or in the historic past. There are truths, or near truths at least, about the physical world, as that, subject to slight perturbations, planets move in regular orbits or that the sun will rise, appear on the horizon, at a certain part of the Earth at a specific time tomorrow. But these are scientific and not really logical findings, acquired by means of observation, temporal measurement and so on, not by deduction alone.[7] Truth, in its logical meaning, cannot, despite the claim that it is potentially all-embracing, properly be applied to external actualities, which exist in states of continual change and so have no unchanging or constant form such as would allow of clear categorization. It is possible, of course, to categorize in broad terms, as species, classes, genera and so on, but those are abstractions only and cannot pretend to be more. Nor is it the case that realities or externals exhibit themselves as particulars, as they are taken to be when cognitive enquiry assumes that it refers to them, when its reference is and can only be to phenomena. For they are interrelative and subsist as modes of becoming in a dynamic, indivisible complex. Hence they cannot be engaged as they are by means of objectification on which cognitive enquiry very clearly depends.

Despite these obstacles to its reach, it is not to be doubted that formal logic serves some purpose, in education primarily, where in its critical form it compels students to think more carefully about the ideas they harbour or project. This requirement constitutes an excellent preparation for those who will later in life have to make decisions affecting the lives of others and the public generally, and more importantly perhaps to criticize proposals made by the other side, in Parliament or the Law Courts, to show how very significant its negative aspect is. But that anything advanced in such conditions as these has the the sharp simplicity of projections in formal logic, which are either true or false without any allowance for doubt, is simply not the case. For what such proposals refer to in any practical discourse are the complicated affairs related to life and action, in which few factors present have a clear-cut character whilst most have confusing ramifications. What in such cases is called for are the most reasonable, cogent and efficacious answers that can be obtained. And as those are generally found through a screening process of elimination, to determine what will stand up, they, although imperfect in a formal sense, have yet to be accepted, since decisions have to be made. The application of logic is then in practical action for the most part negative, even in definition, since in attribution terms rarely have absolute meanings, but are generally circumstantial and based on broad agreement. A training in logic, accordingly, has as its end the strengthening of the capacity to detect flaws in what is proposed; and, in a Socratic manner, *dialektiké* is employed rather than *analytiké*.[8] For truth in any absolute form is abstract or ideal, much too definitive to engage the involvement that has to be faced in directed discourse.

A further point may be that were the obligation to conform to the rules of logic abandoned all discipline on statement would be undermined. But this again can be questioned. It is known that whole cultures have ordered their relations and affairs with a large degree of efficiency without recourse to the rulings afforded by formal logic, and have even avoided certain mistakes that adhesion to them produces, primarily through the adoption of inept presuppositions. That reality is knowable or that truth can be found in respect of what it really comprises, that complete detachment with idealization is possible, give examples of these. Regarding the individual in the guise of the knowing self as having primacy over the general or social interest affords a further instance, based on the assumption that subjective or personal values can be universalized without generating imbalance or a form of social divisiveness. For, seeing himself as a man apart, peculiarly enlightened, the savant tends to forget that he is also a social being enmeshed in the complex of reality about which his ideas may be faulty, often more so indeed than those of the ordinary man who meets the world directly, which the first affects to override as uninformed by analysis. Again, indulgence in sharp dichotomies, characteristic especially of rationalistic thinking, has plainly led to grave errors, since nothing in reality is divisible so precisely; and even in the phenomenal world there are interrelativities, for that itself is a complex when response to its presentations is impressionable or direct, as it normally is. In the field of logic itself, as intuitionists have recently pointed out, the third of the laws of logic is patently very restrictive, since it seldom applies in life in which distinctions are not so sharp. There are shades of meaning in everything, even in what is said, as is evident from the fact that discourse involves debate, which, even among logicians, is continually active, as if all were open to question. Though truth and falsity may at times refer to what is presented in the phenomenal world, that is only sometimes the case, usually with sharp contrasts, the principle behind red and green lights as signals. But the excluded middle is simply an intellectual construct, a product of conception and not, except in special cases, of transient impression, which is infinitely more fluid and mobile with the requirement to adapt to continually changing conditions. In the final analysis there is no sharp division between clear or 'objective' and dim, impressionable perception, which itself suffices to show that precise or clear-cut divisions, allowing of no exceptions, do not obtain in vital response related to conditions as they occur in actuality and impinge upon the psyche.

As for the many refinements developed in latter-day logic, these are not used by or even known to most educated persons. And as for applying them in the field that cannot well be done as they are so abstract and intricate that their bearing on normal discourse would merely be restrictive. Logic's relation to language, which has so intrigued the analysts, as if their studies in some way brought them more closely together, has only shown that the latter, an inherited structure which grew out of relation to life and its need for ready communication, is infinitely more subtle than propositional logic can possibly comprehend. Even Propositional Calculus, the simplest of logical forms, referred to the employment of sentential connectives – 'and, 'or', 'not', 'if...then' – is clumsy as compared with their use in ordinary language, from which they were purloined to be given a certain stiffness, such that accentuation, which plays part in their vital employment, is sacrificed to precision of a rather flat variety. Quantifiers, dealt with officially under a further mode, Functional Calculus of the First Order – 'all' and 'some' for instance – are also common usages which are seldom employed improperly by those without training in formal logic, who, if confusion arises, readily resolve it by a question such as this: Is that what you really mean? Formal logic, in short, although it includes the clear detection of fallacies, some of which are real and so in need of exposure, scarcely enriches discourse in its normal forms, since it merely stiffens it and so limits its flexibility. Latin might have been an appropriate base for it, since it is so concise, although in actual use no doubt, as contrasted with written texts, accentuation and rhythmic stress gave that language a suppleness not now to be detected, unless perhaps in verse. And that was doubtless as true of Greek, the language of Aristotle, as is suggested in the Comedies, though how words were actually spoken we cannot now know with certainty. It would be a mistake to suppose, if Greek grammar lay behind the logic that came to birth later in that culture, that it represented the flavour of the spoken language, which was doubtfully so precise. That formal logic disciplines all thought and its expression, or the second more precisely, is a dubious claim, for its range is very much more restricted. Thought is certainly more elastic than a system which depends on rigid, unyielding formulae can conceivably comprehend; and language, even if strict, contains so many *nuances* that it cannot be caught, without loss of the power potential in it, in so circumscribed a net.

Eminent logicians, Frege and Tarski notably, recognized this point, averring that formal logic should confine itself to abstractions – 'essentials' for the first – and had no real application beyond that so limited world. Indeed, it has to be granted that most words are penumbral with meanings determined by circumstance, when meaning is what counts. And so obvious is this that to eliminate ambiguity, all too common when reference is to external relationships, strict logicians elect to operate with symbols in order to avoid the complications attaching to words as they are applied to reality. If a statement is to be true, true beyond all question, irrefragable, indisputable, free, that is to say, of any hint of ambiguity, it has to be expressed in symbolic equations which make no pretence to refer. For as soon as a symbol – not a sign, for that has some significance – is, in an attempt to give it concrete meaning, replaced by a word with some import, it is related to life with all its complications and ceases to be precise, unqualified, ideal. It is no longer a symbol, related to other symbols themselves without other associations, but an expression purporting to engage external events, which do not as real have that ideal character. Within its own limited sphere, formal logic affords a discipline on discourse as that complies with its rules, to ensure that what is said is related to other notations in an unequivocal manner, so that nothing passes which cannot be shown to be incontestably true, which is seldom the case when words claim to be referential. It may be difficult to abandon what has for so long been accepted, that formal logic refers, when, as formal, it does so only by appeal to certain verbal conventions, the assumption that words precisely reflect actual states of affairs, when that has now to be seen as another dubious presupposition. It is an assumption which grounds this debate, since question is always present when meaning is being considered, a debate which should not in principle be indulged by logicians, unless to negate false claims: since once such a truth is established it surely stands for all time to leave no scope for questioning. An established relation in this form is necessarily final; and this would seem to be its virtue, that an alternative to it is effectively inconceivable. It is something alone that is certain. Striving for this certainty is a highly commendable enterprise, a noble paradigm to set up as the final criterion by which expression is to be judged. But sensible men must recognize its limits as ideal and see that it is little more than an unattainable target if it affects to apply to more than abstract relationships. For, if it does so, it constitutes an improper intervention into directed discourse, which is not ideal and of its nature cannot be so. This may go against traditional acceptances, the product in the West of Platonic idealization, thought of perfect archetypes, in this case of veridicality. But Plato himself did not contend that his Forms had external existence.

Reality is present and is what must be confronted without an implicit idea that it can be disregarded because it is not, as is appearance, cognizable. That ideal representations in some obscure way reflect external actualities, as though the ontic and psychic could be taken as coincident, is another false assumption, for the most part adopted blindly. That logic, or rather philosophy inseparably tied to it, "leaves everything as it is", would seem to render it innocuous. But when it is projected as the universal standard that ought to be accepted in all discursive enquiry, unhappy and confusing consequences follow, if only in the sense that the real is not distinguished from the ideal. Grave problems, with which philosophy has some obligation to deal, since thy are outside the province of science, do not receive proper attention when they are plainly real and are falsified if approach to them is ratiocinative and deficient in sensitivity, cognitive as if they should be objectified. And this is especially the case as logically grounded contentions carry a kind of compulsion to accede to what they project. This entry is not so admirable, then, as it is normally taken to be, since under its dispensation vital interests may well be interpreted improperly, as if they had simple forms which could be defined precisely in rationalistic terms, when that is plainly not the case as they are more deeply considered.

Finally, it might be remarked, if with a measure of caution, for the idea is not welcome, that this distinction between two basic forms of logic, the natural, as that with which reality is confronted in the process of living, and the formal, which can only deal with ideal relations, has some bearing on the direction that philosophy has taken in the present century. For its limits are particularly shown when, in attempts to be practical, it essays to deal with the problems that really concern society, when the attitudes it adopts are so restrictive and narrow that those involved with real issues, practising professionals appear not only better informed but more capable of meeting them. Around the turn of this century, a group of creative thinkers, Bergson, Alexander, Driesch, Bosanquet and later Whitehead, to name the most significant, attempted to cast off a received empiricist heritage and to break new ground in philosophy. Whether they fomented the coming advances in science is an open question. But had their thought been carried forward what followed could have more in tune with developments taking place in science with a better understanding of their implications for philosophy itself. But, for reasons that are obscure,[9] a logocentric upsurge overrode this creative thrust and dominated thought, greatly to impoverish it.

An outcome of this was the advent of the philosopher as a 'professional' speaking a technical language comprehensible only to those who were specially trained, thereby excluding 'amateurs', unless as humble admirers of this new found specialization. This is not important, but what quite certainly is is a failure to grasp what is happening in the world of thought at large. Science without design to trespass on philosophy, has effectively developed a holistic ontology – always latent in its implicit monism – grounded in discoveries in physics, biochemistry, biology and ecology.[10] This implies that reality is an interrelative complex, which cannot be broken into parts without a measure of falsification. That this presents science itself with a methodological problem of formidable dimensions is not at once of concern, since what is now of interest is its meaning for philosophy. For if that is to deal with responsive actualities, with man's relation to reality, roughly to events occurring in the social complex, which reflects the form of nature as itself a dynamic, interrelative manifold, then this has the greatest significance. But that will not be understood or, if grasped, will be resisted as a threat to all that rationalism involves, the presuppositions, for instance, that it clings to so uncritically whilst bound to the approach that it uncritically adopts. Hence, unless it is to remain an effectively marginal discipline, which it is inevitably if it claims to be cognitive, philosophy has to examine its acceptances more closely and to ask itself what it contributes when that is its only end. Perhaps it is content with its present role and, resting on its past prestige, feels no need to change it. If that is so, it denies itself a meaningful place in the movement of thought today and, more seriously, turns its back on the task it is called upon to perform: to study the issues implicit in general evaluation, which science cannot do. Formal logic still has a role, in education specifically; but its claim to be a universal discipline bearing on all expression, is little more than a prejudice harboured to give it authority, which only logicians and those who suppose that it has this extensive power acknowledge as being justified.

*

Natural logic does not fall into similar errors or suffer from the limits that trammel formal logic, since it does not consciously adopt certain presuppostions – as that absolute truth is the end or that there are strict dichotomies rendered so by definition – so that it is not in a similar manner restricted. To presume that as a consequence it is a perfect instrument guaranteed to give the answers that are required would however be a mistake. For it makes no pretence to have any such capacity, accepting that perfection in discourse, as in life, is a dream devoid of substance, an idealistic terminus which, such is the belief, pursued with sufficient persistence will at last be reached. Hence it is not concerned with what interests formal logic as an alethic discipline, but with quite a different end. It is then to the point to consider what that is more closely, since it is scarcely recognized as a means of checking expression, as a power that plays a significant part in discourse. Natural logic, of course, is embedded in natural language, which is said, and not without justice, to be 'in certain respects unclear, imprecise and so potentially misleading",[11] though it would be an error to align these two completely. To support their bias, even so, rationalists sustain this, to hold that natural logic, commonly called 'informal', is inferior to what, almost as an act of faith, they set up as the paradigm. But that is to misunderstand the function it performs, which is not to elicit absolute, demonstrable, indisputable truth, seen to be unattainable in the field in which it operates, but to act as a check or discipline on what is loosely said.

Its purpose, if that term is appropriate for what it was developed or evolved to meet, is to guard us against error in the use of language as that is referred externally. To take a simple example, the use of the double negative is obviously confusing, 'bad grammar' as is said, for when it is employed it is far from certain what the speaker means. Nor does it call for great skill to detect this infelicity. It is then a critical instrument directed towards ensuring that meanings shall be clear, which differentiates its end from that of formal logic, which is to substantiate truth claims, positive assertions. With it, in fine, we return to the logic developed by Socrates – prior to Aristotle's projection of a system aimed to secure conclusive answers.– that is, to the rejection of ideas that will not do, thereby to protect us from mistaken notions about what is really the case. For the last, when thought is of relations in actuality, is an aspect of what has being in a complex and so cannot be described or defined in objective, positive terms in the form that it actually has. The meaning of justice, for instance, is not correctly to be defined in categorical terms, since it is in essence relative, a balance of interest between two or more parties in conflict, and thus is implicitly circumstantial. Law develops rules which are absolute only in the sense of precepts laid down to ensure a measure of consistency the reduction of subjectivity in any judgment made; and that is clearly recognized by open-minded lawyers, accepting that conditions are modifying factors. Its less far-reaching equivalent goes by the name of 'fairness', which is broadly understanding of what is appropriate in conditions, as the adjective 'fair', meaning 'equitable' or 'acceptable', illustrates sufficiently. Absolutes have their place, but they must be evoked with care, for they are blunt and insensitive and do not properly take account of the subtleties of involvement.

This is not unrelated to the role of natural logic, which, since it has little to do with absolutes consciously laid down, is a more sensitive instrument when it comes to the use of discipline in the sense of correction. For, as a check on what is said, it allows for flexibility and accepts that the rules of grammar permit nuances of expression. Its criterion is not in any sense bound to a structure of artificial rulings developed by the intellect, acting as it were in detachment from real conditions, but that implicit in language evolved over many centuries to serve the needs of communication in actual living conditions. In other words, it is meaning, meaning in life, that is, which constitutes its criterion. To condemn it as unreliable, then, is a rational prejudice which presumes it to be directed towards assertoric statement, as though that were the only end, when in fact it is a limited one. Taken to be impulsive and not rooted in careful thought, language may well have that character, but it is still the meaning that has to be conveyed that lies behind its use; and, as that is primary, the role of natural logic is to secure sufficient clarity in communication. Applied as a critical instrument it then refers to expression which has that as its end, an end that may not be achieved unless it is brought into action. For language has to be precise, though not in a rational sense, when it relates to vital interests, in respect of which error may be disastrous, since failure to act correctly, that is to give proper guidance in the conditions prevailing, might carry serious consequences, as the need for warning shows. There is a great difference between propositional error and that which appertains to life, in that the second menaces it and may not allow of recovery.

In performance of this function natural logic is not immaculate, since language itself is not so even when employed in a critical role. But language, whatever its flaws – and to render it rigid is not to bring it to perfection but to render it inflexible – is the means whereby relations are established. And it was to hold some check on its loose or confusing employment for which that logic was evolved, to serve the interests of social co-operation. Thus, it plays a part in life, centrally and deeply, in a way that formal logic does not, since that at best is marginal. Cognitive enquiry, using that term strictly, to refer to the gathering of precise conceptual knowledge, is but one form of response with very limited range, since it can only refer to what can be objectified, separated out from the complex of involvement. Other forms of response, which comprise the vast majority and exert an undoubted influence, are not within its range, whatever its claims may be. But they clearly play a part in life, to bear on what is thought and communicated to others in various subtle ways. Formal logic, itself a form of cognitive enquiry, is powerless to take these into account, notwithstanding that they comprise the very substance of life, condition all that is said, all relations between persons seeking mutual understanding. Although such basic interests as these have been largely lost to view under the heavy cloud of overt cognitive concentration, they have very much greater importance, since everyone is involved in the process of adjustment to changes in the environment, to the pressures bearing on them, subconsciously for the most part, which are better understood as they can be given expression. Of course, that can never be perfect, since in contrast with externals relations are far from simple, clearly dichotomic; but yet they must be established lest confusion should ensue. Although involvements with reality can not be defined precisely – poets, for example, rely on the powers of suggestion – it should be clear to a little thought that, if expression is to engage it, imperfection is a natural and inevitable consequence of ideal limitations.[12] To meet this, natural logic was evolved as a means of securing that this weakness should not be too productive of confusion. And, paradoxically, that is more likely to be the outcome when rigour is introduced and perfection is demanded.

If natural logic refers to what is beyond the reach of propositional logic and relates to what that cannot, some of the characteristics that enable it to do so must be considered more closely. Its relation in this sense is not so much to reality, as if that was where the essential difference lay, as to a human capacity to come to terms with its pressures, to establish a rapport with what it brings to bear. Thus it is related to human sensitivity in a way that formal logic is not and never can be. Let us see what this means. When Aristotle characterized man as a 'rational animal', referring to man generically, it is doubtful whether he meant that men in general were logocentrics, given to rationalizing all of which they were conscious, as if the aim were to bring it under control of the intellect. He rather meant, it seems, that all men were naturally gifted with the power to reason, to act in a *reasonable* manner, in the main consistently. What he referred to, in other words, was a natural human endowment, which, linked to articulate language, was, it seems uniquely, granted to human beings as a feature of the species distinguished as *homo sapiens*. Nor does the adjective *sapiens* mean having the characteristics of the guru or the sage, still less of the learned man; it rather signifies 'sensitive', alert to what is important in the process of living. Sensitivity, then, as opposed to intellectuality, is for the greater part exercised spontaneously, which does not mean incontinently, thoughtlessly, capriciously, but with a 'sense' of what is appropriate in conditions, rooted in part in experience, in part in innate proclivity.

To exert this delicate power, the heritage of a capacity to act with a measure of reason, which though innate is only acquired in fullness with maturation, has to be evoked. And it is of some significance that, when conscious deliberation is brought up to replace it, its grace is often compromised. For with that it is subjectivized, using that term in the meaning which it is given today, and calculation may enter to render it self-centred with ulterior motivation and a loss of rapport with nature. Under intellectuality, regarded as a sublime power which renders man supreme, this further human capacity which lies at the root of culture, for that must have a sensuous base,[13] has been thrust into the background, just as natural logic has effectively been forgotten in the interests of an approach which promises domination and mastery over nature – or more precisely the hope of it. Natural logic, then, is closely bound to sensitivity, since both are general potentials and both are linked to action in life. Both are at base concerned with what is really appropriate; or, in more precise terms, the second with what is fitting in direct contact with reality, the first with what is out of order in communication on a verbal plane. The clumsy or unfitting act is not wholly to be controlled by verbal checking; but, when its repetition is to be avoided, expression to that end is suitably brought into play. And that, if not in the same sense spontaneous, since the thought implicit in critique involves some deliberation, is none the less a power which is present to human beings as part of their natural make-up, developed through evolution as a needed complement to this power of deploying thought. Men may, of course, deliberate in a more elaborate manner, on the reasons for ugly actions, their causes and motivation, and at times should certainly do so, indulging sharper rebuke. But that is not the way in which they normally behave when judgment has to be made more or less immediately; and that, a significant aspect of life, has largely been forgotten when only the rationalizing powers of the categorizing intellect receive consideration. The power to reason spontaneously, implicit in natural logic, though it also has greater scope, as will be seen in the sequel, then calls for some attention, not only because it relates to life as it is actually lived but because it is potential in every human being. If then, it has not been considered with the seriousness that it merits, that itself is reason enough for reviving interest in it as a discipline on expression. Nor because expression is other than propositional, to mean that discipline placed upon it cannot have that form, does that imply that checks imposed are not justly deemed to be 'logical'. Any procedure developed to check statements publicly made is 'logical' if that now so limited term carries disciplinary meaning.

Accepting that natural logic is an instrument with which the ordinary man is equipped to undertake critical reasoning, it differs from formal logic in that that requires special technical training and is very seldom used in a practical capacity. With effectively exclusive concentration of the latter, what the former is potential to achieve as a critical power is little understood. It is not that it is not recognized outside academe, since under other names, such as 'the use of reason', defined as 'good sense' or 'judiciousness', it is plainly something other than 'rationalism' or 'ratiocination'. But that it has not been regarded, in itself so to say, as meriting serious study. Nor is it without interest that 'logical' in English, as in kindred languages, also signifies 'reasonable' when referred to action, which does not necessarily presume deliberation. It might also be noted that the Kneales in their classical work observed that pre-Socratic thinkers showed themselves quite capable of conducting discussion intelligibly without the knowledge or benefit of later formal logic.[14] That also applied in China, where a formal logic under the name of *Mo che* was at one time developed, but was positively rejected as too rigid and insensitive. So with Nyāya in India, "the science of right reasoning", which flourished for a time but fell into disuse until revived under Western influence in the Nineteenth century.[15] But in general, philosophical thought in all developed cultures, including classical Greece, was conducted on the basis of natural logic, *dialektiké* broadly, and *analytiké,* formal logic, if it was used at all, was employed in the interest of sustaining religious belief, to refute those holding other views. In other words, it was a discipline with which to uphold beliefs or doctrines against heretical challenge, not unlike the character it has acquired today, though what is now defended is not a faith, believed to be socially valuable, but an intellectual stance and the presuppostions on which it depends for its continued authority.

*

Natural logic, as has been said, is infinitely more important in a vital sense than propositional logic, since it bears directly on life and the power to conduct it sensibly. Reason, indeed, was needed for appropriate action, and that is always a requirement. Reliability, understood as referring to that on which reliance can be placed, seems in a functional sense to have two distinctive meanings, a verbal and a vital, of which, though they may plainly be considered in harness, the last has clear priority. Implicitly to claim that truth, in the sense of what is the case when reference is to fact or reality, is necessarily verbal is to be blind to what it means in a broader sense, for instance, fitting into place, as in the expression "true to type". For its meaning then is that an action is appropriate in terms of changing conditions, when the test is evidently different from that applied in formal logic. For in that case it comprises conformity with real need in some form or another as that has to be met in the process of living. This has little to do with precision in a verbal sense, even when something is clearly definable, but presupposes a form of it in relation to reality, with the implication that failure to achieve an adequate rapport might well have serious consequences. Grave mistakes may not be made if their effects would be to throw the organism or society off balance, an outcome of much greater moment than falseness in propositions which is readily rectified. If such mistakes are made, as when clumsiness or ineptitude brings about an accident, the sensible aim is clearly to avoid their repetition, by admonition, critical comment applied to what was involved in the situation. Hasty words might well leave an indelible mark. At times men act unreasonably – irrational action is rare – for otherwise that term would not have application, just as errors may be made in mathematics and logic, for man's powers are far from perfect. But generally men act in a sane and reasonable manner, since if they failed to do so on an extended scale they could scarcely maintain their balance in life, which their power to reason sustains. Nor does this apply to the single man alone, for the balance of society depends on that of its members, or the vast majority of them, without whose co-operation it would soon fall into anarchy. It could be said that nature, without apparent intention, demands that the human species, whether by reason or instinct – the guiding principle in the lives of sentient beings generally – respects its implicit requirements, and even inflicts a penalty on any failure to meet them. Man, as a being gifted with the powers of reason, which can readily be abused, clearly had to develop some restraining principle, to ensure that his linguistic powers did not prove too unsettling in a social sense. And natural logic afforded a means of securing that what was said should not be too disturbing to the stability of society, of ensuring that men acted, given the powers of speech, or more deeply of self-consciousness, which is its correlative, in a tolerably reasonable manner.

Action may be guided by thought and thought itself by speech, and is normally so guided. For thought is always active in some form or another – since 'thoughtless' normally refers not to a lack of thought but to a failure to give due attention to what is required in the situation – but it is by no means always deliberative. For, apart from anything else, time may not be given for the full weighing of relevant factors, for leisurely contemplation of all the forces at work.[16] Today it is widely accepted that thought, exercised under influence both of memory and intentionality takes place on subconscious levels, and very much more extensively than on a conscious plane. Below the level of consciousness thought is persistently active to ensure that proper adjustment to external pressures is effectively made. And if we confine attention now to post-gestalten response, it is active in dim perception without prolonged deliberation, as the case with speaking, which is very largely spontaneous. It might then be called 'instinctive', all that that can be taken to mean is that man is conditioned by nature to act in certain ways when under stress or threat. Jumping back in front of a bus which is suddenly seen to appear may well be an instinctive act; but thought, marked by extreme rapidity, is implicit in it, with the evoking of memory of the effects that ensue from any failure to take appropriate counteraction. And though such thought may be dim and in process scarcely detectable, albeit that it can be recalled – "I admit that I was scared" – that it is overt in a rational sense can hardly be maintained. Further, that such response takes place in varying conditions, which may not always be threatening, is suitably considered. For then it has some affinity with the emergence of intuition, which is likewise sudden and effectively unexpected. Thought is always present, at least in waking life; but that it is then fully conscious and in that sense rationalizable is certainly not the case. In fact, if it were, without the relief that subconscious response affords, its presence would overwhelm us and render life intolerable so exhausting would it be. Nature protects us against this by rendering responsiveness predominantly subconscious, so that we may live with tolerable equanimity. All of which is said to show that many assumptions harboured under the dominant influence of intellectuality lead to mistaken ideas about the nature of normal response and so about the grounding of vital communication and of the needs it meets in relation to actualities.

Normally, natural logic is applied on a conscious plane, since it involves communication. For logic, however considered, relates to the use of language. It may accordingly be confused or aligned with formal logic, which claims to discipline all thought, or rather its expression, affecting to believe that that subsumes its practical application. But since that form of logic was a late development, that is an improper assumption, based on the idea that there is no communication which does not depend on laws, those that it projects as though they fully engaged every form of discourse. Of course, there are resemblances between these two forms of logic; but that is scarcely surprising since formal logic comprises a kind of crystallization of a long-developed means of ordering expression. Thus, when a drunk in a pub says "What do you mean by that", he is, though he may not know it, evoking what logicians call 'the doctrine of the terms', as if that were unique to the specific discipline, whereas, as is tolerably obvious, it has much deeper roots. He is not, of course, demanding a rigorous definition, but simply a clarification, or possibly a reason why such and such was said, which might then be put in other words which are clearer or less offensive. But many technical terms employed in formal logic reflect those implicit in natural logic, consistency, contradiction, quantification, negation, to mention the most obvious. The use of sentential connectives is plainly a feature of both; nor are obvious fallacies beyond the powers of detection of those who rely on natural logic. Even syllogistic arguments can readily be applied in discourse dependent on that, and then in rather more flexible forms than those in formal logic.[17] In fact, it was natural logic which first evolved such structures without pretence that they produced irrefragable answers, or any idea that those were readily attainable in directed discourse referred to the complex of becoming. These rules or structures, however, were implicit and not explicit, and the requirement that they should be made so is mistakenly projected. For *nómos,* an ideal or rational conception, can never properly engage *phýsis* or *natura,* real states of affairs that is. The laws of nature, for instance, only refer to clearly detectable regularities on macroscopic levels, underlying which there are, almost certainly, further 'laws' which are so subtle and so complex that they cannot be represented in such terms as those above. That early man made this distinction or indeed was conscious that there were laws at all – though the pattern of the seasons gave some index of them – is not to be contended, and such is the case with respect to other systematic structures. In so far, then, as there are discernible rules of grammar, their perfect formulation, taking into account the subtleties of speech, tone, accentuation, emphasis and so on, not to mention irony, has yet to be achieved. Like language, natural logic has implicit principles, which are in fact the source of the laws of formal logic, which, at considerable penalty, the loss of flexibility, renders them explicit. Some of them are obvious, negation for example, which indeed is primary, since its role is essentially critical. But consistency, though it appears to have a similar status, is a more subtle demand. For if it implies that the terms in a syllogistic structure should be absolutely constant, as in formal logic, something would be lost, a measure of plasticity. Rules there undoubtedly are, but to demand that they be formulated precisely is to remove what gives this discipline its capacity, much as if we were to demand that language should be shorn of all its colour and its richness in order to render it rigorous.

We could, as has been done elsewhere, get along quite comfortably in the absence of formal logic, and in fact most people normally do, since its forms are largely unknown to them unless they are very simple. Conversely, we could scarcely survive to conduct our lives in an orderly manner or to have assurance of balance in society without recourse to natural logic. Its neglect in favour of a passion for rigour seems to be one of the causes of a failure to understand what really conditions life. If, then, a deeper study of its potentiality is a task that falls to scholars, that is not academic in the sense of attempts to *explain* its form, but one undertaken in order better to understand the nature of response to external pressures. For that is cognitive only in a limited sense, so that concentration on knowing even falsifies ideas with respect to what is presented, which can never be grasped as it is for as long as we cling uncritically to the presuppositions that formal logic adopts. Natural logic is a power with which all men are gifted in order to secure that expression referred to contact with external reality shall be tolerably free from factors that tend to confuse. Any attempt to improve on it, as distinct from grasping what constitutes its potency, is pretentious and uncalled for, as pointless as it would be to try to control the weather, which means changing it in one place at the expense of another, since it is a vast interrelative complex. No, the interest is to understand how, as an aspect of language, natural logic relates to reality, as a means of aiding men to grapple with conditions as beings bound together in the network of society. For that relation can never be grasped through cognitive approaches, which cannot reach beyond particularized phenomena generalized in the intellect to produce the logical universal, which is purely ideal. It was evolved to serve quite a different purpose from that of explanation, to meet a vital need that is, which is what it still serves on a linguistic plane. The analysts studied more limited means through linguistic enquiry; but since their approach was rational, analytic that is, they were powerless to grasp what language really referred to: reciprocal requirement to adapt to pressures brought to bear by nature and society, to the second of which, even perhaps the first, men bore a binding responsibility. The unhappy dichotomy between mind, the psychic, and matter, nature or the physical – though 'matter' is a very crude term with which to refer to the second – has to be rejected, since natural logic refers to these external pressures, to the real conditions under which life is actually lived and to which language in depth relates. The problem is then to attain to a better understanding of what these conditions comprise; and, by turning to a means that allows of a deeper entry, philosophy is presented with a task which is other than that of a cognitively oriented science. That may be metaphysical, and its ontological bearing is sufficiently evident. But, irrespective of what it is called, its point is to achieve a better understanding of what really counts in life.

It is not that natural logic affords an entirely dependable instrument, since it can plainly be misused, just as formal logic can. However, it has latent powers which have yet to be explored with a meaningful end in view. If it then presents possibilities and could reasonably be adopted to allow of a more penetrant approach, it would be absurd to dismiss it because it does not produce conclusive, absolute answers, as if those alone were valid. What is needed are better answers to real as opposed to verbal problems; or more precisely, more sensitive means – for the end is not positive explanation but a measure of control over public statement – of restraining inept or confusing projections referred to vital interests. It is of some importance, then, that natural logic be recognized as referring to action or expression related to it in the external world and not to ideal projections which do not touch it at all unless with misrepresentation. Difficult though it may be, then, to relinquish a tradition in which language is used abstractly to produce apparent certitude, truth which is irrefutable, an effort must be made to extend received approaches in order that real problems may be given deeper attention. Such problems are normally met through the deployment of natural language, on which natural logic acts as a control, if it was not the basis on which it was built as a structure. And if it is then presumed, since it is other than rationalistic, to be for that reason unreliable, that, if just, implies that its weaknesses must be rectified, but not, of course, at sacrifice of its peculiar virtue, its invaluable flexibility. However, if those can only be seen in terms of a failure to be veridical, the point of giving thought to it and to what it might achieve, has been missed completely. For that is not to serve the traditional end in philosophy, the eliciting of truth, in abstract form essentially. It is, as has been said, more fully to extend our powers of understanding what is really of moment in life.

*

Formal logic has always, or at least from Roman times, enjoyed an immense prestige, even though that involved the loss of a needed flexibility in directed discourse, because it afforded a guarantee of rigour and perspicuity in certain forms of enquiry. That it ensures that inferences are valid is clearly valuable, for at times there is a requirement for absolute precision, for unequivocal statement with regard to intention and for formulations on which there can be total agreement. And whether such statements, as these are true with respect to external reality is even beside the point; that they are firm and consistent gives them the needed authority. It is often contended, then, that in want of this assurance there would be a weakening of confidence in authority and doubt about its justice, indeed a decay of quality in fields in which the greatest degree of exactitude constitutes the demand, in science, politics, law and balanced argument generally. It is to be questioned, however, how far this requirement extends and how far it is satisfied by formal logic alone, as if other forms of argument played no significant part in it. Its claim on this count, which constitutes the warrant for its prestige, is seldom really challenged, because it has insisted on and propagated the notion that there is no apparent alternative which affords an adequate discipline.[18] Students have been persuaded that this is the manner of reasoning that all responsible persons are obliged to adopt and are never told the real reasons why logicians are so attached to it and make such claims as these. But when those are expressed by logicians, speaking rather more openly in further justification of the sublimity of their discipline, questions are fairly raised. Thus, that formal logic establishes "a relation of personality to the world at large" or that it "brings the mind to self-consciousness", a view at one time favoured as if that were unique to it, are so pretentious as claims that they cannot be taken seriously. Further, that it affords great delight to its devotees "by giving them liberation from the life of instinct", in other words from the pressures that bear on ordinary life – in Jasper's language 'contingencies' – is an even vicious idea, for, if thought is to be responsible, it is precisely those to which it should be turned. The attempt indeed to attain to detachment from the world, to be strictly idealistic, is a very dubious aim and, from a realistic standpoint, amounts to a condemnation, for vital issues are disregarded.

Perhaps this is too scathing; but while such views are held and even regarded as admirable, grave consequences ensue. The test of value, surely, is some contribution to life as it is actually lived in the social context in which all men are involved, and not in the delight of an élitist individual who positively glories in his indifference to that interest. If formal logic comprises a proven means of ensuring that certain inferences, judgments or conclusions are valid beyond all doubt, that is acceptable as a claim only within the limits of that as a requirement. And if this links it to mathematics, which has its ultimate warrant in its practical application, that is a point in its favour. Whether this carries over into science is more doubtful, since what that aims to achieve is something rather different, for the test it applies is not truth but successful experimentation. Moreover, its findings, unlike those purporting to be absolute, are regarded as contingent, subject to revision in the light of further discoveries. "A hypothesis", it has been said, "is sometimes very fruitful without being correct", or again, yet more decisively, "In science the primary duty of ideas is to be fruitful...even more than true".[19] Schiller even went so far as openly to declare that: "Among the obstacles to scientific progress a high place must certainly be assigned to the analysis of scientific procedures, in accordance with its own prejudices".[20] If reasoning is used in science, then, as it plainly is, it must have some other form than that of formal logic. Trial-and-error is not a procedure derived from that in which the aim is a static conclusiveness; for, though experimentation may give the answer sought, it is a dynamic process rather more nearly related to that adopted in artistry, in the build-up of compositions. It can scarcely be doubted, therefore, that since science and other disciplines proceed in an orderly manner, with a nod at best in the direction of formal logic, it is natural logic that they deploy and reliably in the main.

If by logic is meant "a clear, accurate and orderly intellectual procedure",[21] that fairly covers all its forms, notably as its role is essentially critical. However, if the word so defined is presumed to apply uniquely to formal logic, not only is its reference confined to a very narrow sphere but the effect of such a restriction is clearly to delimit the reach of any other procedure. If science, law and other forms of investigation into matters of real significance were tied to formal logic and could not reach beyond it, their work, as scientists have declared, would be gravely inhibited. In practice, both have been unwilling to accept this limitation and have over time developed more appropriate procedures which are better adopted to the problems they confront. Accordingly, to contend that they should be bound within the strait jacket of propositional logic or comply with its presuppositional set is unwarranted as a demand. But neither, of course, does any such thing, holding very properly that the methods or modes of procedure developed and refined to meet continually changing conditions do not call for modifications of a type that would act as a brake on their powers to deal with their specific problems. If natural logic affords the discipline they need, or rather grounds the several procedures which experience shows to be needed in these activities, that is as it may be. For the present concern is not to make claims to universality, since to intervene in other fields without deep understanding of the problems that have to be met would even be impertinent. It is to rescue another interest from the grip that at present confines it to rigid verbal abstractions and blocks any latent power to attend to what has vital significance, with which thought such as this is concerned. Because of this circumscription, philosophy has not like other forms of enquiry given serious thought to the powers latent in natural logic, as a consequence of which its contribution has been minimal. Debate on what earlier thinkers might have said or meant, which is what hermeneutics amounts to, may be very scholarly, and even at times illuminate ideas on what they discussed. In the main, however, that has little bearing on the problems with which society is confronted today, which differ in many features from those that these thinkers had to deal with in the societies of their times, in response to which they applied imaginative thought in a sufficiently disciplined manner. Their problems took various forms, ethical, political, religious and scientific, of which the last is of special interest, since, though initially bound to formal logic, science became mature enough to sever its links with a rationalistic philosophy.

Philosophers, however, have had difficulty in accepting that an escape from a logocentric embrace was possible, even needed, and have persisted in the belief that their role was cognitive or alethic, epistemic in effect or quasi-psychological with the philosophy of mind, however limited and removed from vital interests were the findings they projected. Now it should be clear, if only with obligation to accept a holistic ontology, that as a discipline philosophy is called upon to undertake quite a different task. That might broadly be defined as general evaluation referred to the actual process of living, which is dynamic and interrelative. And that as a problem will not be met by deploying methods devised to serve cognitive enquiry, nor certainly by the restrictive and delimiting form of it, propositional logic. It so seems that it must turn to evolving another approach, that is, to developing natural logic in a manner apt to meet these problems peculiar to it, specifically to discipline statements referred to relations in the complex of becoming. This doubtless presents a task of formidable dimensions, initially methodological, since a disciplined procedure is a preliminary requirement if this role is to be accepted. Then, the problem is to consider man's relation to reality and through that to his fellow men, bearing in mind that that is more than cognitive or material, a relation to phenomena, which is the field of science not that of a meaningful philosophy. For that refers to deeper needs, which have latterly been neglected or seen in a rather restricted sense as bound to certain acceptances which are not universal but tied to various faiths. But that, as a further interest, is not the concern of the present study, the burden of which is confined to an appropriate procedure, discoverable conceivably through forms of natural logic, a deeper understanding of its latent powers.

Chapter Three

The Two Further Forms of Logic

Logic of whatever form exists to distinguish between acceptable and erroneous answers, and that is its *raison d'être* in respect of which all else is subsidiary. As contrasted with formal logic, natural logic may reach such conclusions in less precise and rigorous forms and may accordingly be prepared to accede that in many, indeed in most cases considered, answers cannot be indisputably true. It so, as circumstances impose it, accepts that what seems to be the best answer that can be found in awareness that perfect answers are not normally available. But for quality much depends on how important it is that conclusions drawn shall be suited to the occasion when that demands a measure of certainty and the need to eliminate serious doubt. Both logics are, however, intent on eliciting answers appropriate to the need envisaged, one on a strictly formal plane, the other in relation to problems presented in actual living conditions. In the last case it may happen that an ideal answer is simply not available – though attempts to reach it are always properly made – and that is a point that has clearly to be recognized lest a desire to attain to precision actually leads to improper conclusions, those which do not really meet the situation and so in effect are false. Otherwise said, it is wisely accepted that certain answers, however confidently projected in the abstract, simply will not do in practice, so that the need for rethinking arises whenever doubtful answers, doubtful because they may be impolitic, can be exposed on that or any other score. Another approach must be adopted to ensure that such answers are not permitted to stand. For, though they may be perfect in an abstract sense, they fail to take what is apparently operative properly or fully into account. No final answers may then be established, but circumstances will have been considered, doubtless to complicate the issue but to reduce any likelihood that decisions may be resisted because they are too arbitrary and in that sense insensitive.

Without elaborating on its form at once, the Socratic Method is of interest in this connection in that it shows that logic as a disciplinary procedure can have other than the aim of eliciting final truth when referred to vital interests, which he saw was not available in respect of what they really represented. In other words, logic has two significant purposes, in part in play against each other, significant in terms of what may be achieved when real issues are considered. Such ends may broadly be distinguished as the *positive and negative aspects of application,* which, as will be shown, have quite distinctive characteristics. At once this may seem obvious, since assertion and denial are manifestly different when seen as establishing truth claims or faulting findings that fail to do so. But when their full capacities are more deeply considered and when the idea that adequate answers must always be affirmative is discounted as delimiting, it will be seen that this simple differentiation does not properly meet the involvement. For, from being no more than ancillary to a veridical or alethic end, negation has a potential that asseveration lacks, which is overlooked or obscured when the only acceptable terminus is held to be the eliciting of irrefragable truth, as if negation were but a stage on the way to that consummation. With this as a belief, almost an act of faith in rationalistic philosophy, the real difference between these two modes of approach, seen in terms of potency, has largely been neglected, misconstrued or blurred with effective concentration on finding perfect answers that leave no room for doubt. Regarded as no more than a means to an end, negation is without independent meaning and is devoid of a parallel status, to the point that, taken in itself, in its sceptical form that is, negation is even resisted as if it constituted a threat to the achievement of that sublime aim.

This prejudice is exemplified when *aporía,* interpreted as failure to reach conclusive answers, is applied to Socrates' procedure,[1] which must now be considered more fully. So far, then, from aspiring to find conclusive answers and apparently failing to do so, Socrates rather recognized that in respect of the interests with which he was concerned those were not attainable. It was not doubt or uncertainty that characterized his thinking, although his indulgence in irony may well give such an impression of it. It was awareness of the limitations imposed on the categorizing intellect whenever it tried to engage the complex interrelations of socialized involvement, or for that matter, though that was not his specific interest, any interrelative or holistic manifold. False projections could be checked and were so to ensure that, by refusal to accept them, the interest really at issue was protected against mistaken ideas about it. For when those were shown to involve incorrect definitions, the integrity of what was essentially under review was safeguarded, so to say, from any misconstrual, so that further ideas about it, although they could not be stated precisely, were refined in the sense that suggestions made in respect of its character were tentative only and could not pretend to be more. Then, with the slightest doubt, they were themselves to be dismissed, thereby further to tighten the protective ring of negations about what could not be defined precisely. Although this is implicit rather than explicit in Socrates' approach which did not pass beyond negation, something other than assertoric reasoning was held to be the manner in which realities were to be engaged; and further that suggestion rather than claims to truth was a more fitting and sensitive entry. Sensitivity, schooled by meaningful negation rather than strict rationality was, by implication, put forward as the means appropriate for dealing justly with vital or interrelative issues. This may not be acceptable to those labouring under the difficulty of distinguishing between the phenomenal and the real, who appear to believe that, by dint of application, truths about all relations whatsoever will eventually be found. But as referred to externals such truths are certainly limited, if, as truths in strict sense, they are to be found at all. For relations in reality are too complex, transient, volatile to allow of representation in any ideal form, too fluid to be expressed in any effectively static or immutable truth claim, unless, for reasons to be discussed, that should be by deployment of negation. If then we aim to speak about conditioning realities, events that really bear on life, without misrepresentation or implicit ambiguity, we must realize, as did

Socrates, that another, a more sensitive approach must be developed, that another means of using the reasoning powers that we have must be given closer attention. For that, though it may not produce conclusive answers or result in attaining finality, will at least delimit misconstrual of what is not ideal but real, takes place, that is, in actuality. This point must be considered in very much greater depth, and the power that lies in negation, as a critical or delimiting instrument with a more extensive reach, must be studied much more closely than it has been hitherto, for the need to refine approaches as philosophy turns to deal with real problems is a matter of some urgency.

To gather the full bearing of this it is requisite to give more careful thought to the essential difference between these two modes of approach, when 'essential' means rather more than what is immediately obvious, that qualifying labels are patently antithetical. For, when they are thought of separately and not as indissolubly linked, that difference must be seen as fundamentally functional. and by 'functional' is meant what they are potent to achieve when applied to problems presented, or better, what they accomplish as contributions to meeting human needs. This means giving keener attention to a pertinent question, all too seldom examined: What is logic deployed to do? Traditionally, though that idea of it in fullness is post-classical, it has been to establish or elicit absolute truth, a consequence of which has been to confine it to abstractions.[2] For, when aligned with knowledge, truth ceases, properly speaking, to have a similar meaning and should not be carried over into science as if it had. And this form of confusion, which still bedevils modern thinking, as in the persistence of unqualified empiricism, in the guise of logical atomism notably, has the effect of falsifying ideas about its capacity, to delimit it unduly, so that it remains ideal and no more and powerless therefore to engage real or vital problems.

Observing, then, that this was not, at least in a modern sense, the accepted idea of its employment in antiquity, it is of interest to note that Aristotle, followed by the Stoics, showed interest in not one but three forms of logic: *analytiké, dialektiké* and, as a practical tool, *rhetoriké,* for use in certain types of discussion. Of these, the first alone is exclusively ideal, for the others relate to external events or to the manner of dealing with them. It is curious, then, that the first is projected as the heart of philosophy when it is the second that philosophers, with others concerned with solving problems, employ whenever they engage in directed argument, in which negation used in a critical capacity plainly plays an important part, as, for instance, in trial-and-error, in the shooting down of proposals. Indeed, if a statement bears on life, it is of plain importance that it should be subjected to proper critical test, lest it be inapt and so confusing. For all its vaunted claims, then, to elicit truth as the end, it is not in analytic but in dialectic form that logic is used in normal discourse, primarily to criticize projections too confidently put forward as solutions to given problems. Conclusive answers are far to seek; and, unless in the simplest forms, which scarcely call for argument, those supposed to be so are seldom permitted to stand as too exact to meet the situation. Conclusive answers are far to see; for, as the history of philosophy shows, every development in it, whether metaphysical, ethical or even logical, has been rejected as limited or flawed for some reason or another. When reference is to capacity, then, truth takes second place to what amounts to falsification. And indeed, as one studies texts which deal with the nature of philosophy – *What philosophy is?* – or in parallel *What philosophy does?*[3] – the impression one receives is that the issues with which it is concerned remain unsettled, unresolved, and admit of no final answers because none can entirely escape the consequences of determined critical attack. This is not to deny that discussion of some of the issues debated has evident value. But it is to suggest that, though philosophy claims to be a search for truth, it seems rather to be a field in which projections are largely open to question because no finality is attainable. To see logic, then, as the key to finding irrefragable answers is to harbour a somewhat limited idea of its function, when, even within itself, as theoretical in distinction from pragmatic, directed discourse, its role is rather that of a critical discipline, active persistently in the sense that truth, with claims to be indisputable, is invariably put to question.

Granted that this is not improper as a finding, ideas on the role of logic are due for some revision, notably as logic constitutes an organon devised for and intended to serve some fruitful and meaningful purpose. What purpose that most fruitfully is then the point at issue. If it is to elicit absolute truth and no more, logic has not been very productive, largely because such truths are seldom to be found unless in symbolic forms, in which case they are from a practical standpoint effectively without meaning since they have little relation to life or to real needs. It should rather, it seems, be seen as an instrument devised to ensure that what is said with respect to vital issues shall not be out of order. For in that capacity it serves a meaningful end in that statements which are given publicity can, if there is need for this, be shown to be flawed as inconsistent or as disregarding what is relevant in conditions.[4] Of course, it is far from easy to detect mistakes in what is publicly said, when prejudice intervenes and when divergent ideas about requirements to be met are sincerely entertained. But the mere attempt to do so is of value to society, which is warned, if nothing more, that certain adverse consequences may follow if some policy is permitted to be adopted without question. In the clamour and complexity of comment in modern society, in politics, law, economics, education and even medicine, the philosopher is in a quandary in that his experience is limited, so that on many of these issues he can only speak as an amateur, unless he claims that his specific discipline is unique in engaging all human interests, which is so pretentious an idea that it is likely to bring philosophy into contempt. His role is philosophical, which means that the philosopher is concerned not with highly specialized controversial issues in other departments of life, but with the attitudes people adopt in respect of general life values. Thus, attitudes towards nature, with which men must come to terms, or in respect of the values that they most sanely accept, which bears on the presuppositions that they are inclined to harbour, normally without careful thought about them, are matters on which philosophers may speak with a certain authority, checked themselves by the critical powers, developed through training in logic, in their specific discipline. And it is tolerably obvious that on matters such as these there is a very real need for mature and balanced thinking, as for disciplined critical comment. That postures, some of which are certainly disruptive, can be changed at once is not a serious contention. But the long term task of philosophy is to show that certain views are mistaken or will have adverse effects; and, with that as the aim, gradually to modify those attitudes that tend to be destructive of social balance and refinement. In short, it is a critical power, applied first to mistaken ideas in philosophy itself – with reference especially to presuppositions and priorities – and then, with the reduction of those, to proceed to some agreement, with which alone an influence can be exerted on unhappy tendencies in a disturbed society.

It may be thought that this is an over-ambitious programme, albeit that it affords a meaningful role for philosophy, now uncertain of its purpose and in what its contribution to society consists. For, to put it bluntly, debate on problems in formal logic has no social bearing whatever and very doubtfully aids the work of scientists or statesmen. Neither deals in absolute truths, but necessarily with the real conditions obtaining in nature and civil society. But, as this matter of purpose is somewhat controversial, even one of opinion or preferential inclination, it is better not to stress it. The salient point, however, is not seriously to be questioned: that it is by means of the critical powers latent in negation which philosophy has at its disposal that it may make a contribution of a form of which society is in need. There is nothing unduly pretentious in this – Searle's finding notwithstanding – which relates to thought on traditional problems, logical or procedural, ontological and ethical. What the first now presumes is some rethinking on the methods to be adopted to deal with the second, which appears to be holistic and so does not really lend itself to ratiocinative or cognitive procedures once becoming is accepted as the form of what is confronted. Meanwhile, without sound ideas on what is appropriate in the second, which refers essentially to attitudes towards nature, seen as other than domination, thought about the third cannot properly begin. For it is as a mode of nature, in and through which he acts, that man relates himself to other human beings.

It is not positive logic, then, that is wisely or justly applied to problems such as these. It is a critical power, negation, turned to what is now outdated: the idea that they can be met by recourse alone to strict rationalistic procedures. For they are in no just sense ideal, matters for the subject as the knowing self or as one affecting detachment, since they call for a kind of involvement, involvement of some sort with what has to be confronted, not by a subject alone but by men in general. Indeed, such problems are rather real, in that they relate to externals, to what is confronted in actuality, that is, to the conditions that men must face, as sentient being enmeshed in the process of becoming. Man is endowed with the power to reason, by means of which he is able to gather a measure of knowledge and so in part, no more, to control the world about him. He can also cultivate wisdom, aligned to sensitivity, to reasoning as opposed to ratiocination, the first a natural gift which, if not corrupted, is potentially common to all men. It is something then that relates to quite other interests, those that appertain to life, directly and not obliquely. Those cannot be dealt with ideally, in positive, cognitive terms, simply because they are not in depth detectable, do not have cognizable forms. The upshot is that the powers latent in negation, which does not produce propositional truth but at best determination, have to be developed, lest such important matters as these either go by default or are treated in a manner that is inept and misrepresents them. It is then those powers to which attention will now be given, first to pit them against ideas of what procedure should be adopted in conventional terms and then to consider, provisionally, the forms they might take to render them really fruitful and, as requisite, disciplined. If ideas on the last are as yet but tentative, and they could scarcely be more on first consideration, the interest is then to submit them to critical review. For the only certain conclusion when limits have been shown is that there is an obligation to give thought to a fitting alternative. But further attention must first be paid to the form of these limitations, if only to justify doubt about their reach and their capacity. For the real gravamen against them is not so much their narrowness, which would not be injurious were it not for claims to universality. It is the restrictions they impose, by attitudes towards it, on the development of more flexible and penetrating thinking.

*

Positive, alethic or veridical logic, which is either all that logic as a discipline comprises or an aspect of it viewed in broader terms, aims to establish immutable, irrefragable truth, to show that justified truth claims are demonstrably irrefutable. Inasmuch as philosophy is defined as 'the pursuit of truth', as if that were its only purpose, it plainly rests on logic of this positive form, to which, in principle at least, it is held in a grip that cannot, it seems, be broken without ceasing to be 'philosophy'. And if it was once concerned with truth, or rather more deeply with wisdom, which is certainly not the same thing, though it came to be considered so, loosely, in later times, this is best understood if truth is taken to have two meanings, as something either intuitively or rationalistically gathered, for the first might relate to wisdom, the *sophía* of antiquity.[5] Whether, then, this rational view of philosophy's role, which is almost unique to the West, was held in earlier classical times is certainly open to question. Doubtless, it was Plato's view, although questionably that of Socrates, whose thinking was more sceptical and even presumed a denial that truth, as referred to vital relations, was to be discovered. But by an accident of history, whereas the works of the first and many of his successors, have survived in considerable quantity, those of an opposing school are but sparsely represented in surviving documentation, to give a rather unbalanced view of thought in classical antiquity. This division of stances appears to go back to a divergence of view between two early thinkers, Heraclitus of Ephesus, who elected for Becoming, and Parmenides of Elea, who laid the stress on Being, as the form of what was confronted, the actual, external reality. The first, as a dynamic, indivisible, interelative, indeed holistic complex is not in strictness knowable, if for no other reason than that it cannot be objectified. The second, seen as static, uniform, regular in action and obeying projected laws, is in principle cognizable, in which sense it refers to the phenomenal world as opposed to that of external reality. That the last was not, insights notwithstanding, distinguished clearly at that time is scarcely odd when it is not entirely so today, by those who believe that knowledge refers directly to reality.[6] Without elaboration, then, though this matter seems to merit very much closer attention, there is reason to suppose that these two schools continued to face each other throughout the classical age, to constitute the *lógos* as opposed to what might fairly be called the *alétheia* doctrine. For the first is discernable surely in the thinking of the Sophists – primarily condemned by Plato for that reason – as in that of the early Sceptics, and later in the thought of the Cyrenaics and the Epicureans. It is echoed again by the Pyrrhonists and certain Academics, Carneades and his school; and is further to be found in the approach of Posidonius, who, plainly under influence of the *lógos* doctrine, was sceptical of the reach of ratiocination and espoused what might be deemed to be a holistic ontology. Hence, to hold that 'the pursuit of truth' was the characteristic interest in classical philosophy, is evidently to harbour a rather limited view of it.

It only became the sole end of thought with the rise of subjectivity and with it the movement towards personalized religions in the late Republic and early Imperial times, when resurgent faith could not tolerate sceptical doubt and indeed demanded a *credo,* a truth that was indisputable, to question which was heresy. And thus the cult of the knowable, or truth in an unequivocal form, dominated thought throughout the following centuries. Sceptical protest, in either the form of philosophical doubt or of religious mysticism,[7] was not entirely absent even in scholastic times, to reflect the *lógos* doctrine in some form or another. Its most interesting advocate was quite certainly Bruno, who paid for his boldness with his life. Thereafter, however, that stance became increasingly common, though always strongly resisted by the reigning establishment which continued to hold the cards, wary, even fearful, of this sceptical challenge with a dim suspicion that it could perhaps be right, thereby to undermine all that it held dear. The curious point is, then, that when thought became more secular in the later Renaissance, this demand or passion for truth was carried over into studies of natural events, which were presumed, at least by conventional thinkers, to be rationalizable or cognizable, met by truth claims that is to say, in a not dissimilar manner. But scientists, who were less involved with that alethic tradition, recognised that their findings were contingent or revisable, other that is, than true in a logical sense. However, without pursuing this point further at once, it suffices to note that the cult of truth, despite a failure to find it except in very limited forms, has persisted to this day, with a peculiar upsurge in the present century. Philosophy is held to be 'the pursuit of truth', and thus is rendered powerless properly to deal with issues to which that interest does not and cannot apply.

Jaspers held that there *was* a truth about reality, but in the nature of the case it could not be known. If then, in some sense, truth refers to the phenomenal world, which as strict it doubtfully does, it certainly cannot pass beyond the veil that that imposes.[8] Truth, or rather absolute truth, is not to be discovered when thought is turned to deep or meaningful problems – those of man's relation to reality, for instance – so that, if not quite empty, it is a narrow and limited interest. Perhaps, to give a point, there are occasions when indubitable truth can be found in respect of actual conditions. But even that is questionable if the truth discovered is abstract or symbolic, strictly propositional, when meaningful relations refer to actualities, which are scarcely true or false as opposed to fitting or unfitting from a psychophysical or a social standpoint. Finding fault in arguments is a rather different matter, since that does not elicit truth but merely shows that it has *not* been attained in discourse as that was referential. But failure to find perfect answers, truths that are truly beyond dispute, is scarcely very surprising when discourse to be meaningful is referred externally, to the complex of events which have then to be engaged. And, as that is so, it brings up a further point. Whenever we objectify, we isolate an instance taken to be monadic – torn from its context so to say as strictly to be defined, an act that can only be done when it constitutes a unit. But that is not the characteristic either of impression or of normal reaction to it, which is fluid and interrelative and has to be gathered accordingly. There can for positive logic, then, only be one truth in respect of any presentation. For were there two or more – the very idea is untenable – claims would be open to question, since none would have real standing. The truth admits of no other, no alternative answer, for once that was projected, truth would cease to have character that it purports to have, to be unique and indisputable. Degrees of truth cannot present themselves as absolutes.

Though truth is presumed to refer not only to propositions but also to ideas, to factual statements or findings, to include them is to accept a very loose use of the term,[9] which deprives it of its prestige as presenting absolute answers. For any statement, then, which is not patently false, is placed on a par with one which is logically established. Positive logic either refers, in a rather equivocal sense, to externals real or phenomenal, or it is strictly abstract and confined to propositions, which are other than proposals tentatively projected. It cannot be both and make the claims to precision that it does. As Church observed in support of the second of these meanings of logical truth: "Truth as predicated of ideas today is normally restricted to those that are propositional in nature",[10] though 'normally' seems to imply that it could have other meanings, which surely cannot be the case with the demand for absolute rigour. The Correspondence Theory of truth, as contrasted with that of Coherence, interpreted as consistency, presumes that ideas in the intellect relate without reservation to external states of affairs, 'facts' as is commonly said. But 'fact' is an ambiguous term, since it has two meanings: what has real existence, is done so to say by nature – the basic meaning of *factum* – and an idea or concept of that entertained by the intellect. If either of these relate to findings in positive logic, which itself is open to question, that that word passes from one to the other in a very uncritical manner cannot redound to logic's credit. Again logicians cannot in decency have it both ways: to elicit absolute truth and to refer externally, without indulgence, it would seem, in illicit equivocation. Truth in positive logic means that about which no doubt can possibly be conceived, when such findings, for example, as *cogito ergo sum* may fairly be shown to be limited, in the sense that *sentio* is evidently deeper and relates to all sentient beings, or certainly to those endowed with the gift of self-consciousness. But, then, if the only end is cognitive, deeper involvement scarcely counts. What positive logic asserts as a truth is perhaps, as Wittgenstein said, a 'tautology' and no more; and in any case it is certainly more than a verbal relation, based on the idea that words define precisely. For, retaining its rigour, it can only refer to relations between clear concepts entertained by the intellect, that is, to abstract propositions about strictly formal relationships. Properly, despite Leibniz, there are no 'truths of fact', but only 'truths of reason'; and the Correspondence Theory is one that strict logicians should never allow to refer to what they in seriousness are doing. In practice, however, 'truth' is used, even when limited to their sphere, in a very ambiguous way. For, if logic purports to refer, other than symbolically, 'appropriate' or 'valid' are terms that better befit what is then projected.

Logic as here defined has one and one end only: namely to state a truth which in principle stands for all time. If then it purports to refer in that sense, difficulty arises, as apart from this aspiration to elicit definitive truth. For to be absolutely true, a statement when it refers is tied to the adverb 'now'. That 'grass is green', for instance, is true in a strict sense only in certain present conditions. For when it is dry or scorched or otherwise changes colour with the changing of the seasons or has naturally other colours, this statement will not stand as an immutable finding, quite apart from the question as to whether green as a term refers to one shade only. But perhaps we may have taken a rather unfair example, which might better have been the familiar 'man is mortal', for he has certainly been so up to the present time. Allowing that projection into an unknown future is permissible in this case, that constitutes a truth that appears to stand for all time. And doubtless there are others which are effectively indisputable. In metaphysics, then, concerned with other than what is physical, claims are often made that what concerns it is the perennial, which well may be the case for rather limited findings – as that every event has a cause, or more accurately causes,[11] or other forms of what are commonly called 'first principles'. Those, however, are very few and have validity only when their reference is to that which cannot be conceived as having any other form – that reality is, for instance, an interrelative complex, at least when seen in itself and not viewed idealistically by the objectifying intellect, intent, as all-embracing, to give it rational form. Metaphysical findings, in short, if this is the form that they take, tell us little more than what we already know or accept with a little thought. But further, truth in such forms, though supported by formal logic, is far from certainly attained unless what is said is obvious, and has always been subject to question by sceptics dubious of its claims.

As to whether metaphysics is not unduly dogmatic, as Kant believed it to be, this is fairly said in extenuation: that it is only when it makes no pretence to project categorical truths and is willing to admit that it is simply speculative, that this critique ceases to apply. In freer forms it undoubtedly enriches our understanding. For certainly, if thought is confined strictly to the physical, crudely aligned with the natural, which is inclusive of everything, the psychical and the spiritual, it is gravely impoverished. It is only, then, when it, as assertoric, is tied to strict formal logic, that questions are properly raised, specifically with respect to the proper grounding of ethics, its ontological base, since the promotion of value in some form or another is the end of all enquiry, ultimately directed towards *human* interrelationships. The final justification for metaphysics, accordingly, lies in refining ideas about the form of what is confronted by men when they face reality, which is not in strict sense cognizable since it has more than a physical character.[12] In this sense ontology performs an important function, since it is concerned with apt presuppositions, assumptions, that is, about what is not known but which have nonetheless to be made – perhaps in different forms with regard to what is under review[13] – as the ground on which meaningful discourse must rest. No ethics, indeed no science, can be developed without reasonable assumptions, sensible ideas of what is confronted in response, and so conditions all action, and thought, in a fundamental manner. Nature is the determinant, not some intellectual principle.

There is always a certain tension, then, present in philosophy with respect to the role it performs. Is it to establish truth, which cannot but confine it to the sphere of abstractions, or is it to develop disciplined speculation – not then to further knowledge, which is the role of science, but to deepen understanding on what conditions human life? If absolute, irrefragable truth, sustained by recourse to strict logic, is regarded as its criterion, it has a restricted field and takes second place to science, with which it cannot compete if that is all it can offer as knowledge. Presumed to have higher status because it refers to first principles, which were surely discovered hundreds of years ago, so that little more can now be said about them, philosophy now makes desperate attempts to provide itself with a role that differs from that of science, one which is still significant. And hence it is now intent on developing refinements in the sphere off verbal abstractions – though these are of little interest to others than themselves – thereby in effect to remove itself from any vital concerns. But a deeper understanding of those, which is roughly what 'wisdom' means, demands that this exclusive preoccupation with formulae be modified or abandoned, and that it is clearly recognized that more sensitive approaches have to be adopted; or otherwise said, that procedures cannot, without restriction, be exclusively rationalistic.

When Bradley spoke of 'degrees of truth', he was, from the standpoint of formal logic, indulging sceptical thinking. His Absolute was not the Absolute of Hegel, but had quite a different character. For it was not idealistic and linked to the slippery notion of *Geist,* but rather referred to reality, to what was at that time given the name 'ultimate reality' – an almost forgotten expression. Indeed, he was thinking in what would now be called 'holistic' terms; and in as far as truth, when more than an intellectual construct, refers to external reality, he recognized that it could never be conclusive – an idea, incidentally, that echoes Leibniz's *vraisemblance.* "What exists in the world", he said, "has external relations", other, that is, than those developed in the intellect. "Every idea", he also said, "is at last referred to reality", that is, to the whole, his Absolute, to the underlying complex of dynamic becoming. Hence, if truth is claimed for any statement made about it, that 'truth' is necessarily "relative and imperfect".[14] And this applies not only to truth claims about reality, but also to those referring to the phenomenal world, which is as much a complex though we are aware of aspects of it. For when objectification is applied to what is presented, initially in impression, what is received or recorded involves a measure of exclusion. Further, if what is given is given to 'dim perception', which is primarily impressional, it is surely the case that impressions are wider in their embrace – as tacit knowledge indicates – than are any effects recorded in 'clear perception', which are essentially unitary.[15] The upshot is that truth, in the only form in which it is justly regarded as absolute, is and cannot but be restricted to abstractions. Indeed, if truth must be absolute, it is necessarily limited, whereas, if its meaning were wider, as with degrees of truth, that notion of it would be replaced, complemented perhaps, by the idea that it could reasonably be relative. If then, that reading of truth challenges, undermines indeed, the basic presupposition on which formal logic rests, that is less of a disaster than might be supposed. For that opens up possibilities of discussing real relations with a measure of flexibility.[16] Bradley, allowing absolute truth to be one of its degrees, was referring truth to states of external reality, with the suggestion, for which 'truth' may not be the happiest term, that ideas about real relations could be *reasonably* expressed; and, as a further point, on which he did not speak, subjected to critique in a sufficiently disciplined manner.

Leaving that for the moment, however, this last point has to be made. That the difficulty in pinning down the proper scope of the discipline referred to expression, logic, to be distinguished from others such as experimentation, springs from the loose use of terms. It cannot be doubted that 'positive' is the antithesis of 'negative' and 'assertion' of 'denial', so that as contrasted terms these are wholly warranted. But confusion clearly arises with respect to the meaning of 'truth', which is regarded both as absolute, pure and wholly independent of ordinary contingencies, and as referential, that is, as referring to what is presented externally and so is indeed contingent. Perhaps we should use another word to designate the second, or better add qualifications to distinguish findings *rationally* elicited from those that are rather *reasonable,*[17] which do not claim to be perfect but 'valid' in conditions – though, like several other terms, that has been purloined to refer only to propositions. But the need for distinction is evident. For, for as long as the ambiguous use of the key term in this discipline is employed uncritically, for so long will there be doubts about the arena in which logic valuably operates. But more, whilst there is confusion as to whether truth refers externally, or alternatively does not, there cannot be logic, a discipline on statements referred to real events and developed to meet them properly, as they are in themselves. That cannot have the structure of propositional logic which is confined to formal relationships – 'essentials' in Frege's vocabulary – since that is not the character that real relations have. What form it then should take is at present open to question. It is one, however, that cannot be disregarded if proper attention is to be paid to more complex and vital problems, regardless of whether they permit of veridical answers or not. This as an issue has now to be raised, and if a sufficient answer cannot be given immediately, it yet remains a question that has to be considered if philosophy is to make a meaningful contribution.

*

Negative logic is best understood as a critical instrument, active in that capacity in many aspects of life. But as such it has never enjoyed the esteem that is accorded to positive logic, directed towards a respectable, admirable, even exemplary end, cognitive achievement or its apparent securing. It constitutes an enterprise which is apparently looked upon as the highest form of endeavour to which the human mind can aspire. With such a status philosophy claims to stand above the sciences, as the supreme, most eminent, exalted sphere of scholarship, since it outranks and, as it pretends, governs all other disciplines.[18] Any questioning of its virtue is tantamount to a failure to acknowledge its supremacy over all other approaches, as if scepticism of its reach were churlish or perverse, a denial of all that the West has given through its application to humanity, as affording it a grounding for rational advance. To be positive, to seek truth – which differs from being truthful, which everyone sees as a virtue – is respectable as a pursuit, and has been so regarded for many hundreds of years. To doubt that that is attainable in respect of meaningful issues, as sceptics have always done, is, if not disreputable, held in little regard, as constituting a refusal to accede to the hope of continual improvement, material though it should be, through the augmentation of knowledge. And that scientists, pursuing their essentially cognitive aims, are far from certain that formal logic is the most fitting procedure may for the moment be disregarded, since the doubts they have expressed seem to have made but little impression on logicians intent on eliciting absolute truth.[19]

It has to be admitted, of course that the rising revolt against established norms and customs, presumably inclusive of rationalistic procedures, might itself be taken as a form of negation, further to warrant suspicion of it. It is a feature of modern life based, a little paradoxically, on the finding that such modes lack a rational warrant, to believe that they may be disregarded, disregarded with impunity; although a more likely reason for their rejection seems to be that they represent the traditions of a now outdated establishment. But the purported end of this movement seems rather positive than negative, since it is to bring 'a new society' to being, to establish which the vices of the past, adherence to its norms, must be swept away, eradicated completely. To what end, however, is never quite clear, for what is to replace them is but vaguely envisaged – loving kindness, universal peace, absolute equality and freedom from all restraints, as though passion counted for nothing and would with these changes 'wither away'. A negative aspect enters, taking the form of protest; but that is excused as a means to an end, this undefined Utopia. Logic plays little part in this, since any idea of discipline, of adequate definition or of the setting up of criteria – unless 'political correctness' may be said to provide one – is not a feature of such movements, which are rather distinguished by what passes for liberation, "doing one's own thing" as is said. The form of that, however, has no discernible structure, but is rather individualistic, to the point that little agreement on what is ultimately desired is apparently achieved. In short, this has little resemblance to what is of concern to serious thinking directed towards a deeper understanding of what conditions life and redounds to its improvement, or what, to put it in negative terms, thereby to avoid any idealization, constitute real obstacles to social or cultural advance viewed in a sensible manner. Negation, then, is not an approach likely to have much appeal for idealist rebels today under sway of liberal propaganda, since it has clear associations with past proscriptions and inhibitions and so hampers the development of the autonomous individual seeking to express his unfettered personality.

Yet negation is at the root of ethics and morality, social and personal discipline, and has always been so from the Ten Commandments onwards. "Thou shalt not murder, nor steal, nor covet thy neighbour's wife", or in modern terms, blackmail, rape, sell drugs, corrupt the young, be sexist or, in rather less heinous terms, drive through a red light. And the reason for proscriptions such as these is obvious. That such acts, and many others which the reader can name for himself, are justly regarded as vicious because they tend to produce disturbance, to destabilize society, which despite the powers that can now be brought to bear, is always in fragile balance, which is undermined at penalty. Positive demands are generally more questionable because there lies behind them a tincture of ideology, as if subjective ideas were being foisted on others, who may for that reason reject them. That could also be the case for negative interdictions, such as some imposed today. But justly projected, in freedom from prejudice in favour of personal predilections, they must be seen to have clear warrant, plainly to be needed for placing checks on what are truly disruptive tendencies. One has to pay one's taxes, of course, and meet other obligations, which clearly have their warrant in the interests of the whole. But the effective ruling is rather that one shall *not* refuse to do so, so that society is empowered to exert the needed restraints. Indeed, with failure to take apt action with sufficient firmness it threatens its own survival and, in terms of its leadership, loses its authority. Those who hold positions of responsibility have, if need be, to grip the nettle, to make unpopular decisions, prohibitive in character, since those are in the long run the interests of society, the ultimate criterion, whatever may be said. Negation plays a part in life – quite apart from self-denial – and tacitly for the most part since its powers are largely latent when conditioning norms are respected. With its application as an underlying power restraint would not have to be exerted as otherwise it has to be, as an implicit requirement for securing relative social harmony. Its value lies in sustaining the norms, which, rather than coercive law, are the key to civilized balance, even if that should seem to ride against the cherished ideal of absolute personal freedom.

Leaving the meaning of that in its broader sense – for it is merely mentioned here to show that negation has social bearing – to be discussed in greater depth when the time for that is ripe, let attention now be turned to its value as a discipline in the sphere of directed thought. Logic as an organon constitutes a discipline which provides a check on statement in order to ensure that it is *not* improperly projected when some significant issue is under consideration, particularly when that may exert a pernicious influence on attitudes. Attitudes are not verbal in themselves, nor are they always conscious even when held by philosophers; but what is said at times clearly conditions postures. And though they may be given open verbal form, that is secondary to what they really involve as influences on underlying thought. They are states of mind which are either wholesome or deleterious in the effects they have upon society, as socially valuable or the reverse. They are therefore subject when exposed to suitable critical comment based on that criterion. But that, unless in moral philosophy which turns on conscious choice and personal motivation, has not been well developed in recent times in the schools where negation has been confined to the sphere of propositions, to verbal relations rather than to any further interest. In formal logic negation functions as little more than a means of exposing flaws in truth claims – F against T in truth tables – the falsification, that is to say, of propositional statements purporting to refer by appeal to verbal conventions. This – though it may be a little odd to cite a vitalist when making such a point – was shown by Bergson when he declared, as though it were an all-embracing finding: "Negation, therefore, differs from affirmation properly so called, since it is affirmation of the second order".[20] For that can mean no more than that negation comes into play only *after* an assertion has been made. And that that restricts it unduly scarcely needs to be said. It constitutes a failure to grasp what is really potential in it, which was better understood by Kant when he laid it down that "Negative judgments – those that are not merely such as regards their logical form, but in respect of their content – are not commonly held in high esteem. They are, on the contrary, regarded as the jealous enemies of our insatiable desire for knowledge, and it requires almost an apology to tolerate, much less to prize and respect them". To which he adds: "All propositions indeed may be logically expressed in negative form; but in relation to the content of our cognition, the peculiar province of negation is solely to protect us against errors".[21]

As used in this context, however, 'solely' calls for some modification, as does confinement to 'the content of our cognition', since both presume restrictions. For, seen more fully, negation is the very key to advance, in thought which is not to exclusion cognitively directed. This advance is less achieved by the inspiration of genius, drawing ideas from the air as it were, since those do not emerge *ex nihlo,* but from the recognition, which grounds this inspiration, that things are not as they should or might be. For that is the first requirement for thinking about any form of refinement. Negation has its essential root in some dissatisfaction with current states of affairs or attitudes adopted, with what is accepted uncritically in the field of philosophy, in science and elsewhere. This is shown by the procedures that science sees fit to adopt, implicit in the idea that its findings are contingent, revisable in so far as they can be seen to be inadequate. This is not so clear in the field of philosophy, but a reading of its history surely confirms this point: that certain doctrines or approaches are seen to be untenable, even if few are wholly abandoned or discarded, but simply fade away. Without a firm criterion – for abstract truth does not provide one if discourse refers to realities – philosophy is tied to its past in an unbreakable bond and rather refines on what has been said by reinterpretation. For it is generally recognised that the ancients had powers of thought quite as great as our own and were freer from the biases implanted by education which perpetuates prejudices. And this to the point that at times scientific findings – holism, for example, or again Gestalt psychology, both of which have surely philosophical implications – tend to be unheeded because they threaten traditional stances. Even so, though it is in this sense retrospective, philosophy may be said to advance in a rather roundabout way.

Nor is it then that anything goes, that any available doctrine may be preferred to another, or that fashion determines attitudes to bring about a change – as, for instance, from Bradley to Russell in the early years of this century. It is, with the finest thinkers at least, a felt need to think more deeply, to refine on current ideas which seem to be deficient in some salient sense, which doubt, that is negation, brings out to demand more thorough, deeper thinking. The classical case is that of Kant's reaction to Hume, who "woke him from his slumbers" and compelled him to rethink the ideas that he had up to that time harboured. But of course, there are many instances throughout the course of history, from Heraclitus' reaction against the ideas of his predecessors, as too materialist to his thinking, Bonaventura's doubts as to whether the rationalistic approach adopted by Aquinas fully engaged the needs that the faith was developed to meet, Leibniz against Locke, Schopenhauer and, differently, Kierkegaard against Hegel, to Bergson against the Positivists. And this list could be extended to cover a range of examples in any given period. Some disagreements were battles between opposing schools – nominalism and realism – which have always been a feature of the Western tradition, discovered more especially in the dialectics of scholastic education. But disaccordance has often led to creative thinking, if in a rather different way from that developed by science. For philosophy has in general advanced, or at least refined its doctrines, by subjecting them not to practical test but to rational critique, a process that continues, although it becomes increasingly clear that that, as verbal only, does not relate to actualities. Even so, without the spur of persistent sceptical questioning, of negation that is to say, it would have been less creative, and might have sunk, as it sometimes did without this irritant challenge, into little more than mere internal bickering. Negation, "the jealous enemy of our desire for knowledge", has performed a valuable function in stimulating fresh thinking, much to the dislike of those who cling to established precedents, to logically grounded certainties. It is the means whereby those with the power to do so feel the need to consider presented problems more deeply, to refine on certain acceptances which are seen to be in need of re-examination.

Finally, and this is a point of considerable significance, negation appears to reach into the realms of reality – though that should mean no more at once than engaging the problems with which men at large are confronted in the exigencies of life – in a way that a rationalistic approach, aspiring to positive verities, manifestly cannot. It is evident, of course, that 'rational' moral philosophy, involved with clear definitions, makes attempts to concern itself with mundane or practical problems. But in so far as it adopts rational means to do so, aligns the moral self with the knowing self, as if such an approach were fitted to meet extra-cognitive issues in their extreme complexity, it is trapped in subjectivity and presumes, with the intersubjectivity which it is obliged to evoke, that personal needs and interests can thereby be universalized. As a consequence of this it fails to see the criterion which should operate in the sphere to which it gives attention, which is social or general, effects on the social whole. For that, as much as nature, is a dynamic, indivisible, interrelative complex, which cannot be particularized or viewed in objective terms without misunderstanding of what is involved in relation to it.[22] In no just sense can rulings have ideological forms or properly be regarded from an individualistic, an idealistic standpoint, since what is confronted in viewing involvement in society is too complex and interwoven to be defined with any show of precision or adequacy. It is only properly thought of in its organic entirety. But this is not the occasion to make that point more fully, as in relating negation to ethics. Enough to note that society is an interrelative manifold, such that its actual form, as a network of interrelationships, cannot be specified or described in positive, cognitive terms without misrepresentation. The only thing that can be said without equivocation is that certain acts, murder with rape for example, are intrinsically iniquitous which is a negative finding. And it is wrong not only because it destroys an innocent life, but also because of its greater social or general effects, the devastation it generates, not only in families so bereft but in others who see it as a threat. Society can only be regarded as a whole, in which its members are involved less as individuals than as social beings caught up in a network of relationships and, on reaching maturity, in a mesh of responsibility.[23] As deployed in terms of this whole, negation comprises a power for detecting what is not fitting, what rides against social balance and so tends to produce disturbance. The manner in which this might be done, to the end at least of securing a reduction of imbalance, will be given thought in the sequel, in which the latent powers of negation will be explored more fully. For those have been sadly neglected in rationalistic philosophy directed essentially towards cognitive ends and achievements and largely disregarding those which do not have that character.

For as long as logically centred truth is held to be the only proper end of enquiry, with effective indifference to any wider interests, for so long are such interests neglected by philosophers because they are not amenable to rationalistic treatment. If then attention to them must mean a different idea of the role or purpose of philosophy, that must be accepted if real problems are to be met in the forms that they actually have. Positive truth, or, if that is preferred, the elucidation of concepts,[24] may still be sought or explored as an academic enterprise, doubtless intriguing to those who cultivate that interest more or less uniquely. But vital interests, plainly, have evident priority over veridical inquisition, which has little application to what really counts in life. And preoccupation with the last, as if it were the whole of what should be the concern of philosophy, may well be one of the reasons why that form of enquiry is viewed with sublime indifference by the public at large, and even with scorn by scientists. It is vital or human need that affords the real criterion in philosophic enquiry, as compared with which the truth, as understood by strict rationalists, is almost empty of content. Without the recognition of this as the warrant for its enquiries, philosophy may well sink into ineptitude, as an academic plaything without real bearing on life. This will happen at once, of course, for an ancient prestige protects it and people are overawed by its traditional repute, just as they are overawed by the marvels of modern science, its cosmological theories, its claims to have discovered the origins of the Universe. But already there are signs that it is losing its erstwhile standing, and so because it fails to attend to what really concerns society, vaguely perhaps but more certainly as disturbance becomes more evident: its balance in a more subtle sense than that secured by law, its general tone and quality with their spiritual dimensions.

Chapter Four

The Latent Power of Negation

To form a better idea of the potency of negation, point is served by enlarging on the comparison made between the positive and the negative forms of logic in terms of what they actually achieve, which up to the present time has been dealt with rather vaguely. For it should as a discipline be actively employed in the sphere of philosophic enquiry as that it is concerned with real problems of life, where it has hitherto been given little study with the consequence that misunderstanding of them has commonly ensued. When, for instance, assertion and negation are regarded as but aspects of one another, related to a criterion which only applies to the first, a limited view of logic's scope is necessarily given. Logic as an organon should discipline all projections whatsoever, not those alone of propositional form. If its only end is the eliciting of truth, as if all statements had to be rationalistic or cognitively oriented, that is to harbour a restricted view of what it is potent to accomplish. Everything said, at least in as far as it exerts an influence, ought to be subjected to disciplined critique, and whether it is projected as definitive or suggestive, it should not be allowed to pass without that check. That is indeed the warrant for logic as an organon, as a discipline applied to directed discourse, its ultimate justification if it is to serve a purpose truly related to human needs. And those, to any broader view, are certainly not confined to cognitive findings alone, still less to alethic conclusions of essentially abstract form, but relate as much, or rather more, to action undertaken in the real, the actual world, in the form of adjustments to what it brings to bear. To have an exact idea with respect to verbal relations is doubtless a part of this ever-present need, but it is only an aspect of what is required of thinking when that is seen as a power with which men in general confront the realities of existence. Thus, to confine it to what can be shown to be strictly true, is to limit its scope unduly. The interest is rather to ensure, in as far as that is possible, that what is said about the conditions in which life is lived and which bear on everyone shall be apt to the occasion and not confusing or misdirected.

This said, it is reasonable surely to give thought to a broader view of logic,which is necessarily verbal, and especially so when *lógos* in its best known sense means 'speaking', though it was not in early times limited to rigorous precision in the employment of language. That is an ideal, appropriate on occasion, whereas the real, or rather any direct response to it, seldom has that narrow and restrictive character. And though it may be difficult, and constitute a rather formidable problem, to contemplate the complexity of what is confronted in life, that cannot be disregarded because it does not have clear rationalizable form and cannot therefore be defined in rigorous positive terms. It is yet a point, however, that statements have to be made about the involvement that everyone encounters. Those may be loose in a formal sense; but, as they are directed towards and bear on what is significant in life as it is lived, they too must be subject to critique, applied even more decisively. If broader contentions can only be given propositional form, in that way to render them stiff, rigid and inflexible, a loss of their meanings must be the result. All is not so simple, so open without reserve to strict rationalistic engagement; and to claim that in principle everything is to misunderstand involvement, though that is not well understood today.[1] Need, not truth, is the touchstone by which all projections ought to be judged for their value as contributions, to be checked in as far as they fail to meet that requirement, because otherwise they might misrepresent the issue. Let us then examine the reason why logic as now conceived cannot properly touch problems such as these because of a self-imposed restriction.

Its aim is to state a conclusive truth about what has been selected for examination, predicated in formal language, and so without allowance for doubt or any degree of 'tolerance', which normally has to be accepted, so complex is what is generally confronted. Only one answer, the truth, is judged to be acceptable, and that is itself a limitation. In other words, since truth can only have one form on any given occasion, a single point must be established, or, in metaphorical terms, the arrow launched, which corresponds to a projected truth claim, must strike the bull precisely in the centre. For nothing less will satisfy the requirement prescribed. With the excluded middle, any shot that fails precisely to hit the mark, any finding that does not comply with the ideal standard set up, must be dismissed as false without extenuation. No modification of this ruling is permitted, although a sentence may be reframed to render a claim acceptable. 'Apodeictic' meaning, at least for Aristotle, 'certain beyond dispute' – though that was not its original meaning – is a term applied to what is necessarily true, albeit that there are other modes, assertoric and problematic, of which the last affords a 'let-out' with claim to refer externally, though in principle a contention must even then be evidential. But, if the end is truth strictly so considered, that cannot justly be problematic, since doubt is plainly implicit in any such a finding. Positive logic, in short, can only have one end; and if many value logic allows of degrees of truth, it is, if irrefragable truth is held to be the only proper end, not unjustly regarded as deviant.[2]

Negative logic, by contrast, has a much wider field, since it refers to the whole of what is confronted with the exception of that which falls within the realm of what can be distinguished as true. To continue with the metaphor, the sphere to which it applies is everywhere outside the bull, the inner and outer circles and even the ground on which the arrow may have fallen. The bull has not been struck and that alone suffices to bring negation into action. This means that negation reaches into further fields, and indeed, as will be seen, it penetrates effectively into many aspects of life, or more precisely into what is said about relations in it or with circumambient nature. Were the arrow to strike a spectator, and statements are sometimes as wild as they have ideological form, this point would be exemplified. A false statement would not, of course, be disastrous in that physical sense, but its effects might certainly be so were no proper check placed on it. Accordingly, negation has to be brought into play, firmly if what is said is gravely misplaced or mistaken, whenever there may be occasion to evoke it. For false statements can, especially when they claim to be logical or rationally supported, disturb or confuse as much as a misdirected arrow, if in a somewhat different manner. 'That will not do' is a typical negative expression, which is certainly not confined to truth claims shown to be false, since it refers to errors generally committed, which as social may well have repercussive effects. In fine, negation refers to action no less than it does to speech, albeit that it must have that form when used as a logical instrument, in which case it is fairly applied when anything is seen or even felt to be wrong, to be disturbing of equipoise.

*

So much for its greater reach as compared with positive logic, which would scarcely have to be mentioned were it not that that has almost been forgotten with exclusive preoccupation on the eliciting of truth. But that does but brush the matter, and so the time has come to consider the powers of negation in themselves, that is in relation to real as distinct from ideal problems, which are even themselves confused, as when formal logic purports to extend its reach to externals. For terms in use are ambiguous. Thus, though 'false' and 'that will not do' are more or less synonymous, a difference between them appears, it is not precise, to be this: that whereas the first is usually taken to refer to what is said in rational discourse – though it may refer to equivocation in such forms as lying – the second rather refers to what is done in the form of inappropriate action. Nevertheless, they are fairly regarded as interchangeable, for 'that will not do' as justly refers to erroneous statement and 'false', if not to action generally, when the appropriate term would rather be 'mistaken', at least to certain forms of it, cheating for example. Indeed, we commonly speak of false coin, false pretences, false colours and so on, implying that something spurious is being imposed upon us, so that 'false' related to action means something reprehensible not simply something mistaken; and negation applies to both. Happily, such heinous acts are relatively rare, whereas those that are mistaken are more common and less conspicuous, and so call for different treatment. Even so, they may well be as disturbing in their effects. Thus, even if something is felt to be wrong in a sense that may not be precise and is certainly subjective, that too is a realm of negation, which cannot be dismissed because no definition is possible.

If we sense or judge that an act is right in the conditions prevailing, we cannot say that it is true without a misuse of words. Indeed, when it is right and so fits into place, there is no occasion for comment, since, if all is as it should be, that would be redundant. It fits, and that is all that need be taken into account. It folds into some harmony, 'the whole', 'the implicate order', and meets the need of adjustment to the immediate environment. For attunement to the complex of whatever is presented to the responsive psyche constitutes a successful relation to conditions, adequate rapport with the pressures bearing on it, either in a natural or a social sense. This is seen especially in response to artistic form on a sensuous level, when the rhythmic pulse unfolds in a harmonic sequence, to play on the receptive nerves in a satisfactory manner. And thus do we establish rapport with an aspect of reality. But response, and so attunement to continually changing stimuli is not always so auspicious, nor is adjustment to such pressures always so successfully achieved. So measures have to be taken in order to sustain a measure of poise or balance, be it only homeostatic. Nor is adjustment always easy, since pressures may be so abnormal and so great in scale at times that, though we recognise that they are untoward and disturbing, it is difficult to make the requisite adaptation.

Forces that are disturbing may be said to take two forms. Some for.them are natural, earthquakes for example; and over them we have little control. Those, looked upon with detachment, must be seen as transient states, temporary readjustments of the balance of nature, which, given time, will be resolved into new formations of dynamic equipoise, 'steady states' so called, subsisting as before in tensional equilibrium. From a human standpoint such effects may seem disastrous. But to a broader outlook, if that may be sustained without philosophic pretentiousness, that is as it may be, since nature also has to adjust to pressures within itself, much as the body does to exhaustion or changes of temperature. It is idle to suppose that we can do much about such events, beyond removing ourselves if we can and returning when the danger has passed to restore the damage done. Others, meanwhile have their source in human passions and conflicts, which, unlike natural upheavals, which bring about new balances, may be repercussive to leave an imprint on the psyche, permanently to warp it. Little can be done to circumvent the first, designated 'acts of God' essentially for that reason, for man is playing with fire in attempts to control the balance of nature. That is not the case for the second, since, if only in part, efforts are sensibly made, and have been throughout the ages, to limit the effects of disruptive social action by developing and encouraging saner dispositions. But it is less to extreme forms of anti-social behaviour that attention has now to be turned. For those are better dealt with by coercive law than philosophy. That should rather concern itself with general dispositions or the attitudes adopted in social interrelationships than with excessive violence, unhappily an aspect of modern social life, which is not unrelated to those attitudes themselves and a failure to redirect them into more appropriate forms. Despite the fact that man is by nature a creature of passion, strengthened by his intellect, he yet in normal conditions lives in tolerable balance with nature and with his fellow men and adjusts to various pressures with comparative ease. It is only when some disturbance is noticeably disruptive or potentially menacing that he is called upon to do something decisive about it. What, then, is this recognition if not that something is not as it should be, which is a negative finding, later to be considered as 'responsive rejection' when the presence of something untoward imposes on one affected the need to take suitable counteraction.

*

With this the scene is set for carrying this point further, for that counter-action is taken in a complex which is larger than what is immediately having an effect, or so at least as it involves more than its immediacy, as does any act which may have further consequences. Negation invariably refers to the whole of what is presented, against which, as balance is threatened, it is properly projected. When, then, Leibniz put forward, to be much mocked for his pains, an ontological theory of pre-established harmony,[3] he made a point that merits attention in this context: that what is confronted in nature, albeit that man is a mode of it, is other than that which distinguishes human life as such. For the first is the ontic base on which everything else depends, in respect of which man, in as far as he can, must try to come to terms. That doctrine may have something of a theological character, but if it is read as projecting continual creativity rather than as reflecting the mechanics of his time – that the clock once started ticked on without further intervention – it may be better understood for what it really implies. He was not, of course, referring to human inter-relationships, as Voltaire glibly supposed, since rational beings do not easily live at peace with themselves and others; they are distinguished by their restlessness until, as with Candide, age brings a measure of tranquillity. His reference was to nature, which, despite convulsions, tends to subsist in a state of dynamic equilibrium. And indeed, if it did not do so, life, in the absence of continuity, could scarcely be maintained. Or if he was referring to man, which does not seem likely, it was to him in his role as a subconscious agent, mediating stimuli without the intervention of consciousness. For he is then at one with nature, with the natural pressures to which he adjusts quite readily, thereby to maintain his balance, psychic no less than physical, in the changing environment. Inasmuch as adjustment presupposes counteraction, we might well think of the process of initial stimulation as a sphere in which negation is applicable. But as response on that level is outside conscious control, negation very clearly cannot operate there. It is on the plane alone of conscious registration that it can be put to use. And there alone is there as need for it, since thinking is subject to error in a way that direct response, involved with vital need, is not, unless on rare occasions.

Pre-established harmony, considered as an ontology, which is rather more sensitive than an atomic reading, bears relation to another Leibnizean doctrine, that of his later *vraisemblance,* which also has meaning here. Its essential meaning is that any statement referred to external reality can never have more than likelihood, for it cannot in strictness be true.[4] This implies that all positive statements, unless they are strictly abstract, are in some sense precarious, since when they refer to what cannot be said conclusively, defined or explained that is, they are and cannot be other than speculative or suggestive. They may have greater *vraisemblance,* but that does not mean they have attained to the status of truth; at best it means confirmation in as far as such a projection cannot be refuted and coheres with other findings. The only thing that can be said with any show of finality is that

'that cannot be the case', and so because there is a detectable flaw in the statement, and inconsistency perhaps or a failure to take the whole of what is relevant into account. To give a somewhat crude example, since it is no more than empiric, one cannot without reservation assert that a certain colour is red, when it may be puce or copper or tinged with some other shade, even when it is to all appearance pure. If it is said, conversely, that that colour is *not* green in any of its hues, doubt in terms of the spectrum is evidently excluded. And if this example is far from the best, for distinctions that are more opaque are not readily to be cited, it illustrates in some sense the lesson of *vraisemblance* as it bears on declarations; that, though assertoric statements are generally open to question, those of negative form, when properly directed, have a certain finality. 'That is not the case' implies that what has been projected is wholly without *vraisemblance.* Of greater interest, however, are more equivocal cases, as when a claim to likelihood – truth at once discounted – can be shown to be unwarranted for any of several reasons. For then we must either despair or give thought to more fruitful approaches. Spinoza had this in mind, it seems, when he said in Letter L *determinatio negatio est,*[5] to mean that the only statements which could be accepted as final when referred to external events were those of negative form, declaring in effect that a non-fitting had been detected. Nor is it a truth that has then been found, it is a delimitation.

This is best shown in artistry which relates to direct response. A falsely struck chord, for instance, is immediately recorded, for reasons to be discussed more fully in the sequel, whereas a flawless harmonic flow, in which chords are not distinctive, meets normal responsive requirement. To introduce intellection into sensuous response is to disrupt, in effect to destroy, the grace of the rhythmic unfolding, developed through the chords that lead up to any one in the sequence and follow from it to move towards a compositional unity. And though some may claim to follow the sequence chord by chord, to have the power to study the components in a painting or the subtler details in architectural form, they indulge in intellectual acts, warranted with professionals, but not the normal forms of response to artistic presentations. Postures such as these are altogether too precious; and, if they are projected as the only proper way to 'appreciate' the arts, they are not only pretentious but in effect deny that spontaneous or nervous response has any value or meaning. It is to bring some order into the flow of events that comprises the virtue of artistry, addressing all sensitive persons, such that the romantic idea that it exists to excite, not infrequently leading to decadence, is to deprive the ordinary man of any easy relationship to it, and thus to undermine the development of a *general* culture. The intellect properly comes into play when something is out of order, for that is the basic reason why it evolved in man, by comparison physically weak. For what is out of order or menacing constitutes a threat, and powers are required to meet it to the end of maintaining balance, and even sustaining life.

Harmony is the key in this, since it is that in respect of which negation has its warrant. It is not to be engaged by recourse to objectification, by means of which the intellect gets a grip on what is presented, or rather a fragment of it; since that action as deliberate involves a breaking down, particularization, of the sequential unfolding. It is only when that is dissected, analyzed, decomposed, that the intellect, at sacrifice of sensuous involvement, is able to act at all. And here it might be observed that even when certain harmonies are brought to being by men, as in artistic creation, they do not have their origin in intellectual action, as rationalists suppose, but are rather the product of nervous sensitivity, of sensing what is fitting in a compositional whole, followed up by a quasi-conscious critical standing back, to detect and so negate what is not acceptable. That this critical dimension is intellectually tinged is sufficiently obvious, but it operates in this case in terms of an interrelative whole related to nervous needs, those of those who are likely to be affected by infelicities. It is not in that form devoted to the eliciting of truths or of developing explanations, since harmonic structures are not of their nature explicable. And if results are 'true' that means no more than fitting. The detection of what will not do because it may have adverse effects is perhaps 'the beginning of wisdom'. For unless certain acts are seen to be socially disruptive, and are for that reason condemned, the balance of society is implicitly threatened. It was an accumulation of undermining forces, of attitudes adopted by irresponsible people, particularly in the leading groups lacking a social sense, that brought past cultures into decay. And that is not a thing of the past; it is always a latent threat. Of course, it is a feature of the human make-up to have the power to ride against nature and thus perhaps against long-term social interests, and in part to accept the penalties of any attempt to do so. Nor is it denied that this might be productive of certain benefits. But to assume that every act of this masterful form is meritous is even sentimental, for the effects produced are not invariably advantageous. Heraclitan conflict may be the very substance of life, but a distinction must be made between that which is so to say natural and that engendered artificially by over-ambitious egotists. For the first must be accepted whereas the second can be controlled, if not by the agent himself then by society as a whole alert to a menace to its stability. It may be that the notion of sustaining harmony, though of course behind it lies all prescriptive morality, is seen as mundane or banal by those enamoured of excitement, as if it made for mediocrity. But since, as perfect, harmony is no more than an ideal when referred to human society, hope of its full attainment can not be seriously entertained. The aim, exerting critical powers, is to reduce disturbing conflict, which means to distinguish between what enhances life and what inhibits that enhancement, and to act on that detection as fully as is possible. Negation is then a means by which disturbance may be reduced, and so by its application to whatever is likely to generate undue social friction.

*

As a critical power, however, its readiest application is to the sphere of ideas, which are projected supposedly in the public interest but which, as influencing attitudes in unfortunate ways, may actually render them pernicious. What that then involves is a matter that merits attention, and particularly so as agreement on what words most fruitfully mean is the key to understanding of the nature of social involvement. A point to be understood, then, is the meaning of the word 'general'. Under idealistic thinking it has a rather narrow import, which is regrettable inasmuch as a wider meaning has to be given to it if human need in a social sense is to be understood. For when that is only seen as having a conscious form and as relating only to the conscious individual, the knowing self so said, essential features of it are effectively lost to view. In cognitively oriented thought that need is assumed to be the eliciting of truth or, in more modest terms, the accumulation of knowledge, as if those were alone significant. Questions are then fairly raised in such forms as these: truth in respect of what and knowledge to what end? If the answer is abstract relations or logical universals, assumed to constitute generals, that is justly regarded as a restricted idea of what is at issue when this point is raised. If the interest is extended to cover knowledge of natural relations, richer ground is reached, but a limit is yet imposed since that can only be material: value plays no part in it. 'General' is fairly understood, on a human plane if no more, as referring to the interests of all men whatsoever, to what is common to humanity; and to hold that that is confined to cognitive acquirements is surely rather crude. It is ideas such as these that call for critical comment, less directed at science which does provide certain insights with bearing on this matter, and is in any case more modest and tends increasingly to be sceptical, than on those bound to the motion of rational control, a form of reductionist thinking. It is evident, then, that when it comes to human interests and needs considered in greater depth, that is in their subtler forms, that science does not proceed with its usual confidence, since its field is the material, the observable and the measurable, not the psychical or the spiritual which are neither clearly detectable nor in any strict sense measurable. And this is the case especially when they do not enter consciousness and are only to be observed when they are in some way frustrated and so have external effects. Claim to explain their nature in rational terms is so questionable that critical thought is justly applied to any attempt to do so. If then they cannot be reached by rationalistic procedures when those are presumed to be all-embracing – "There is nothing in principle that cannot be known to science"[6] – the idea of the general, when this claim is unchallenged, is evidently restricted if it is fairly defined as referring to all interests, irrespective of whether they are overt or not. And to deny that these deeper needs are a meaningful aspect of life, on the score that they are not definable or cognizable, is plainly to be blind to what life in depth comprises.

The procedures that are employed in cognitive enquiry cannot but confine it to the phenomenal world; and hence the tendency to restrict the idea of reality to what is clearly cognizable, with the consequence that response to it is taken to be ideal and so tinged with subjectivity. The 'knowing self' is a telling term, for what it plainly implies is that knowledge accrues to the subject and is peculiarly his finding. Of course, it can be generalized on a rational plane to become a logical universal or, in more effective form, something widely accepted by means of confirmation through repeated experimentation. Nor can it be denied that that renders it universal, until subjected to challenge, on a cognitive plane. When, however, thought is referred to subtler interrelationships, those of psychic and social life, its personalized dimension is evidently a feature, as the moral self evinces. Recognizing that there is need to generalize their rulings, which have ultimate social bearing, moral philosophers appeal to what they give the name 'subjective generalization'.[7] But that as a doctrine is questionable, since what is promoted with it is tinged, if not determined, by the attitudes of the thinker or the class that he represents, by a rational bias for instance. This attains it apogee in the projection of ideologies, foisting ideals on others, which are the more delimiting when formed on the belief that they rest on formal logic or scientific evidence, statistical for example, which gives them an authority not easily resisted when the first is held to be "a court from the rulings of which there is no appeal".[8] Indeed, the cult of the individual, autonomous, self-sufficient, though there is obligation presumably to comply with the rulings of logic, has its roots in the doctrine of the knowing self, which is the characteristic theme of idealistic philosophy. Apart, then, from the fact that the self severs itself from others, whom it tends to regard as objects, it severs itself from reality, which it can only see in terms of what is presented to consciousness. But that is scarcely reality seen as the ground of the general in the sense that everything is related in or to it.

Consequences stem from this, as apart from any failure to meet the world as it really is or to come to grips with what may be called the 'general in actuality' and its bearing on human relations. For, if its effects are social, those, when that cult is dominant, are misrepresented, perhaps with serious consequences. The self-centred individual loses a social sense, a sense of the general as referred to basic human need. It is all very fine, even noble, to urge the development of self-discipline in a Millean manner; but the effect of stress on the self on less enlightened peoples is productive of results which are less sublime. For what it rather gives scope to are self-assertion, aggressiveness and attempts at domination, in extreme form criminality, disregard of the interest of others, especially the most vulnerable. Happily, ordinary people do not read moral philosophy, perhaps to misinterpret it, but in the main persist in accepting traditional norms, such irrational notions as honour, tolerance, courtesy, though finding it increasingly difficult to sustain them when their opposites are so prevalent. Even so, this doctrine is slowly corroding society, as the cult of self-expression is vitiating artistry and the growth of a general culture, which is for the first time feasible.[9] Negation might then be brought to bear on such a deleterious doctrine, which has flourished almost unchallenged because idealistic philosophers are capable only, it seems, of seeing value in personal terms and are apparently blind to any greater or social interest.

Carrying this point further, attention is fairly turned to the presuppositions adopted in idealist thinking. Nor will thought at once be given to its accepted criterion, of truth as opposed to need, notwithstanding that that is itself a presupposition in respect of the aim or of what is commonly taken to be the ultimate end of enquiry. No, more blinkered assumptions are the present interest. To meet cognitive requirements what is confronted must be knowable, or at least potentially so. Hence, the 'world' must be seen as made up of particulars, of 'objects' as is said. This becomes a little absurd when the world itself is thought of as 'objective', though then the term is being used in a different sense than when it is referred to objectified particulars. This idea has roots in the Cartesian dichotomy, in which all that was not subjective, clearly mental that is to say, was objective or external, 'out there', 'mind-independent'. Nor is it without interest that such expressions as these are used by rationalists themselves – by Russell for example – to indicate the quandary that lies in their approach. For if 'the external world' is independent of mind, properly of the intellect,[10] a problem clearly arises: that of the relation between the ideal and the real. This has never been solved except by recourse to very dubious means, by claiming that reality is to be interpreted as that which the intellect can grasp, namely phenomenal being. But phenomena so seen are essentially in the intellect, which gives them the form of objects or intellectual constructs created by itself in the act of objectification. For in itself the phenomenal world is an interrelative complex and accordingly indivisible. It is only in dim perception that the mind, as opposed to the intellect, responds to the real world in the form in which it is presented as an interrelative complex, to aspects of which living beings react in a continuous process of adjustment to the pressures brought to bear upon them. That, as related to what lies behind phenomenal presentations, complies with the modern development of a holistic ontology, which presumes or infers that all in the real or external world is indivisibly interrelated, that nothing exists alone. That 'holism', as a term with a rather different meaning, related to cognition, was introduced by a philosopher is now of little moment, since its present meaning is derived from scientific discoveries and later an understanding of their implications, so that it is outdated except for cognitive enquiry, which is not the essential concern of a meaningful philosophy. For that must confront the whole as it bears on human life.

This relatively recent development has an interesting aspect, in that after more than two thousand years it involves a reversion to the doctrine of becoming, the idea that all is in process of continual change. Proposed by Heraclitus and resisted by Parmenides, who advocated Being as the proper ontology, it had a checkered history, unlike that of *tao,* to which it had a certain resemblance. Being – that word is normally capitalized – was held by him to be motionless and unchangeable, and this, he contended, was reflected in the nature of thought and reason. Accepting this constancy – later called 'the perennial', and not unallied to 'uniformity' in science – he held it to be the Ultimate Reality and accordingly the Truth. And though this may be crude as an interpretation of the Eleatic's thinking, that he aligned Being and Truth, knowability in effect, against the Heraclitan Becoming is undoubtedly the case.[11] Why he did so is clear. For, as becoming is in principle unknowable, no truth – as *ming-shih* contended[12] – can be propounded about it. This resistance to that doctrine has had a very profound effect on later Western thinking, even to the point of allowing a rather warped view of the thought of classical antiquity, not to mention that of China. By an accident of history considerable documentation of what might be called the *alétheia* school or persuasion has survived, as with Plato and his successors, whereas that relating to the *lógos* school is so sparse as to allow to the presumption that there was no significant alternative to the first. There is evidence, however, that the second persisted throughout the classical age to oppose this rationalistic approach. That the Sophists saw fit to challenge its pretensions is well-known – and Socrates was one of them, rather, it seems, a negativist than "the first of the rationalists"[13] – and that the Sceptics, the Cyrenaics, the Epicureans and even some of the later Academics were sceptical of its reach suggests that the logocentrics were far from having it all their own way. But with the later triumph of personalized religions and with them demands for *credos,* any doubts about which were heresy, the idea that the end of thinking was truth, truth that was irrefragable, effectively overrode any other view.[14] And so the cult of truth, and with it adherence to Being as that to which it referred, dominated thought throughout the following centuries. A curious effect of that sway over thinking was that in the course of time, when thought became more secular, the idea that the end was truth, unequivocal truth, was carried over into philosophy, not indeed without protest, though that that was conveniently brushed aside. Science was rather more sceptical, since it came in time to see that its findings were contingent, or otherwise said revisable, not true in a logical sense, so that its aim was rather to promote reliable knowledge, which is certainly not the same.

Inasmuch as this ancient ontology of becoming implied that reality as such was not in strict sense knowable, as classical sceptics contended, doctrines which held that it was were in effect discredited. But this critique did not extend to the world of appearances, which was in aspects knowable, given certain limitations, as when that knowing aspired to be definitive and complete. Truth, or rather strict knowledge, was only later acquired, as opposed to merely asserted, by adoption of a means of breaking down into parts of that which was presented. And although it was sometimes claimed that the knowledge so acquired referred to external reality, it certainly and with no small success engaged the phenomenal world, so successfully indeed that as a process it has ruled more or less unchallenged into modern times. With the recognition, however, that nature was indeed a dynamic, indivisible, interrelative complex the situation has changed. That this raises a formidable methodological problem is apparent to scientists. Philosophers, meanwhile, in their role as logocentrics, refuse in effect or are reluctant to recognize what this change really means, since its obvious implication is that the approach that they adopt – which, despite their claims, is not that adopted by science[15] – is no longer valid, except in a narrow sense. Yet they continue to refine it as if that were their justification, dimly aware that were they to accede to this ontology they would have to abandon, or modify, their traditional role, together with many doctrines that they still hold in esteem and do not see to be untenable, logical atomism for instance.

*

Science has long tended to be monistic in its approach, as its laws imply, though the idea that the world it explored was in process of ceaseless change, mutable and fluid, always moving towards new forms of dynamic equipoise, was not fully realized until recent times. And experimentation has always referred to the extra-phenomenal world, albeit that what is discerned clearly cannot be other than phenomenally recorded. It may be difficult for philosophers to accede to what is implicit in this, unless perhaps they are metaphysicians. For metaphysics postulates, in principle at least, an ultimate reality, a world beyond that accessible to cognitive enquiry. Every effort is made to discount such a disturbing, corrosive view, by arguing, for example, that the phenomenal world either reflects the world external to it or that it is ultimate itself. In fairness, however, it should be added that that unduly simplistic idea does not pass entirely unchallenged. It is doubtless difficult to accept a world beyond perception, since that goes against common sense and allows of no verifiable knowledge. It is even more so to grant that ultimate reality is almost certainly different from what Bradley called "our reality",[16] counterpoised to an Absolute which is certainly not Hegelian, although it is often taken to be. It was for him external and beyond an empiric grasp, so that claim that it had a different form could never be more than speculative. But it stands, if only speculatively, because, for similar reasons, it cannot be disproved or shown to be unwarranted. Nor is this idea without well-established precedent. For, throughout the course of history, thinkers of repute have entertained the idea of it – as with the *ding an sich,* for instance – and presumed it be different, if only as an insight. And there is indirect evident that this difference of form is likely. Nor is that surprising when the phenomenal world is effectively brought to being by the conscious mind and is patently different from that to which the dog responds to generate 'his reality', related to something which comprehends both forms of responsiveness. As instruments permit us to probe beyond naked perception, on which past ideas were formed, a world is revealed which differs from that to which we normally respond; the subatomic world with its interrelative charges. Furthermore, it is now established pretty convincingly that the world to which we respond directly, in immediate reaction to undetectable stimuli, is almost certainly dynamic, a continually changing complex, as that what is recorded consciously is but a fragment of what is received in response to external pressures. A fragment, a transient unity, is scarcely to be equated with the whole from which it emerges, so that an inference may be drawn that there is some difference between what is encountered in instant response and what is recorded in consciousness.

Again, we are now aware that living beings depend on a combination of gases present in the troposphere,[17] which is analyzable only by recourse to certain means which differ from those adopted in the normal course of living, in which some of them are detected only by means of smell, notably when a gas is particularly offensive. We are not conscious of these gases unless some are very potent, and when they are so the nasal organ provides a warning signal that the usual relations to nature are not being maintained. But indeed, as will be shown, it is only when something is threatening – sweet smells may be an exception – that we become aware of it in the normal course of living, when consciousness is brought into play to advise us that adverse forces are present, so that we may take appropriate counteraction. Other instances could be cited to show that there is no good reason to think that the external world has a form resembling that perceived. What it comprises is hinted at by such clues as these, which refer to aspects of it only. It would then be unwise to project intuitions about it or even the findings of modern science as sufficient answers with respect of its form. Nor will that now be done, though highly responsible persons bear witness to what permits of no physical explanation. Hence, we cannot simply dismiss the findings of the mystics – that all is one essentially – for no other reason than that they cannot be sustained as truths or be rationally confirmed. However, as the present point is simply to stress that the world that lies beyond perception, the truly external world, must be taken into account, it is enough that its character is defiant of explanation in positivistic terms, which is only disturbing to cognitivists as something beyond their reach. It is a conditioning influence beyond the veil of *māyā,* and since it is that to which direct response is made it should be of some concern to philosophers as they attempt to understand man's relation to it. To which it might be added that many creative thinkers, not only those who were sceptical, have recognized that some power underlies appearances, so that to dismiss the idea of it, or rather to be blind to the influence it exerts, is grossly to misunderstand the nature of involvement, which is plainly more than cognitive. There is a world beyond the reach of cognitive enquiry and failure to acknowledge what it represents constitutes a failure to take a responsible attitude to man's involvement with it as an influence persistently affecting him.

How logocentrics find it in their power to brush aside or discount such pertinent insights as these can only be accounted for in psychological terms. That a passion for precision, a need to cling to ideal constructs, is so strong as to overrule any other consideration, regarded as ancillary, renders that comprehensible as the only acceptable answer. And the fact that this attitude disregards, as it seems without awareness, that man's relation to the reality he confronts constitutes the essential problem is an important aspect of it. Vital interests are forgotten, sacrificed indeed to the search for an elusive truth, which is claimed to be referential, even when it affects to be absolute. This is a strange development, only to be compared with the fanaticism sometimes displayed in politics and religion, and is just as destructive of careful balanced thinking, since it is rooted in prejudice and constitutes an endeavour to foist ideals on others, regarded as unregenerate if they do not accede to them. Nor do its advocates recognize that little of moment accrues from their arcane activities, since investigation of that form bears little or no relation to what signifies in life; or, if it does in any sense, it satisfies no more at last than material interests. It is in a somewhat reluctant recognition of this that attention is now being turned to pragmatic affairs, though intervention in such fields is vitiated by its tie to rationalistic procedures, which cannot properly engage the contingencies of life as involvements with reality. Such, then, is the state into which philosophy has now fallen that doubts about its role, its function or contribution afflicts it quite severely. Should it then abandon the procedures to which it is heir and has refined so carefully, and with that the only apparently acceptable system of discipline, *or* should it continue in the hope that with sufficient persistence, ratiocination – not to be confused with more flexible reasoning – will in time produce answers that are adequate and complete, relate, that is to say, to real or vital problems? And, if it elects for the first, what course should it then pursue to ensure that discipline is sustained?

To propose a return to the time when philosophy lost its way, with the apparent disregard of such creative thinkers as Bradley, Bergson, Driesch, Marcel and others of that period,[18] to pick up and develop the doctrines they projected, may be asking too much. But at least what was then put forward, on, for instance, the relation between knowledge and reality, with the corollary that the last was infinitely richer than 'objective' ideas about it, might modify approaches and open the way to a more meaningful application of the powers available in the deployment of thought. The key to this is acceptance of a world beyond perception, with the recognition that relation to it, initially in the form of immediate response, constitutes the problem with which philosophy, in contradistinction to science, is uniquely equipped to deal. There can be no effective ethics unless man's deeper relation to nature, which in some sense influences everything that he does, is understood in general, realistic terms, in its social forms especially, as involvements with contingencies. It is vital and basic relations, which are general in the sense that they bear on all men, not sophisticates only, that lack as yet for proper attention. That a change from what is apparently firm, definable in precise terms, to something more fluid and volatile may be difficult to accomplish; and hence a reluctance to forgo rational explanation, notwithstanding that its limits are apparent. But this is now demanded lest philosophy becomes sterile and has no real part to play in thought as it is now developing. If an escape from the cul-de-sac in which it now seems to be trapped is to be effected, this dim recognition that a new approach is needed must be strengthened with the acceptance that there is no alternative than to accede to the doctrine of becoming, of 'holism', that is to say, in modern terminology. For that demands rethinking on all the problems faced, logical, epistemic, ontic and axiological. Taking the first alone at once, the need is to find a procedure to discipline what is said on the problems that this raises. That is the initial involvement, since without its consideration extended thought is unrestrained, loose, subjective in what may be called a pejorative sense.

*

This is doubtless deplorably sceptical, undermining the ground on which philosophy now rests and questioning its conviction that rationalistic procedures, which are strictly ideal, can somehow engage externality, interpreted as phenomenal in a vain attempt to do so. But then, if negation is applied other than internally, it operates in this way: to question the validity of idealistic approaches as they pretend to this extension. Echoing ancient ideas, which now take on a new vitality, it is scarcely to be denied that what is now confronted is a holistic complex, which in the nature of the case is beyond the reach of cognition, that is, of objectification. Sceptical thought is applied today, as it has always been, to whatever calls for critical attack, primarily the notion that man as a logocentric can detach himself from nature, view the world as external when he himself is a mode of it.[19] Knowledge has without question greatly enhanced human life, but not without a number of concomitant penalties. But clearly it touches no more than *aspects* of reality, so that if it is urged as the only relation to it which is rationally acceptable – or rather oddly 'meaningful', as if meaning were limited to what is registered in consciousness – that actually inhibits a deeper understanding, which, rather than knowledge, is wisdom. It might be noted in passing, as having some bearing on this, that *skeptesthai* originally meant 'to think with greater care', 'to probe more deeply into the nature of human need', which is plainly more than material and constitutes in its fullest sense the ultimate criterion for the application of thought. And in such sense as that Socrates was a sceptic. Any failure to do so, then, which means to rest content with received approaches, in which attention is turned to idealistic findings and *not* to deeper social concerns – to believe that, for example, realities accessible to rational enquiry – is justly subject to critique, since it plainly will not do. And to hold that this is unfair to those so earnestly trying to elicit truth, perfect answers to the problems that men confront in actuality, is simply special pleading; for that is plainly to be blind to what need in depth comprises.

Idealists are really men apart, living in a world of intellectual constructs and failing to grasp that the problems to be addressed by thinkers are those of man's relation to ultimate reality and through that to his fellow men. To question the credentials of those who make such efforts to rise above contingencies into the realm of pure thought seems on the surface graceless, harsh and acrimonious. But the sceptic is not to be despised, as if he were merely churlish, wanton and destructive. For in insisting on deeper thinking he, if given attention at all, compels a closer examination, with respect, if no more, to purpose, that for which thought is deployed to warrant its intervention. Thought is too easily turned to what satisfies subjectively and accordingly tends to disregard the greater or general interest, problems related to life. Those are extremely complex as subsuming spiritual interests or, if that term is ambiguous, those that are extra-material, which cannot be disregarded if thought is at all concerned with what really concerns humanity, men in general as distinct from a few sophisticates. One reading of the purpose of the sceptics in classical times is that they were contending that ethical issues were either neglected or misconstrued[20], as was nature itself, when attempts were made to define them in rationalistic terms. Scepticism, then, is not a kind of devilry, maliciously undermining serious disciplined discourse. It is, conversely, a stressing of the requirement to think a little more deeply, a questioning of the attitudes which inhibit a proper approach to fundamental issues. For, though it is supposed – by Hegel, for example – that intellectual action is peculiarly spiritual, as in a certain sense it is, cognitive enquiry, even as veracious, can only refer to what is comprehensible rationally; and that can only mean the observable or the material. Scepticism, in short, is a weapon with which illusions, prejudices perhaps, are shown for what they really are: attempts to escape involvement with the living actuality. It is that with which the ground is cleared of such obstacles as those which stand in the way of richer and more flexible thinking.

Though negation has an evident function to perform on the plane of 'higher thinking', as with the rejection of false or improper truth claims, its power is more richly developed on what are presumed to be 'lower levels', in the sphere of action in the form of direct response. But that is where, with truth as the only respectable end, its latent potentiality have been given so little attention that it almost amounts to a scandal, since its effect is to leave comment on vital matters either personalized or subjective – 'emotional' in the language of the logical positivists – or, even more unhappily, to crude and insensitive rationalistic engagement. As vital action refers to the fluid social domain, the delicate balance of which may in some forms be disturbed, in part through mistaken ideas of what value in that sphere comprises, it is perhaps the most important problem philosophy faces, one on which it should certainly bring its disciplined thought to bear, but so in a sensitive manner. For the values by which men most sensibly live do not comprise a matter with which science is fitted to deal. And to attempt to meet the problem posed by this concern by recourse to like procedures is to view it quite improperly. Indeed, it is to act as if philosophy were no more than a branch of science, as logic affects to be, as if it lacked the capacity to develop its own procedures in the face of new found problems. It also presumes a failure to see that the consequences of viewing what it confronts in strictly rational terms, which are without the test of experimentation subjective, delimits its reach unduly. If culture and refinement are the prerogatives of a few when linked to intellectuality, as they are with this dispensation, it is scarcely very surprising that a coarsening is the outcome. Moreover, when a culture turns essentially on knowledge, as cognitively grounded it cannot but be productive of unhappy consequences. It is socially divisive; but, rather more than that, it is potentially threatening if the control of society lies in the hands of a few, manipulating knowledge, by means of computers for instance, in a way that can only be done by specialists or 'experts'. A consequence of this, of which signs are already appearing, is that the humanities will be obliged to give ground to a dominant technology. And indeed, as that becomes the field of those 'who know' – and to urge 'appreciation' is itself a form of patronage, as if there were no such thing as natural sensitivity – that on which a culture of any depth and universality finds its proper ground is gradually corroded. Scepticism in respect of what is now occurring – oddly, because with freedom from unremitting toil and serious deprivation, a capacity is released to develop latent powers – is not then misplaced.

It is pointed, then, to reiterate that negation, unlike assertion, has application to the whole gamut of response. It applies on every level of life; and, in contradistinction to positivistic rulings, which tend to be ideological and in that sense subjective, negation properly deployed may be considered impersonal, inasmuch as its criterion is the quality of life, viewed in its totality. It has, of course, to be deployed with responsibility, and one of its roles is to secure that this need is observed, by negating that which does not comply with its final criterion: that the interests of society always have priority. It is not to be denied that responsibility has at times to take a rational form, as in the weighing of conscious choices as they have effects on the lives of others. That, however, is but an occasional requirement, which, if universalized, can only make excessive demands on the ordinary man – at times to produce false rectitude as subjectivity enters. It further involves a failure to see that the bulk of responsible action has to be taken spontaneously, and so must be inbred, as "the ethic", as Aristotle said, "planted in us by nature".[21] Hence, the problem is to ensure that proper attitudes are developed, which at the present time is just what is not being done. Urging the cultivation of unqualified self-discipline – often a form of preaching to the already converted – is doubtless an admirable doctrine which meets with universal approval. But it may, and often does, lead to less admirable consequences. For, when the autonomous self is held to have priority over the socialized being, those who are not given to reading edifying texts tend to understand it in a rather different manner, as authorizing indulgence in aggressive self-assertion, as permitting unbridled rivalry, as giving a licence to an insistence on one's 'rights', regardless of those of others. In the creative arts, 'expressing one's personality' has in practice led to an upsurge of vulgarity, from which, as works are public, there is no escape unless through blindness to the environment, which is difficult for the sensitive. Thus do admonitions warp when they demand too much and presume that certain attitudes, exemplary as ideals, can simply be universalized without concomitant penalty. Nor is this statement cynical; it takes men as they are, with human strengths and weaknesses, to be tempered as they impinge upon society at large.

Critique of such doctrines as these, if it amounts to no more than that they should be modified in realistic terms, which means with stress on their social effects, is certainly in order. But criticism of ideas held without reservation must certainly go deeper and be referred to the presuppositions on which certain doctrines rest. Some of those go back to the time when the fate of the personal soul, preparing for salvation, was the supreme concern, refined by the idea that *all* were "children under God". But as the self replaced the soul as the pivot of attention, without that needed generalization, a unifying principle was effectively undermined, to leave the ordinary man without an anchor in society, a process gathering speed to render life much harsher, a 'rat race' as is said. It cannot be denied that in a material sense life has become much easier; but that should not be evoked as a warrant for concentration on hylic, hedonistic interests. For without attention to deeper needs, sympathy, for example, or a sense of continuity, which are always present, a 'sense' of man's total nature is blurred, with many unfortunate consequences. No doubt, the mind-matter dichotomy has played some part in this, to generate a distinction between the subject and the object[22] – in fact a projection from the self, though that is scarcely recognized – and has grounded a growing tendency to think of men as objects to be manipulated cognitively. Doubts about the validity of assumptions held uncritically, of which the above affords an example, are justifiably raised, for what is at stake in questioning them is no less than the health of society. And if commercial exploitation, which even threatens the balance of nature, not to mention the human environment, is held to be the prime value, aided by cognition or its complement technology, it is fairly to be asked how far, in placing the self above the whole, the intellect over all else as the paramount human quality, idealistic philosophy bears responsibility.

*

Negation asserts nothing positively, although of course it determines limits, which might be regarded as a form of affirmation, or of 'negative knowledge' so called. But that is a mere play with words, for 'knowledge' so acquired is not a positive augmentation of the type which science seeks, but rather an indication of the requirement to think more deeply. Falsification in that sense is held to be the key to advance.[23] And so seen, it is certainly salutatory, in that it compels the philosophic enquirer to study his brief more thoroughly, in recognition that matters are not as simple as he had supposed. Negation in its sceptical guise traditionally had its warrant in refuting dogmatic assertions, defined as "uncritical positiveness in asserting the truth of a doctrine". Or, as Kant expressed it in less sweeping terms, "... the province of negative judgments is to protect us against error". Since some dogmas, however, sometimes sustain deeply held beliefs, it is wiser perhaps to distinguish between those that are pernicious and give warrant to violent action aimed at upholding power and those that bolster psychical balance, which, as they serve that purpose, should be treated with greater sympathy. Thinkers should be capable of defending their opinions, or rather of accepting justified critique. Meanwhile, the beliefs of those who are not members of that class must be seen in different terms, to be challenged in like manner only when they have clearly disturbing effects, as when fanatics make demands which led to conflict and turmoil, which are obnoxious when upheld by political tyrants. And thus it falls to negativists to exercise discretion, to distinguish between dogmas that are relatively innocuous, even beneficial, and those which militate against the quality of life. It is not without significance, then, that, unlike assertions, which are always a little suspect when referred to human relations, negative judgments refer only to what is disturbing and clearly seen to be so. They do not attempt to influence normal response to conditions, except in so far as that involves setting up personal interest against the interest of the whole, which is a form of perversion. Negation applies to what is plainly inadmissible, in broader terms 'non-fitting', not in the external world itself where disturbances presume changes brought about to produce new forms of dynamic equipoise, but to the human psyche, in part the products of such changes. Nor is it, as philosophical, properly concerned with personal disturbance, which is better dealt with by those who are skilled in dealing with subjective problems. Its concern it with effects on the social whole, the maintenance of balance without recourse to force.

And that must bring us back again to the social bearing of mistaken ideas as to what value in depth comprises and how they influence attitudes to public roles adversely. Its deployment in this sense begins in the field of reflective thought, philosophy itself, basically in questioning dubious presuppositions as they have influence on the postures adopted in society.

Negation seems to be active then on at least three levels, of which that is only one. It operates first on strict rational or logocentric planes, where it checks propositional statements claiming to be true, or, in greater depth, the assumptions on which they rest. Nor is truth always clearly defined, since it is used ambiguously. For it is taken at once to refer to relations In the abstract or, more questionably, to those in the phenomenal world,[24] as if its reference were the same and had a like precision in two very different spheres. Secondly, it is active on the plane of reasoning, where it is referred to what is said with regard to practical matters, wherein it differs from the first in that no judgment then is ever really absolute, so complex are events on this plane of relations. Judgments there are always in some degree provisional, the best perhaps attainable in the conditions prevailing. Any decision resulting is then arrived at dialectically, through a process of trial-and-error, in other words pro and con, in which negation plainly plays a significant part, related to actualities in as far as they are observable. Thirdly, it is applied to what is experienced in life, or better, as will be seen, to immediate confrontation to pressures directly affecting us, in order more fully to understand what is in depth disturbing. But this is not the time to elaborate on that point, the use to which it may be put on this deeper stratum, except perhaps to say that the interest is to distinguish, in as far as that can be done, what constitutes a 'non-fitting' at this basic level. It may be possible, then, to act with greater firmness against it. And so there is a sense in which, when brought to bear in further fields, ethics for example, it performs an even more potent role, since subconscious response, in which ethics is grounded, is the very basis of life. And this we contend can only be done, or done in part at least, by studying the non-fitting as it affects response on this plane of immediacy. Up to this time no attempt has been made – despite the clues afforded by Gestalt psychology – by philosophers to investigate this realm of direct response to reality or to study the implications of what has now been revealed.[25] These are basically ontic and ethical, but they also bear on procedures, which must clearly be different from those devised to serve strictly cognitive ends.

In fine, if the proper end of philosophy is a deeper understanding of man's relation to nature, when nature is seen as something beyond what is phenomenally presented and is more than simply physical, since it also embraces the psychical aspects of life, then all that is implied in response to externality must be taken into account. For otherwise whatever is said about this fundamental relationship is merely superficial, a playing on the surface, as if in that way it afforded sufficient ground to intervene in the realm of human affairs with their ultimate social or interrelative connotations. An instance given above is the manner of reacting to what is stigmatized as dogma, which from a rational standpoint can only consist in showing that an assertion is not well grounded in observation or, in science, experimentation. Though logically immaculate it cannot stand because it is in some way incomplete. Under the rulings of formal logic, any belief can be shown to be false regardless of its value in any deeper sense – from an angle, paradoxically, that may be false itself in terms of human need, in that it fails to engage what has real significance. Failure to take account of the nature of sensitivity, a universal endowment as intellectuality strictly defined is not, reveals a crudeness of outlook which is even deplorable, and especially so today when it is widely accepted that what is ultimately faced, nature or reality, is a dynamic complex of which man is a mode. It is only as sensitive – sentient is more physical – that contact with nature, seen as external, is made. Sensitivity, clearly, is an aspect of man's nature; and it is not without interest that 'nature' in most languages – Chinese and Turkish no less than those with which we in the West are familiar – has double meaning. It is used to refer to all that there is *and* to the characteristics of the various species within it, to imply that there is an intimate affinity between man as a sentient being and what he confronts directly. Philosophy must clearly, then, if it is to contribute in real or meaningful terms, in other than a rather vague and narrow cognitive sense, equip itself to become more sensitive and to recognize that it is not an elusive truth or some positive explanation but general evaluation, interpreted as a concern with what human need or value in deeper sense comprises, that should constitute its interest. Its ultimate concern is effectively with harmony, that of man with nature and through that with his fellow men, that is, with something that cannot properly be particularized but only grasped in terms of the detection of what is non-fitting or out of place, apparently goes against such harmonies as these. Harmony is never, of course, completely attained by men, however virtuous and sensitive some of them may be, but it is always the final criterion, any movement towards which or, better, any reduction of that which tends to inhibit its promotion as the basic value, constitutes a sensible aim. The initial problem, then, is to devise more fitting procedures, which of course shall be no less disciplined; and with that, as the primary problem, the next chapter will be concerned. Nor will that produce complete answers, which can only be brought to being by means of prolonged attention on the part of others, those who see that this is indeed a philosophical problem worthy of pursuit. All that can be done on the present occasion is simply to indicate the way in which thought on such an issue might further be developed, with *determinatio negatio est* as the key to understanding.

Chapter Five

The Logic of Incongruity

Negation, as has been seen, has several roles or functions, or rather spheres of action, which, in so far as it is related to natural logic, to the deployment of reason, may be taken as two, those referred to what is overt and to what is more elusive. All, however, have this principle in common, namely the checking of statements which are not suitable to the occasion. All operate, furthermore, on a rational plane and could not well do otherwise, since the fully conscious intellect has to be evoked, for denial or doubt no less than for asseveration. Even intuition must be subjected to critical comment on the value of what it suggests or puts forward as a proposal. For though the mysterious power of seeing relations directly is normally well-fitted to engage the occasion correctly, it is certainly not sacrosanct, a gift so to say from heaven, despite its arcane origin, and is at time mistaken, largely because the prior knowledge that informs it and was needed for its appearance may itself have been so. The intellect then examines it, subjects it to suitable scrutiny, looks at it quite coldly, without being overawed by its enigmatic emergence. As any writer knows the ideas that spring to mind as he develops his thesis have to pass through a process of critical appraisal, conducted with as much detachment as is possible. And the same applies in artistry, where initial inspiration has to be examined with a critical eye. Its proper place as a factor is within a whole, the composition of which it will in due time form a part – the depth of a shadow, for instance – as is the case with a word, which, if incorrectly chosen, may have an adverse influence on all that is written thereafter. Thus is intellectual power related to inspiration, to give what is received at once, impinges on awareness, a meaningful place in some greater whole, an envisaged composition. Any idea that creation is the outcome of inspiration unsupported by further study is a romantic myth which is certainly not accepted by those who consciously aim to achieve some worthwhile result. Genius was said to be "an infinite capacity for taking sufficient pains", which surely means applying conscious critical powers to what has been gathered involuntarily. Indeed, the purpose of training in any discipline whatever is not to foster powers of creative inspiration, which is a gift without a clearly definable origin, but rather to strengthen critical power, itself the key to achievement of any depth or maturity.

Negation inevitably plays a part in any critical comment, when it is not inspired by mysterious powers of insight but simply by what is presented which is seen to be inappropriate. It is directed against confused or inept expression, which it shows to be mistaken or, more generously, misplaced. Though scepticism, then, is commonly resisted when the end is positive truth, it, notwithstanding all attempts rationally to discredit it, has never been wholly crushed, convincingly refuted, and indeed emerges again and again to curb rationalistic pretensions. Its real interest, however, is not merely to limit those, which, when strictly idealistic, do not carry much weight, but to give its attention to failure properly to deal with what is really significant – for Socrates ethical issues, justice, friendship, and so on. From this such trivial forms of it, linked to the cognitive interest, as knowledge of other minds or of past events, are sensibly excluded, since they turn on nugacious questionings, on academic concerns as if those had any real bearing on life. Scepticism rather throws doubt on claims to state truth or strict knowledge about relations in actuality, in the external world. As serious it relates to thoughts about reality, that which gives ground to life and does not properly fall within the sphere of explanation, much less in that of truth. In this sense it continues to prick the bubble of pretentiousness; and if the fashion of the times, "the insatiable urge to know", attempts to brush it aside as unworthy of attention, more deeply as a challenge to all that rationalism holds dear, such fashions in philosophy, as in dress or ideology, are transient or temporary. Sceptical stricture, conversely, does not pass into desuetude but is always latent, ready to spring into action when occasion for it arises.

Although negation plays part in any critical judgment, it operates on a wider plane, which is not ideational only nor confined to cognitive truth claims. As it then relates to action rather than to speaking, it is less to be aligned with sceptical contentiousness than seen as a means of securing a better understanding of what in depth conditions life. And in this sense, paradoxically, its findings have what amounts to a positive bearing, though only indirectly, for they are not explanatory, even if suggestive. They indicate a way in which action might be taken, or better one by which mistakes or failures may be avoided. The interest at this level, then, is not so much to refute rational misconceptions, or rather their expression, since that is idealistic. It is to extend a critical power into wider fields, into realms that are not empiric or perceptual but real in the deepest sense, as involving contact with reality. Thus, when it is said that there are two forms of negation, that does not refer to those in use in formal and natural logic, applying roughly similar principles, explicit in the first and implicit in the second, but to the introduction of a wholly different approach.

*

Accordingly, when reference is to two logics of negation, what is in mind are two planes or stages on which they are applied, which presume, as will be seen, two different modes of procedure. One is concerned with ideal or declaratory statement purporting to refer, though always a little precariously, since what is confronted is complex and not easily defined. Even so, on this verbal plane, a sentence may be corrigible in an internal sense, as when it uses terms improperly, is ambiguous, fallacious, incoherent or self-contradictory. And this is properly pointed out, to demand at least its reframing, if not to damn it completely. The other is concerned with what takes place in direct response, even though what that involves can only be grasped in a limited way, that is, because it is disturbing. In neither of these forms, however, does negation pretend to offer any explanation, but simply to detect and correct what is out of place in two quite different spheres.

The logic of negation is then used as a generic term which subsumes two forms of its application, fairly to be distinguished by giving them different names: as *the logic of inconsistency* and *the logic of incongruity,* referring to verbal contentions and to direct response respectively. A comment is needed here to make this distinction clearer, for in ordinary language these terms are at times used interchangeably. And yet there is a difference of which dictionaries take note. 'Consistent', and so 'inconsistent', though they may refer to persons and the principles they adhere to, are more commonly used of expressions, and normally so in philosophy, where in formal logic the second relates to its second law, that of contradiction. 'Congruous', conversely, rather refers to states of affairs, to events or to appearances, to what is presented phenomenally, presumed in common language to refer to external existences, as indeed it does, though then they are not objects but ultimate realities. Thus, colours may not be congruous, fit together comfortably, or events may be incongruous with normal expectations, a snowfall in summer for instance. And the same applies to actions, when they are judged to be inappropriate either in time or in place. But this word is seldom or never used in philosophical discourse. A faulty sentence is not designated incongruous; it is held to be inconsistent, and so by a long tradition, to mean that the terms employed do not hold together, are either contradictory or a variance with some principle. In any case, however, in conformity with the principle that terms must be defined in the manner in which they are to be used in any given context, these two will be employed in the meanings here distinguished: one to refer to what is said, in rational discourse specifically, and the other to what is detected as failing to fit into place, that is to say as 'non-fitting' in response to stimulation.

The logic of inconsistency calls for little elaboration, since, as plainly linked to the second law of logic, it is generally familiar. Indeed, it is included in the accepted list of fallacies, and there, if not in all, quite clearly in two forms: the fallacy that is positively called that of inconsistency, which relates directly to syllogistic argument, and the fallacy of *tu quoque,* which rather relates to actions and beliefs which are incompatible with assertions made. But the basis of most fallacies is some form of inconsistency, some failure to relate contentions to one another, to produce a valid inference. Under their formal names they may not readily be recognized, but they would not have been distinguished into their many varieties unless flaws in logical discourse had been detected to distinguish them. Even natural logic discerns the more obvious among them, such as self-contradiction; and indeed, all those that are not peculiar to logocentric discourse. But they are not always detectable in ordinary conversation, and to bring them to attention is perhaps the primary role of strict formal logic, that wherein it justly claims to stand above natural logic, indeed to afford it a discipline, to sharpen its critical powers. Contradiction is usually obvious, inconsistency is less so and may have rather subtle forms which escape attention if alertness is not present. And yet it could be harmful when public statement is made in a slovenly manner, to generate confusion and misunderstanding of aims, which, when it comes to decisions affecting the lives of others, may have serious effects. No one can get round an exposure of inconsistency, and that is quite decisive in the Courts of Law, where a witness making such a mistake invalidates his evidence. Inconsistency is rare in symbolic logic, since that does not refer, so that the relation of words to one another with their implicit ambiguity, does not enter into equations, which can be inconsistent of course if a symbol is wrongly used, though that is a patent fault which is seldom allowed to occur. Errors may be made in mathematical computation, but those are less inconsistencies than mistakes in calculation, which are readily rectified if the outcome is not as it should be. To simplify the issue, then, the logic of inconsistency may be taken to apply to logocentric discourse aiming to eliminate whatever stands in the way of sustaining truth in propositional statements, which if they are flawed, cannot be alethic. To this it might be added that any statements made, positive or negative, rational or suggestive, have to pass the test, if they are to be accepted, of internal consistency, not only when they claim to be truths or to be explanatory, but simply to be intelligible, coherent, unequivocal.

The logic of incongruity is not so simply defined; for not only is it outside the normal conception of logic, a stranger in its midst, and even an unwelcome one, but ideas in respect of it are as yet but tentative and very far from firm. The first thing to be noticed about it, then, is this: that it relates to content in contradistinction to form, not that the last is excluded, as if what was being expressed were immune from any form of checking, that is of the application of the logic of inconsistency, but that what is referred to is not properly to be verbalized. This calls for a little refinement, since 'content' in this context has a rather different meaning from that which it has acquired in idealistic discourse, in which it means something held in, gathered by the intellect, usually referred to, loosely, as the 'mind'. 'Reference' under another approach – to be considered later – one in which response relates to realms beyond the cognizable, is always in some sense questionable from a rational standpoint, inasmuch as truth claims rest on objectification, involving the extraction of something from its context with a measure of distortion. A subjective factor is introduced as an object so formed is analyzed into parts in a particularizing process. Hence when the term 'subjective' is used in it modern sense[1] its relation is exclusively to idealistic thinking, to what has ground in the intellect, in consciousness and not in any realm of response below it. And so it will be used, to eliminate ambiguity, as this thesis is developed. Content may, meanwhile, be considered as an influence on the responsive agent having effect directly, as something which in that sense cannot be objectified, extracted for inspection because it is normally transient, although its effects may be lasting. It then refers to what is received immediately, when its meaning differs from that which it is given in rational aesthetics, where content is taken to refer – and has been since talk on the arts became a special discipline – to what allows of a rational or intellectual entry. What a picture represents, 'means' or in recent parlance 'states', its relation to its period, to other works and so on, are typical of this understanding of content, which refers essentially to conceptual interests. And if this is a little confusing when those alone have standing, it can only be said, in defence or extenuation, that content carries the import here of what affects us generally, in any way whatever. This includes response to form, which in a classical sense implies a play on the sentient nerves, if adequately and successfully, in a harmonious manner. Thus are these two aspects of response to be distinguished, though normal usage may find this alien to received romantic interpretations, in that this has meaning only on a plane on which clear consciousness is not present. Content, to such a reading as this, refers, or so essentially, to what affects us sensuously.

The difficulty, if there is one in accepting this definition, is rooted in a failure, with exclusive concentration on what the intellect can grasp, seriously to consider what lies beyond its range: direct response to stimuli. Once this restriction is overcome attention may be turned to what deeply conditions life, response on preconscious levels. But to refer to such levels as these, there is need for a further vocabulary, necessarily based on familiar words, but extending their meanings to engage extra-cognitive interests, for which both form and content have different connotations. For, in this case form means shape or shapeliness linked to a rhythmic unfolding, and content means the influence that that has on the recipient, referring very broadly to both external and internal changes, to cause and to effect.

Put in simpler terms, content on this level means the content of an impression, which, although that is commonly taken as necessarily conscious – for nothing is granted significance unless it is rationalizable – is normally vague and evanescent except when it is disturbing. Even so, it has substance as exercising an influence. But that is plainly different from any effect with roots in an objective finding, which is ideal and subjective, confined to fully conscious reception, the limitations of which have already been noted and need not further be stressed. It is to overcome those and to penetrate more deeply, if only to understand what artistry implies in universal terms, that thought on extended meanings has to be undertaken, in order to direct it towards what really counts in life, what influences people generally and not only a self-conscious few. And since it has hitherto been supposed, because they are not definable, that interests such as these are without significance, it is time that that view was changed. If, then, the extension of meanings given to various terms is part of what has to be done, that is not improper. For what it really involves is a return to basic meanings which are by no means obsolete. 'Form' still means 'shape' or, in such expressions as 'well-formed' or 'elegant', 'shapely'. And 'formal' in its more rigid sense is but a derivative rooted in what originally meant 'graceful', 'comely', 'eurhythmic', as in natural movement or in easy manners.[2] It only later came to mean 'conventional', 'without spirit', as in perfunctory performances, stiff and rigid attitudes lacking flexibility. As "the constituent of a conception", 'content' again is derivative, since at base it means 'holding in or with', a 'reception' as might be said of what is taken in impression, which is just as fair a reading as that which aligns it with conception. To illustrate this concretely, the content of a symphony might be given consideration. It could comprise the chords or notes of which it is constructed, accessible in principle to close examination or, alternatively, to the influence it brings to bear on the hearer, which presents itself sequentially, in effect as a play on the nerves,[3] which is surely more natural, the normal form of response. To introduce 'incongruity', then, is to employ a term that refers to real events, or rather to adverse effects on reception at basic levels. This has little or nothing to do with verbal formulations, but evidently relates to vital response to stimuli, which is normally harmonious – for life would otherwise be intolerable – but is on occasion discordant, in other words incongruous. The implications of this will not be considered at once. Enough that what is now of concern is something wholly different from what interests conceptualists, striving to define what is definable or explicit and disregarding that which cannot be so engaged.

Given permission to use these terms in the manner set out, the way is open to explore a more basic aspect of life than that which rationalists can reach. It is important, then, to note that, if positive explanation is the only end of enquiry, these matters must go by default. For there can be no explanation of what is not observable or, better said, is not to be analyzed or objectified. When *psyché* is used in its basic sense as the principle of life, usually understood as the spirit that informs it, it is scarcely proper to limit the ideas we have about it to its physical characteristics. For, although there can be no life without a physical matrix, its psychical characteristics cannot be divorced from that in the manner of Descartes or of Husserl more recently. Indeed, we must now accept that there is an interrelation between these animating elements, not only on conscious planes, quite certainly granted to humans, but also on subconscious levels, which, as shared with animals, were presumed, if regarded at all, as outside mental life, and so were viewed as bodily, physical to exclusion.[4] But if the two are, so to say, aspects of one another, then this interrelationship is not a simple matter which can be comprehended by exclusive study of one aspect or the other, but an indivisible complex which must be viewed in that character. If life in its total meaning then defies strict explanation, which can only have a rather limited reach, what it involves in responsive terms can only be understood through response to external pressures as they produce disturbing effects. This is the key to what at base conditions life, and it is detectable only through the study of what disrupts or undermines its equipoise. That itself has both psychical and physical correlates or effects, though those as has already been said, are not properly separable. For what is disturbing or untoward and adversely affects the system – the psychosomatic whole, which constitutes the nature of every sentient being, at least of higher species – must be seen as an infusion and not as something compounded of elements or parts. The restoration of balance then calls on all available powers, developed through evolution as means of achieving that end. Some of these powers are cognizable and the tendency has been to concentrate on those that are in that sense explicable, though it is evident enough that explanation cannot engage all that is detectable, inasmuch as its aim is positive, which confines it to causal consequences that allow of quantification. Others are more subtle, since they have psychical features, in which case disturbance is deeper and so in some sense spiritual, or at least has that tone as a factor.

In fine, it is through the study of what is out of order, interferes with the normal state of psychosomatic harmony, that deeper understanding of the nature of response is at all achievable. But the implications of that, both in respect of findings and of checking their value as furthering understanding, cannot be discussed at once, for that involves other considerations to warrant its projection. Sufficient now that the congruous or harmonic aspect of response to the environment, which is its normal form,[5] calls for no explanation, for that would be redundant, were it possible at all at these basic levels, because in such conditions relations are as they should be, attunement has been attained. Conversely, the incongruous, though it and the forms that it takes cannot be explained, allows of some detection for reasons to be discussed. And that, to reiterate, is the key to a partial but nonetheless valuable grasping of what produces disturbing effects, and further to the manner in which statement which are referred to these deeper relations may themselves be subjected to check.

*

Before going further, however, some elaboration is needed, for up to the present point disturbance as an influence has been rather vaguely conceived, as if it affected persons only. What then, in more comprehensive terms, constitutes the incongruous to which this logic refers? The simple answer, of course, which echoes what has been said, is that it is whatever seems to be so disturbing as to threaten balance, homeostasis in the body, equipoise in the psyche, reflecting an ancient dichotomy. However, its full effect does not end in the life of the individual, since the influence of externals, although of course they bear on him, does not exhaust itself in effects upon the self, modern bias notwithstanding. It also has repercussive effects, which impinge on society generally. Moreover, these reverberate to increase personal stress. In such sense they may justly be considered as having priority, to be disturbance's most significant form when its nature is up for review. It could be argued, of course, that social pressures are external, just as those produced by nature; and that is not to be denied. But, whereas the latter have in the main to be accepted as the given condition of life, those with social origins are in some sense controllable – the aim precisely that warrants moral and ethical studies. And since the end of ethical thought consists in the reduction, through applied prescriptions, of what stands in the way of attunement, the study of the incongruous is clearly related to it. But at last it is even arbitrary to separate these two pressures, as though in Cartesian terms we were dealing with different worlds, the psychical and the physical; for the concern is with what disturbs regardless of its origin. Both impinge on the psyche, at large on subconscious levels, and neither on those levels is overt or really explicable, definable, that is to say, in a positive sense. Society may be man-made as nature clearly is not; but it is scarcely consciously so and indeed takes the forms that it has, transient fashions apart, through a process of evolution, adjustments to conditions over long periods of time. If nature tends to harmony, however great the disturbances that are generated at times, societies, as history shows, have been gravely thrown off balance with the collapse or decay of great cultures, which is a further reason for strengthening stability, now on a universal plane, by attention to what disturbs it. All societies whatever, whether primitive or advanced, strive, if they are wise and have some sense of consequences, to abide by certain norms or rules, which are flouted at penalty. And although against more obvious threats to balance and cohesion, law can be evoked to control anti-social behaviour, that is limited as a means and must rest on something deeper, the development of a 'social sense', dependent on the attitudes adopted by its members. What values society lives by or, rather more precisely since those are not strictly definable, what tends to frustrate their attainment, should be the concern of philosophy as it essays to deal with real problems. Nor is it ideologies, which tend to be subjective and even generate conflict, which constitute the modes by which balance and cohesion are suitably sustained. It is rather attention to what inhibits their attainment, especially as they involve attunement to a whole, which is not, without misconstrual, divisible into parts.

'That will not do', though apparently related to convention, has in fact a deeper meaning than that word bears when referred essentially to formalities. For conventions are themselves, when something more than etiquette linked to passing fashion, the products of conditions imposed on men by nature, which persist because they work and have proved of value over time as a means of maintaining balance. Relation between the sexes – recognition of women's needs, or relations between youth and age, acknowledgement of experience and of greater frailty – have been developed in this way and in a basic sense are common to all societies.[6] Indeed, they are so much so that affronting them as if nature, in which they are finally grounded, could fittingly be denied is a dangerous game, which usually proves destructive and is itself a form of disturbance. Nature is the determinant and that is forgotten at penalty. Thus, when thought is given to what is basic in human nature – its 'essence' as might be said – man's relation to nature, which has granted him his intellect to deal with more pressing problems, must be taken into account. Though some of these problems presume grappling with inconsistencies, the more vital, beyond question, relate to incongruities, refer to what is out of place in relation to life itself and to the psychosomatic needs which accompany actual living. No doubt, these needs embody many disruptive features, largely the products of passion, which is natural in itself, though rational in aspects. Jealousy, envy, greed, overweening ambition, which conventions, norms, prescriptions and religious admonitions have been developed to bring under some control, are factors always present and are at times so strong that they tend to break all bounds, producing conflict, tyranny, war and other savageries. Their elimination is an ideal, their reduction is a necessity, and all that tends to foster them is justly subject to check. All societies have endeavoured by various means to control them, risking in failure to do so their own degeneration, which is threatened whenever implicit norms are challenged with impunity, almost at times as if that "added a spice to life" – a view that is comfortably held by those who are not themselves at risk. Formerly, powers of destructive type were limited or confined to relatively few, those with the means to indulge them. But that is no longer the case today, since now such powers are widespread and a sense of responsibility no longer holds them in check, to allow of a certain balance between exuberance and good sense. Self-expression, ennobled as self-determination, justifies the destruction of otherwise innocent lives, wrecks any hope of arriving at reasonable solutions, which, though they can never be perfect, allow at least of the prospect of living together in unity. Hence, with the cult of autonomy, it is of greater moment today that such destructive passions are brought under greater control, not so much by political means, introduced when the damage is evident, as by developing attitudes that are more in tune with reality, sounder ideas about what is socially destructive.[7]

It is necessary, then, to make a distinction between two forms of anti-social behaviour, that which is clearly criminal and that which has another, a rather less obvious character. For the first is overt and in that sense controllable or containable by means of legal coercion and rather less effectively by moral admonition, *prima facie* the only means of dealing with subtler forms of what may be no less destructive. But address to persons in that way is effective only when they are susceptible to it, and it is further under handicap inasmuch as moral values give considerable scope for dispute. That there are moral absolutes may very well be the case; but whether they can be defined in strict rational terms is certainly open to question when there is no criterion which has universal bearing in which they could be grounded – the sacredness of human life, absolute truth or whatever is projected as the paradigm – for exceptions are surely present. But the problem is not well seen in such personal terms as these. It should rather be understood as that of the balance of society, sustained, or if fragile restored, by means of a gradual process of modifying attitudes, particularly those adopted by the dominant classes, the Jesuits' 'heads of state'. However, it is not those today who exercise the real influence, once held to be a trust, but rather those who control what constitutes the 'mass media', whose interest is rather to entertain than to give responsible leadership. This should not be pressed too far, though it is a point of some moment that therein lies the key, to suggest that that is the class to which attention should be addressed, for at present responsible thinking is characteristic only of responsible persons and not those with the sole idea of competing for audience figures. If we harbour the belief that all is as it should be, that we have no obligation towards the future, that materialistic attitudes aimed at increasing prosperity afford the only apt criterion, we are living in a fool's paradise, fiddling whilst Rome burns. Disregard of the attitudes adopted by society under the influence of 'thinkers' or smugness in respect of those that are presently fostered as if they were all that were required renders ethical thinking futile, as if to project prescriptions were an infringement on personal liberty, on "freedom to do one's own thing". There is a problem to be faced, and if it is disregarded we have only ourselves to blame. If the quality of society is a matter of some importance, then it should be given the attention it deserves.

Anti-social behaviour is endemic in human society, but happily something finer is also characteristic of relations between persons. Decency, trust and courtesy, a sense of the needs of others, are intrinsic features of the human make-up, and so much so that they survive even under repressive regimes, where, as if in silent protest, they may well take steadier forms than when freedom is exalted regardless of the consequences. Paradoxical though it may seem, the decay of a social sense is more likely to occur with stress on the cult of the individual, under which the agent is even encouraged to act as he alone see fit, largely in indifference to the needs of others. This is not, of course, to advocate arbitrary control which is even delimiting socially. It is simply to suggest that deeper thought be given to the later effects of libertarian advocacy, when that does not so much relate to democratic politics as to social relations.[8] The postures characteristic of self-centred orientation, rivalry, competitiveness, personal advance achieved often at social cost, are bound to produce resentment in those without the power to attain what seems to be so desirable, and so positively engender dangerous and unhealthy divisions in society. Nor is it pointed to argue that these have always existed, since that is merely to blur the issue, which is the problem presented today, when for the first time in history all might share in a culture which was once confined in its finer forms to a few. A human potentiality, sensuous and spiritual, for oddly those are related, could be released were it understood that equality on that plane has other than intellectual or economic forms. Intellectualism is indeed, as Hartman so wisely said, a divisive factor,[9] and the notion of 'lifting the masses' to that exalted plane involves both a form of patronage and a grave misunderstanding of what is really of value in life. But then, as a cult of rivalry is promoted as that on which emphasis is to be placed, any idea of quality related to something more subtle – 'tame' as might be said – can scarcely be entertained as a meaningful aim.

Put in philosophical terms, this idea of rivalry does not, it seems, apply. For officially the aim in that discipline is impersonal, to elicit truth which is free from any tincture of subjectivity. But the notion of the knowing self, rooted in and sustained by idealistic thinking, is by no means unrelated to subjective stances and may be said to ground them. Moreover truth, the purported aim related to verbal niceties is not a matter of much interest to a wider public and as such has little bearing on what is of moment in life. For verbal play is one thing, doubtless intriguing to those whose delight it is to indulge it, vital interests are quite another and only in part engaged by words when those are essentially abstract rather than referential. Ideal relations are not the same, and are certainly not more important, despite a stress on their sublimity, than those that are real or vital; and indeed, the more ideal they are the further are they removed from the complexity of the continually changing reality. Quite another criterion has to be envisaged if value is the concern; and that presumes a different approach, because, if the aim is still positive, it is so but indirectly, as the enhancement of life on planes that abstractions cannot engage. Perhaps this is a little obscure, but what it means is this. That a general end is attained, in as far it may be, not by idealizing what is presumed to be desirable, which is always debatable, but by the delimitation of that which stands in the way of a refinement, by attempting to establish a better relation to nature and through that with other people. The proper approach, accordingly, is negative rather than positive, applied first to dubious doctrines and the attitudes they countenance. For unless their adverse effects are exposed any more subtle entry is blocked by persistent advocacy of doctrines which place the emphasis on what is not only irrelevant but positively obstructive of what is really required. But as that is not clearly to be defined and so has no rational standing, it cannot be simply put forward without deeper thought on what is involved in relation to reality.

*

This preoccupation with value may seem rather far removed from logical concerns, notwithstanding a hint present in the last paragraph. But if that is the end of enquiry in contradistinction to truth, there is certainly a relation between logic in negative form and value considered as general, in that the first refers essentially to its protection. It is requisite then to understand what value in that sense means, means when its import is other than that of material advance and when it is not rationally quantifiable. In depth or in general it accrues through attunement to the environment in natural or social forms, which means in the latter especially in relation to others. As both of these aspects of what is confronted are interrelative structures, any idea that either allows of rational definition involves a failure to understand what is involved in confronting a holistic complex and man's relation to it as the ultimate source of value. Undoubtedly there are values that can in some sense be defined. Those, however, are broadly peculiar to the person, a matter of personal preference intellectually tinged, as when critics disagree, praising one work or doctrine rather than another. It is therefore not so much to value seen in these general terms as to *dis*value to which attention is properly given. For that, as involving restriction on adequate attunement is, conversely, something definable, precisely because it interferes with implicit rapport. Clearly, disvalue takes many forms, those that are natural for instance, illness and other disasters, earthquakes, floods, droughts and so on. Those have in general to be borne, as have taxation, recession and other economic events, which, though not exactly natural, have somewhat similar traits, since they are more or less unavoidable. Others, however, such as ugly or garish surroundings, gratuitous rudeness, crass and uncalled for violence, excessive noise and even unrestrained vulgarity,[10] are within our power to control, if current postures allow of it. And it is in effect to guard against these unsettling intrusions that prescriptions and norms, which have for the most part negative forms, have been developed in all societies, and so for quite sufficient reason: that such attitudes as these threaten social harmony. The ideal is that anyone indulging these proclivities should be faced by disapproval generally exerted. For there are such values as decency, honour, trust and courtesy which are scarcely rationalizable, on which society depends. To know how to behave certainly differs from knowing that such and such is the case; for, since appropriate action is effected in a complex, it involves a measure of 'sensing' what is apt in a changing world.

Fully to understand involvement in this sense, it is requisite to grasp how men, and other sentient beings perhaps, respond directly or spontaneously to what they really confront. And 'directly' is the key word here, for to hold that the phenomenal or the perceptual world is that to which we respond *immediately* is a mistaken view, adopted by those who are stigmatized – oddly even by logical atomists – as 'naive realists', bound to "the vulgar prejudices of simple common sense",[11] but free, of course, from the prejudice that sublimates absolute truth. Perception is only effected *after* a filtering process, which alone allows of it, has been undertaken. That is a form of selection from a greater whole, aspects of which are arrested when the end is conception, wherein the process differs when it is but dim perception which has a dynamic character, involving response to the flow of events and not an attempted detachment from them. This deeper response, though established by scientific findings, may be resisted as an idea bordering on sophistry, because it projects a world beyond explanatory reach. But, apart from the *ding an sich,* which is generally familiar, neurology now shows that much – some 90% of response it is said[12] – takes place below the level of consciousness, and Gestalt psychology further shows that a process must take place to shield us against the distraction which would otherwise be the consequence of a full awareness of the showers of stimuli persistently playing upon us. The philosophical bearing of such findings as these has received but little attention because the tendency has been to concentrate on the clearly perceptual as that which can be analyzed with a measure of clarity, as if what cannot be so were devoid of meaning. But if philosophy is concerned, as it most certainly should be, with man's relation to the world he confronts in immediate stimulation, these findings are surely operative, and indeed all later effects are evidently conditioned by influences from below and the values they sustain. Put in another way, the world that is studied by empiricists, the so called world of 'facts', is grounded in a deeper world, justly to be distinguished as infra- or extra-empiric. It is further to the point that when we speak of response as sensuous, in distinction from perceptual, it is that plane to which we refer as the very basis of life. To disregard it, then, because it cannot be brought into consciousness, or better said be objectified – notwithstanding that ideas may be formed about it – is to disregard this vital aspect of response, and so to misunderstand the nature of value in general.

Without attempting to describe this filtering process in depth, what is at once of concern are the forms of dynamic response to the process of becoming, the characteristic of nature. These forms appear to be two, apart from response which is clearly conscious: dim perception, which has likewise scarcely been studied, and wholly subconscious response, which might be called 'sensation', were that term not so ambiguous.[13] Why then, it may be asked, does this last form of it comprise so extensive a proportion of all response that is made? The answer lies in the way in which nature affords us protection against its profuseness so to say. For were we fully aware of all the pressures it brings to bear, we should be so distracted that we could scarcely act, much less think with clarity, so that life would be intolerable, in the words of a well-known *apercu,* "a blooming, buzzing confusion".[14] Happily, nature protects us against such a calamitous outcome by so arranging matters that that does not occur. For the mind, with roots in *ma* or *man,* meaning 'interiority' – the organism poised against externals acting on it – acts on unconscious levels, aided in this by psychical powers, mnemonic and intentional, and so orders stimulant pressures as to select from among them those that are significant in relation to present needs; mediating others, the less important majority, below the level of consciousness. It is a feature of conscious reception that it can only with comfort gather one thing, a unitary whole or relationship, at one time. Hence, the stimulus that has the greatest significance for us is, through this screening process, presented to consciousness as a whole, commonly called a *Gestalt,* as something with which we are able consciously to deal. As conscious, accordingly, we relate to external events only when a Gestalt has been formed in respect of a stimulus selected subconsciously from many, which may be received as a grouping of unitary form.[15] After that act it is possible to proceed to objectification and subsequent analysis of what has been objectified to inductive generalization. For particulars are Gestalten viewed in a certain way.

Objectification is relatively rare, at least in any strict sense. For, when living directly in relation to nature, when immersed so to say in the dynamic of becoming, a somewhat different process takes place. Gestalten are not held, frozen for inspection, but are received sequentially, one following another in very rapid succession, as when, for instance, in driving a car, the eyes are constantly scanning the way that lies ahead, searching as it were for what might have significance, a bump or a bend in the road or another car approaching. When walking this alertness is to the presence of others, to obstacles in one's path, to oncoming traffic, and so on. Of course, there are constant switches from dim to clear perception, as when there is need to cross the street in the face of fast moving traffic, or again when something of interest catches one's attention. But such rapid calculations as these, of speed, direction and change, even though they involve a form of objectification and a measure of analysis, are scarcely to be equated with the deliberation required in rationalistic thinking. Their purpose is not to know in an epistemic sense, but to act with appropriate adequacy. Hence, quite apart from subconscious response, which is the basis of all of it, there is a world in which dim perception operates, which is significant philosophically as evidently related to those aspects of life which call for conscious sensitivity, based on memory rather than on strict or definitive knowledge.

Greater significance, still, attaches to that response which involves direct contact with reality, which, though it cannot be observed, as to some extent dim perception may be, plainly exerts an influence on everything we do. All nervous response, as to rhythmic form, is grounded on this plane, where it is more or less common to men, though that should be said with caution because such response is so complex, so intertwined with the psychical, that it cannot be said with full confidence, notwithstanding that nervous response is more likely to have broadly similar traits than that which is subjective. But any attempt to characterize what is not fully observable in physical terms alone, which can only describe, at times with the aid of instruments, what has concrete form, plainly leaves something out of account, although it is influential. Indeed, it is common knowledge that sensuous or artistic response defies rational explanation. This complicates the issue, or would do were the concern to establish similarity on this responsive plane as distinct from supposing it, with a measure of justification. The crucial point, however, when thinking of response at this basic level, is that, when we are on it we are directly involved with externals, pressures from which are absorbed and mediated quite naturally. In fact, we are in harmony with reality itself, acting much as animals do, if rather more acutely, without deliberation, that is, as might be said, 'instinctively'. Nor does this mean that we, as we so respond, are then no more than animals, as if that lowered our status. It simply states an obvious point, that we share some characteristics with other sentient beings, modified by those which are peculiar to our species with greater psychical powers, inclusive of sensitivity, noting that that is as natural a feature as are the others. Direct response is conditioned by the conscious powers with which we humans are endowed, exemplified in mnemonic and purposive proficiency, the capacity to learn from more varied and richer experience acquired in the course of life.

Let us then be clear about this, which has largely been forgotten, that sensitivity, which is innate in the human make-up, is at the root of all refinement and the grounding of any culture which is fairly considered general. Indeed, if seen in other terms, those that are intellectual, or rather strictly so, what is present to everyone may well be overlaid, replaced by artificiality. Contrary to the common belief, fostered by intellectuals with essentially cognitive interests, response in artistic or rhythmic form is sensuous at base and not in deep sense intellectual. Hence to intellectualize what is really involved is not only to misunderstand wherein its general value resides as an enhancement of vitality, but to deprive the ordinary man of his power to respond directly, or rather to confuse that power with rational irrelevances. Enjoined to look for a meaning in intellectual terms – its provenance, what it represents, who the artist was, his psychological attitudes – its essential value is effectively lost to view.[16] Practically all societies have cultivated the dance and the music that accompanies it, normally without attempts to rationalize its forms, to show that response to rhythm is innate in the human make-up and so revealing the need for, the will as it were to harmony through relation to nature, balance in bodily movements linked to the nervous system. Sensuous or nervous response – when the first does not mean 'sensual', which involves a conscious, subjective, concupiscent stance – plays part in every aspect of life, in delicacy, in sympathy and other forms of relationship, which are even coarsened when self-consciousness intervenes.

*

All this may seem to be a digression, since logic scarcely enters it, concerned as it is with response below the level of consciousness. But, if we are to discuss the relation of thought to worlds beyond the reach of formal logic, the matter of ensuring that discourse referred to relations in such further worlds shall be subjected to proper discipline takes on some significance. What has been said has then been said to show, a necessary preliminary, that on these 'lower' levels man is at one with nature and in harmony with its pulse. This is man's normal state, as is seen when he makes quasi-conscious adjustments such as can be observed, easing himself in his chair or modifying his step as he climbs up rising ground, should be sufficiently obvious. For nature forms the body to deal with changing situations, reflected in stimulation which is mediated successfully below the level of consciousness. Thus, to refer to the lowest level of awareness, if a fly settles on one's cheek one acts with no more than a flick of the wrist in order to drive it away. Conversely, if the intruder is a hornet or a wasp, which presents rather more of a threat, one proceeds with greater caution and waits perhaps until one can drive it out of the window or otherwise dispose of it. And so the greater the menace the greater the need for thought as to how to counter it, thinking rapidly perhaps but none the less with clear consciousness. In other words, reflection is called upon for guidance whenever something untoward has to be confronted. It is evoked to bring experience to bear whenever pressure is so great that it cannot be countered effectively by the means that nature provides to meet less disturbing influences. Elsewhere such adversative action has been labelled 'responsive rejection'[17], since that is that in which the need for counteraction originates. As a prelude it is active on all levels of response as a form of negation when counteraction is called for, from flinching through tasting something questionable or sour to repudiating a truth claim. In sum, negation is called into play whenever there is need to take apt action against what is in some way disturbing, in the first case to the nerves, in the second to the psyche, in the last to the intellect acting in full consciousness. So logic, referred to what is incongruous or disturbing, is introduced to detect what is out of order, whence it is carried further as need arises to criticize what is said about what has been detected. For, although detection is usually just when it is spontaneous, as soon as description is introduced a subjective element enters. And it is that subjective element which may falsify or corrupt a proper notion of it, which means its likely general effects. Negation has then a double role on the plane of instant reception, both to detect the form of an impression justly and then to ensure that what is received is properly reported. For the end of all such action is to determine what disturbs, basically on this level, in order that its effects, which constitute general influences, may be countered effectively in awareness of the involvement.

Clearly, this presumes the deployment of conscious thought applied on the plane of immediacy, now given special attention because it has not as yet been fully studied. What signifies, then, is that such thought, in effect applying negation, is evoked when something is other than it should be, threatens to disturb or positively does so in some way or another. Let it be understood, then, apart from internal disorder or disconcerting introspection, that disturbance has its seat in the external environment, for even some mental disturbance may be said to have such an origin, in what is said or read for instance. What is external in that case, to intellectuality no less than to sensitivity, is ultimate reality, even if what is registered has a phenomenal form. Thus, responsive rejection is made against some form of stimulation, deeply brought about by change in the truly external world. A point of some moment, then, which is highly significant here, is that it is by negation alone that the intellect makes contact with reality immediately or directly, that is to say without the delimiting intervention of objectifying processes, which can never reach it. Something is out of order and so much so that the intellect is immediately aware of it and has no time, if there is need for instant counter-action, to resort to deliberation about what it represents. And this contact with externals is direct because the intellect is, so to say, woken to attention. For though thought may be being given to some philosophical problem or other passing matters, something really disturbing throws that into the shade. Attention has to be turned to what is more compelling. What has then to be emphasized is that when the intellect is obliged to act directly in this form of responsive reaction, it does not objectify in the normal sense of that term, extracting an 'object' from the complex in which it exists, but reacts in quite a different way. For what is presented to it on such an occasion as this *objectifies itself*, stands out against the circumambient harmony, which is the normal state of relation to reality, both in man himself and in other natural beings, reflecting nature itself as it moves through a series of subtle adjustments to maintain dynamic equipoise. Something is out of order, and the intellect, as a power given to man to allow him to take more decisive action than 'instinct' with its more limited range allows in the animal world, has to do something about it.

This clearly takes two forms on the human level: that of personal interest, the need to sustain one's balance in the environment about one, and that of which responsible men must surely take account, effects on the body social. For many disturbing forces have social repercussions, with which the ethicist at least ought to be concerned. Indeed, these repercussive effects are precisely the ethical problem – in contradistinction to that which the moral philosopher faces – as influences on the social whole which may disturb its balance, if not immediately over time.[18] What those are likely to be and what can be done control them is very much the concern of the responsible thinker. But leaving that aside for later consideration, let us attend more fully to the salient point in this. A state of affairs is operative in the complex of reality as an event with influence on society generally. Something in the manifold holds a potential threat – not necessarily physical, as if that were alone significant – in that it tends to disrupt the harmony on which the sustaining of balance depends. A 'non-fitting' is detected apparently as it is when contact is immediate; and, as its effects are disquieting, it addresses itself to the intellect as something standing out which unacceptable. And that it is on which action has to be taken, fully in a general sense, as if the recipient in that case represented all men, as in some sense he does when his response is spontaneous. For response of that type has the virtue of being extra-subjective until it is rendered personal by interpretation. And that is where negation as a critical power comes in, for the aim is to gather what is received in freedom from irrelevances. As then we are thinking of man's relation to reality, the ultimate environment in which he is enmeshed, the interest is to consider anyone so involved as characterizing humanity, not as an individual. And this is a crucial point if the logic of incongruity is to be a general discipline, properly employed on this specific plane to discipline suggestion as that is made in respect of basic relations to nature.

*

Turning to detection first, the point to be noted in this, which, though it has been said before, bears reiteration: that what disturbs must be grasped in the form that it actually has without the introduction of subjective ideas about it, which are unavoidable when it is interpreted and viewed in rational terms.[19] Assuming that response to it is free from that involvement, there are complications in this when something is disturbing, as to where precisely this disturbance is located. For, although detection is a psychical event, such that disturbance is inward, its ultimate source is plainly in the external world exerting stimulation. But leaving that immediately, since it is a complication, it is well to bear in mind, in the intellect precisely, that, though causes have obscure origins, in that they are related to changes in the complex, their effects upon the recipient as a conscious being are plainly more accessible inasmuch as they are recorded. However, if any effect must be gathered in the form in which it actually occurs, a problem is presented: How is this to be done, when it seems to run counter to normal conscious reception, which invariably involves some interpretation? And this demands attention. An established form of philosophy is known as 'phenomenology' or, rather more precisely, as 'transcendent phenomenology', to distinguish it from other uses of that term, will then be given consideration. Its central concern was to attain to what were called 'pure ideas' with respect to essences, by refining and restricting the approach or perspective adopted. That was to be done by excluding all the psychological factors which accompany normal approaches, all the presuppositions usually implicit in rational enquiry. In order to achieve this purity the *epoché* – with various meanings in Greek, of which 'the suspension of judgment' is perhaps the most apt in this context – was called upon as a means of excluding all that was irrelevant to the interest, thus to ensure that what was attained was indeed a pure idea.[20] Presentations were to be viewed as it were in themselves, for what they represented in depth prior to any attempt to apply interpretation to them, since that took place only *after* the subjective self, now to be distinguished from the transcendental ego, had been introduced. This, in a rather brief summary, was the doctrine of Husserl, which was carried further by Heidegger, his pupil, whose aim was to apply it to psychological states, in order to elicit their deeper core or essence. So proceeding he disclosed such deeper states as *dasein* (being there or in itself), *sorge* (concern) and *angst* (anxiety, dread or despair), which could not be detected by simple observation but only be delving deeply into man's essential nature, viewed without preconceptions about what it might or should be. Merleau-Ponty, less involved with such morbid states, carried the suggestions implicit in this doctrine into the study of dim perception, even subconscious response, to show that it involved more than bringing things into consciousness by clear use of the sense organs, and was linked to intuition or other hidden factors.[21] In short, though this was initially a rather arcane thesis with limited application, it was the means, as its author intended it to be, of deeper penetration into aspects of response to external pressures. Hence, there is some warrant for further thought on possible applications.

As developed by Husserl himself this doctrine was idealistic in the strictest sense of that term, since the end was the pure *idea*. But it is not unreasonable, justly to be considered out of order or fantastic, to hold that it might be given a more realistic form, in which ideas are not so much pure as referred to relations to reality with a minimum of distortion. Detachment, understood as the exclusion of irrelevant factors, might then be seen as having two distinctive forms: detachment from the world, or better said contingencies, of which the pure idea as strictly ideal affords a sufficient instance, or detachment from the self from its subjective stances and their attendant presuppositions, always present in consciousness. What is of interest, then, is to relate reaction, both physical and psychical, so blended that they cannot be separated properly, to the external world to which direct response is made. In this sense the *epoché* has a different reference, for what is excluded or bracketed out is not what blurs pure thought but what is involved in ideas about what is received immediately. Then, since reception is in this sense spontaneous, a form of responsive rejection on a nervous plane, there is some reason to believe that what is received in such impressions as these is broadly common to men, whose nervous responses are certainly rather more alike than those derived from conscious, that is filtered thought, conditioned by selection and subjective interpretation. In the final analysis the only forms of response that are indisputably common are abstractions of a rather elementary type, the rules of formal logic for instance. That A is A and not B, that certain conclusions follow from premisses justly projected, cannot but be accepted by any reasonable man, though disagreement may yet arise about the excluded middle. But divergence at once occurs when thinking is referred to more complex interrelationships; and indeed, were that not the normal case, there would be no ground for debate. In fine, to demand demonstrative proof about common human traits is to demand that thought be confined to rationalistic issues, that reference to realities be excluded from enquiry, with the upshot that no assumptions about relations to or in that further sphere can with reason be entertained. Meanwhile, when we stumble and try to recover our balance, we all behave in much the same way; and it requires no small effort, as also mental training, to remain quite calm in the face of danger or disaster. As normally made such response is effectively common or general because it is natural and spontaneous. It is not "sicklied o'er with the pale cast of thought", which would render it subjective and peculiar to the person. Hence, 'general' in such sense as this, as 'the general in actuality', has a meaning wholly different from that of 'the logical universal', which is strictly ideal and does not refer directly to real events at all. And the first is that to which attention must now be given, difficult though it may be to grasp what it comprises.

The general in actuality, then, is that which touches all men and so exerts a common influence, to which, however, they are not normally fully alert until it has a disturbing character. And if in the realm of consciousness that influence is modified through subjective interpretation, a core may be presumed to remain as specific to humanity.[22] On the present occasion, however, no attempt will be made, which is not in any case possible without misrepresentation, to investigate any positive aspect of this relation. Interest will be confined to what alone is accessible, clearly disturbing effects. For those, as has been noticed, impinge on the conscious intellect when they are sufficiently strong. Then, and then alone, can that be activated meaningfully in this further world. No doubt, some physical aspects of the general in actuality, of this underlying world, have been discovered by modern science, passing beyond the world presented to naked perception with the aid of elaborate instruments. But that is not now the concern, which is to mark its effects on men in the only way that is feasible, that is by means of the study of what is clearly disturbing. Certain forms of disturbance are evidently cognizable, such, to give an instance, as the striking of a false chord, or, in rather less subtle terms, referring back to the obstacle that caused the stumble or accident. But those are incidental events, which, though they may have influences, in shock or remembered agitation, are now used only as illustrations. They are not then the present concern, which is rather with general effects as they with greater subtlety affect the body social, all persons in society or, more deeply, their attitudes. Obtuseness on the part of those with the power to influence others, thinkers who fail to recognize that responsive rejection quite certainly leaves a mark, as does a demand to accede to what is rooted in prejudice, priority placed on the self, delimits understanding. For, as influences, these postures have repercussive effects, which are for the most part general, less physically, of course, than as psychical dispositions.

Thus, when we speak of disturbance, two forms are being considered: that produced by nature, including involuntary action, and that produced deliberately, by those who may themselves be under influence of the first, or rather lack the ability to comply with what it imposes. No doubt, this presents a formidable problem to which no final answer or solution is attainable. Even so, attempts to penetrate more deeply into possible causes, or rather more convincingly, into their subtler effects, are likely to be more meaningful and accordingly more productive, despite the difficulties presented, than resting on the surface and dealing only with the obvious. Man's relation to nature, to the general in actuality, specifically in its human form conditioned by externals, affords the only proper ground for deeper understanding of what his involvement comprises, both on a personal plane and on that of social life, which gives the first its ultimate meaning. For problems such as these present are not simply cognitive, as if knowledge were the only relation to externals; they are infinitely more intricate, complex and elusive.

The question then arises as to how what in this way is gathered, comparable with the means once called *via negativa,* is to be expressed or communicated to others in the form that it actually has. For, unless that is rightly done, the experience adds nothing to an understanding of its implications for others than the recipient himself. It well might add to the total of his own experience, to render him a wiser man made aware that such acts should be avoided in future or met with better preparation. But, if that is the only approach, its public or general influence cannot then be studied by those concerned with its further effects. If it is to be conveyed as it was initially experienced without the distortion attendant on subjective interpretation, the question remains as to how that is to be achieved. Nor is that as a question easily to be answered. Let thought, however, be given to such a suggestion as this. In artistic circles a certain expression is used, or at least implied in the judgment of work at once presented to a quorum of experienced and fully sensitized artists. 'Reference' is then a term that means something other than what it means in cognitive enquiry, although in both the expression is used to apply to whatever is presented, in cognition to some aspect of the phenomenal world, viewed as something objective, in artistic response to rhythmic form, seen in a less objective manner. It does not in that case have a similar character, since what is received is not in the accepted sense an 'object' but a dynamic complex, in which, strictly speaking, there are no parts as all is interrelative and flows together to produce a compositional whole, temporally extended in some manifestations.[23] Artistic form is essentially 'sensed', since response to it, as sensuous, is nervous, not intellectual. With experienced artists, trained in the classical tradition, steeped in such responsiveness and attuned to all its nuances, no words need be spoken in face of what is presented, for a nod of approval, a grimace or a shrug of the shoulders suffices to indicate the effect produced. Speech is even redundant, for if the form is as it should be there is no occasion for comment. Moreover, as constituting an indivisible complex, form is simply not amenable to analysis. It fits, it holds together as an impartible whole, or it fails to do so, when whatever is at fault is not simply to be defined as it may be rather subtle. A weakness is felt and that is enough to show that the form is some sense wanting. Of course, when flaws are obvious – that red is much too bright, that note too highly pitched, that movement misplaced or clumsy – a critical comment may be made, though that is plainly not required when there is general concordance. Reference presumes a sensuous projection, which of course involves perception, awareness of what is confronted, but not of an objective type, which rests upon induction and severance from a context. It involves direct response to a rhythmic structure which is sensed immediately, in principle without undue preconception, unless that should be of classical taste bred into the system, or possibly innate. As *ch'i yün shêng tung,* the first principle of Chinese painting implies, a sense of life movement, its spiritual pulse, is required in creativity, reflecting the vitality that characterizes nature.[24] We respond in this way, directly, even if we are not artists, in many aspects of life, without the intervention of the fully conscious self. For on this level of response that only comes into play when something is untoward or threatening and calls for decisive counteraction, in order to restore equipoise or balance.

How, then, does this relate to ethics, to the question, that is, of man's relation to his fellow men or, more to the immediate point, to comments on that question when relations are not as they might be? And the answer is this: that that presumes a similar sensitivity applied in a further field. Inasmuch as ethics has a greater public bearing, words have to be spoken and findings to be expressed, immediately to a quorum of trained and sensitized ethicists, who will either agree that an impression received – that there is a failure to fit – has justly been recorded and is ethically significant or will reject the finding as subjectively tinged or without a general relevance. In this sense the recipient reflects and must reflect what has general bearing and he has to convey it in that form to others in the quorum, who then consider its meaning in depth. It is surely not impossible, then, that ethicists, just as artists, be trained in the needed sensitivity, in place of, or in addition to, the rigour required in projecting rational contentions, limited in that they fail to take contingencies into account and so fail fully to touch reality. For the interest in this is not explain, that is to give cognitive form to these delicate interrelations, to view them in positive terms. It is to discern those forms of response which tend to be disturbing in their repercussive effects. For, to be warranted and free from any subjective elements, prescriptions should rest on this base. The attitudes adopted by persons in society should in the last analysis be related to what is natural, that is to sensitivity, and not to artificial ideas of what the enlighted presume to be desirable or 'correct'. For spiritual values are sensuous and so have little relation to intellectuality, notwithstanding a long tradition which much appeals to those who cultivate positive knowledge, apparently in blindness to its evident limitations, as the key to enquiry.[25]

Ethics properly rests on norms, as Aristotle held when he spoke of "the ethics that nature plants in us". These norms, although innate, are confirmed and strengthened in the process of maturation, so that they are later readily complied with, unless deliberately affronted, at times without awareness that they ought to be adopted. And prescriptions must relate to them if they are to be accepted as given obligations. Norms are scarcely to be rationalized, given conceptual form unless with a measure of self-consciousness which distorts what they represent. It is for this reason perhaps that they have not received proper attention from those who aspire to rationalize everything.[26] But inasmuch as they are vital to society, its quality and its tone, a better understanding of what they achieve and contribute and how they relate to man's involvement with reality calls for deeper consideration, and so by other means than those which are powerless to engage them. If 'reference' cannot be applied as readily as in artistry, it remains the case that some means of detecting what tends to disconcert has to be devised. And that must involve sensitivity. All attempts to rationalize, to proceed through explanation, amount in effect to exulting the subjective knowing self almost patronizing the simple, incapable apparently of thinking for themselves, quite apart from the fact that no positive explanation fits, or precisely fits, the world of vital action. And this at least is certain: that, when all is in order and harmony is sustained, comment is superfluous and explanation unwarranted, since that can only result in crude misrepresentation. Applied negation is then the only sensible means, related to incongruity reflected in response, the only disciplined method of ensuring that what is intended to further understanding shall be subjected to proper check. To say that 'I am disturbed' is simply to be subjective, to express a personal feeling, which may represent no more than pique or irritation, not unjustly ridiculed as the 'boo-hurrah' doctrine. Thought on response, or rather now on an aspect, responsive rejection, must in some way be generalized and face a further questioning. Hence, as appropriate comment, negation must be related to the complex in which disturbing events have their essential meaning and relevance.

It is, it might be added, undoubtedly the case that interpretation is easier to criticize precisely than is suggestive statement, since it operates within the field of consciously registered knowledge, of 'factual findings' so-called. None the less, it has to be done, since suggestion, which is usually less confidently projected, may also be mistaken. The expression of an impression, fleeting and evanescent, is something rather different from an empiric statement dependent on induction, if only because it is not deliberately extracted from a totum, an act which presumes the employment of fully rational powers. For anything that grounds it, which is something so to say that objectifies itself, is intimately related to the whole from which it stands out, of which criticism of it must certainly take account. That is to ensure that its relation to reality shall be general in form. That means that in a receptive sense what is in this way gathered has characteristics common with those of other human beings, on the fair assumption, tenuous admittedly, that all with similar nervous systems are similarly affected. What is said about an impression then has some resemblance to reference in artistry, which, if it is misdirected, will immediately be checked. For that is the form of classical training in the arts – as the ballet master's use of his staff sufficiently evinces – which rests on just such an assumption, not proven because it cannot be, but needed as an acceptance if critique is to be applied. The incongruous, accordingly, has a general meaning in relation to human response as that involves some form of responsive rejection. Its discerning is meaningful, then, in as far as it seems to have general bearing, though that can only be justly established as critical thought is brought to bear on its implications – just as in criticism applied on the basis of sensitivity in the various arts.[27] Thus the logic of incongruity is not without precedent since, if not rationalistically developed as a procedure, it has been so in those fields from the earliest times, in ancient Greece, in China and in Western classical culture.

*

Negation is then a discipline that operates on that plane no less than on that of formal logic. And even, it seems, more decisively, for what is then at stake is vital need or value on a basic level, unrecognized at present because it cannot be clearly recorded. Value in this subtler sense has to be protected, in a somewhat Socratic manner, against false ideas about it, at times perpetrated innocently, inasmuch as subjectivity is difficult to exclude; but, as mistaken, subject to negation none the less. The need for such a discipline has not yet been recognized, notwithstanding this index of its potentiality, and so because rationalists believe that they alone are judges of what has meaning and value and that what they cannot engage – sympathy, for example – is without significance and can therefore be disregarded. Alternatively, which is even worse, they attempt to deal with such subtle involvements as these as though they were rationalizable, amenable, that is, to cognitive explanation. Plainly vital response, when it is not corrupted by such clumsy intervention, is quite beyond its reach; and, in so far as its finer forms – grace, sense of the fitting, courtesy afford sufficient instances – are potentially common to all men, it is the key to general refinement, something clearly called for. Difficult though it may be, then, to think in such terms as these when so much militates against them, when the expression of personality unfettered by any principle and materialistic attitudes dominate the scene, that is no reason for neglect of the problem this presents.

Negation has therefore a function of real moment to perform, both in criticizing such pernicious doctrines, which have the effect of vitiating advance to a greater degree of cultural maturity, *and* of providing a discipline patently needed for checking extra-cognitive statement. Rationalism, with its end in positive explanation, has little part to play on such a plane as this, since what is of interest in it is not some positive finding but the detection of what disturbs in a fundamental manner. It has no power to explore the real nature of response, which can only be done, when reaction is immediate, by discernment of what is unfitting or out of place. Such sensitive detection is, as conscious, doubtless rational, though not so in the sense of being rationalistic, but rather in that of grasping the form of an involvement, fairly described by contrast as an act of reasoning. The evoking of *epochái* should not damned as a fantastic idea, difficult though it may be to put them into practice, but rather as a means of limiting what is received to what is really relevant. It comprises a means of achieving deeper penetration, of grasping pressures in the forms that they actually have, without the intervention of a filtering process which can only lead to distortion and a measure of subjectivity. Society has suffered from that, inasmuch as the attitudes that it has been enjoined to adopt have falsified ideas about the constituent of value, which has been so personalized as to blind us to the forms in which it is common to all men, the self-centred perhaps excepted. Nor does this refer to artistic response alone, but to culture and refinement in the widest sense, to all those relations which are graceful and spontaneous. To grasp what stands in the way of their fuller development is one of the roles of negation, which makes no attempt to elicit positive explanations, but merely to liberate latent powers from what obstructs their flowering. Without this penetration, approaches are idealistic, and the many confusions those have brought and still are bringing about need not now be stressed.

When thought is turned to an aspect of what should be of concern to ethics, the quality of life in a general or social sense, in some way under-pinned by negative prescriptions, matters are more straightforward or closer at least to traditional acceptances and procedures. For now the interest is addressed to greater effects than those that have been considered up to this point, to those called 'repercussive', which only manifest themselves in as far as we are aware of them.[28] All effects have causes, of course, and attempt has been made to elicit some of these in the form of what is disturbing or threatening. In other words, disturbing effects are causes in so far as they can be recorded consciously, seen, that is, to be such; and what those produce as effects it is that has now to be studied. But since, as based on impressions, projections may be vague and so do not admit of wholly convincing answers, albeit that those are more so the more acute the threat, findings do not have the firmness of those of abstract or factual form. Moreover, repercussions have their being in a complex, so that inductive procedures, those on which traditional empiric enquiry rests, do not apply in this. An empirical, or rather an observable, element enters into reception even so, not of course in the sense in which it does in empiricist philosophy, but none the less in relation to a form of conscious experience. One of the aims of science, dealing with hylic relations, is to predict precisely when such and such will take place because found facts reveal that it will – that an eclipse of the sun, for instance, will occur at a given time; and that is what is meant by the expression 'reliable knowledge'. But no such firm findings as these can be found in what is under review in the study of human relationships with their psychical dimensions. Moreover, the 'facts' available, discovered from what has occurred, are not phenomenal particulars but complex social events, which are interrelated in the most intricate manner. Experience is evoked, but now it must be distinguished from that gathered by means of analysis and referred to specific instances. Reference is then to impressions received throughout the course of life, recognitions that certain effects tend to follow from certain acts. Projections from such impressions as these, as all historians know, even when referred to what has happened in their lives, tend to be highly speculative, inasmuch as the acts of men are related to motivation, which is unobservable, contextual and volatile. Accordingly, clear prediction is scarcely the target in this, even if certain relations are tolerably well established. But after events have taken place and their consequences have ben studied, in retrospect which allows a measure of detachment, there is some power to understand the sequence of cause and effect. When an effect, however, has yet to come to being, and so is unobservable, it can only be conjectured, suggested as likely, not known.

However, that certain fell consequences will almost certainly follow from certain misplaced acts, or from mistaken theories when those are practically applied, is more easily noted when experience shows that as some mischance has happened before it is likely to happen again – an accident, for instance, for want of a warning sign. And that is better seen as attention is turned to pervasive or general effects rather than to those which are linked to individual acts, since the last are much more varied. That such and such was not sensibly done because it produced disharmony, proved politically, economically or socially disturbing, is better understood when its effects are widespread and so to be distinguished from the idiosyncratic. History shows many examples of this, revealing themselves over time, exemplified in the adage, made as it were in passing: "He who knows no history becomes the victim of history", meaning that some understanding of trends as they have certain effects is requisite if decisions affecting the lives of others have to be made by those who exercise authority. And 'affecting the lives of others' implies 'having adverse effects'. With these, again, negation, as referring to what will not do, emerges as the instrument with which to proceed in this. For the point of any such study is to learn from past mistakes, which leave their mark more clearly than do actions in conditions in which they so to say enfold. If certain things are done or, as is now as meaningful, if certain attitudes are adopted, thoughtlessly in effect, the likely outcome will be to generate social imbalance – easy divorce, for instance – and so to inhibit advance to greater harmony and refinement. People are often blind to the consequences of their acts – discoveries in science are not always beneficial – and regrettably indifferent to the quality of society, as if the idea that that could be raised, other than materially, were utopian or visionary, whereas in less exalted form it is even a necessity, as it bears upon the future and what is passed on as a legacy. These are not the attitudes that ethicists should adopt, even if they are those of certain modern philosophers, more concerned with the meanings of terms detached from real conditions than with current actualities and their repercussive effects. "Philosophy changes nothing" amounts to an irresponsible, not to say a conceited remark.[29] For then it is no more than an academic interest, only obliquely, and then in a manner that is inept, concerned with real or vital problems. It cannot simply disregard the responsible role that falls to it as a concern with value, which may be taken to mean the guidance of society in terms of what is valuable, needed for its quality. For even if all is apparently well, and there is some reason to doubt that, the problem of the attitudes adopted by society and their effects on those who will follow and inherit their residue cannot be disregarded, since such concerns are primary.

Particular interest turns on these accepted attitudes or, to come nearer home, on the doctrines that foment them and are doubtless one of the causes of the present unrest. Undermining the norms on which society rests, a type of sceptical thinking what has nothing to recommend it, undermining a social sense in the name of personal freedom, which paradoxically has the effect of increasing the need for coercion, are attitudes to which attention should be given if, as opposed to personal whims, social needs have priority. Such questioning is negative and disciplined by a criterion, which must stand whatever is said: that the interests of society should always be taken as paramount, the ultimate warrant for any projection or proposal referred to human concerns. Theoretical enquiry seldom seems to be so, since formal logic, the discipline it so narrowly accepts, cannot furnish more than a verbal check, which is abstract and so without relation to realities. It is not, then, as a positive aim, achieved by admonitions based on explanatory findings, that social amelioration is likely to be effected. It is rather by the detection of what delimits or inhibits a grasp of what in a social sense value really comprises. If values are mistaken and have conduced to a social malaise, to "emotional insecurity, ... alienation, spiritual homelessness and a growing anomie",[30] we sensibly search for the reasons for this state of affairs, less in attempt to explain them when they are as complex as they are, than to reduce them by discerning the manner in which they appear injurious – by studying effects, that is, rather than clear causes. This is plainly more easily done inasmuch as what disturbs impinges decisively on consciousness. the disharmonious stands out, objectifies itself, unless it is pervasive, as now it tends to be, to render detection more difficult. Even so, what has that form can at least in part be detected, gradually to attain to a deeper understanding of what indeed is baneful, particularly in attitudes and the doctrines that encourage them. The task is fraught with difficulty, but it has to be undertaken if we are at all concerned with present tendencies in society. Nor should we expect that such studies as these will lead to some form of perfect achievement, a fully balanced society, for that is no more than an ideal dream unrelated to realities. A modification of attitudes seen as having adverse effects would be sufficient an achievement, a reasonable aim in the sense that it could conceivably lead to a meaningful outcome.

A caution is necessary here, which is that, as an organon, negation should be applied with delicacy and discretion, lest it should turn into bigotry, puritanical imposition on the lives and interests of others. For that would be ideological, with roots in personal prejudice. That may perhaps in theory redound to social elevation, but that is from far what is implied in a general culture grounded in sensitivity. And 'generalized' is the key word here as relating man to nature – in which sense alone is his character justly held to be general – and developing his potentials now limited by demands that, as in artistic response, he shall conform to subjective, rational ideologies, as if those were the road to perfection when in fact they lead to falseness. To aim at changing the nature of unregenerate man is bound to meet with resistance because it is asking too much. There are limits to what the ordinary man is ready to accept when he is not obstructive but simply desirous to live in a normal and sensitive way. If making him a paragon, rationalistic and detached, is the positive objective it is likely to come to nothing. Change can only be brought about without justified resistance by means of a procedure more closely related to nature, to the needs – for harmony, continuity and a measure of trust – of the natural man. And that can only be done effectively by the removal of what stands in the way or obstructs an acceptable development, in order to release the latent powers within him to live more gracefully and sensibly. The aim should be more modest, since only then can it be met by the normal sensitive man. A gradual weaning away, in as far as that is possible, of what can fairly be shown to generate disturbance is the warrant for this suggestion of how properly to proceed. An idle hope, perhaps, but not necessarily so. For, if philosophy is to be more down to earth, more meaningful, to serve a serious purpose, to exercise an influence on attitudes adopted, it should not be beyond its latent powers to do so, to deal with vital problems in a more sensitive manner. And it might be remarked in passing that, within the frame of social balance, needs that are more personal are more easily met. It has not merely then to detect what is justly subjected to check, but from that discernment to study how best by judicious prescriptions to reduce or to delimit that which militates against greater social harmony, maturity and refinement.

*

As an instrument negation may then be applied in various ways, which may be listed thus. First, to question the validity of certain accepted doctrines and the assumptions on which they rest, in which sense it is related to traditional sceptical thinking. Second, critically to study the effects that such doctrines have and how they generate disturbance, particularly as an influence on an uncritical public, powerless because they seem to emanate from authority to see wherein they are destructive of value and social maturity, as materialistic and as conducing to divisiveness, rivalry and friction. Third, to detect, in forms below what is at once apparent, what forces tend to produce undue disturbance and disharmony and the manner in which they do so to have general repercussions. Fourth, to apply critique to any findings about them, to any suggestion projected in respect of what has been in this way elicited, that is, to any proposal of a prescriptive type, basing this on the Chinese idea that prescriptions should always be minimal, put forward only when there is quite evident need for them.[31] Finally, to study repercussive effects in thought of their likely consequences, that is, continually to review the value of what has been done, its efficacy in view of what is envisaged as the aim: to secure more balanced and saner social relationships. For criticism must be persistently applied, as a tuning to ensure that balance is sustained. Negation, to repeat a pertinent saying of Kant, is evoked "to guard us against error", when error in this context is less falsity in expression, which is readily rectified by the logic of inconsistency, than mistakes in understanding actual social conditions, to which the logic of incongruity, referred to disturbing effects, applies in a deeper sense.

The hope of finding true answers in respect of what really counts, of explaining what has being in the dynamic of becoming, is simply wishful thinking, for too long entertained by rationalizing philosophers. Philosophy must give heed to the realities of living, to the deeper, spiritual needs of men and the society in which they are enmeshed, present more particularly when its tone is secular, which it has either neglected or falsely attempted to rationalize. For only then will it make a significant contribution to contemporary life, as that moves towards a future to which it has some responsibility. Linked to cognition and science, almost as if it had to be to enjoy respectability, it is aligned, though thought of that will be deplored and even strongly resisted, to a materialistic approach, to which, as aware of its grossness, it should be opposed. For, as tied to phenomenal findings, and truth has no other meaning unless it should be abstract or vaguely metaphysical, it is indeed but hylic. Formal logic, however refined, is but a means to that end. For truth is surely cognitive, if only in aspiration, claiming that as its justification, on, or so it is believed, a higher level of knowledge, as abstract, not contingent – which means, of course, that it is not really related to life.

If philosophy can contemplate changing its present stance, though as yet it shows but few indications of that, negation, with its more modest end, is the procedure it has to adopt, develop and refine in quite another manner. For the problem is how to deploy it in the most effective way. But that should present no real or insurmountable difficulty once it is accepted that it must reach beyond a propositional role, even if the means whereby that is to be achieved have yet to be devised. For the logic of incongruity cannot pretend to be more than a preliminary suggestion which, if it affords a clue, has plainly to be refined. That presumably constitutes the problem of the future, exposed but not solved in this book, which at best prepares the ground for further investigation, by showing where the purpose of philosophy properly lies. It may then have turned the soil in which creative seeds may generate, to take – once a methodology has been developed to provide it, to secure that deeper projections shall be subjected to proper critique – an active part in dealing with the issues confronting society, and man in his relation to an ever-present nature.

Conclusion

That there are grave weaknesses in this doctrine – doubts about the meanings given to certain words immediately discounted – cannot readily be denied. And no doubt it would be easy for rationalists, if they really regarded this thought as a threat to their authority, to pick it to pieces on their own terms. But that would not of itself discredit it, since those terms are valid only for those who are attached to them and harbour the belief that no approach other than their own is acceptable philosophically. That intellectualism involves subjectivity and that sensitivity does not, or rather need not, is so foreign to rationalistic thinking, holding the last to be emotional, is an obvious obstacle to acceptance of this thinking, although it is crucial to its proper understanding. A little thought, however, shows this finding to be just, since the first is clearly conscious whilst the second need not be so. Indeed, if subjectivity in its modern and rationalistic sense applies necessarily to the knowing self, it can scarcely be regarded as a characteristic of subconscious response or even of dim perception, into which self-consciousness scarcely enters. The knowing self could, of course, be taken to subsume knowledge by acquaintance, when it would be other than knowledge by description, which is the interest of cognitive or explanatory enquiry, of intellectualism that is. Hence, if that distinction is clear-cut, which is rather doubtful, the subject is only *fully* present when the last comprises the interest. Deeper responses are for the most part impersonal involvements, from which self-consciousness is largely absent, and with it presumably the knowing self, however ambiguous 'knowing' and what it implies may be. Denial of this statement has to show that this distinction is not valid, that the knowing self, with its interest is knowledge by description, reaches into deeper worlds, as also that the procedures it adopts to serve its ends do the same, which would give the term 'knowledge' an elasticity which would remove all strictness from it. It could, again, be argued that the mere evoking of subconscious response or of dim perception – in effect Leibniz's *petites perceptions* – would, since they are not cognizable in any strict sense, be to abandon a rationalistic approach and to render thinking about such matters as these illicit. But plainly, now that science has spoken, to show that much takes place below the level of consciousness and further that that exerts an influence, it cannot be brushed aside as a matter of no moment and so must be considered in some other terms. In sum, if what occurs in psychical form below the level of consciousness cannot be the subject of positive description, then it must be approached in another way, by negation that is to say.

A further point may be even more telling than that projected above. For, if what is confronted in immediate stimulation is external actuality – the 'ultimate reality' of traditional metaphysics – and not the phenomenal world, which is but an interpreted representation of it, ideas about it cannot be dismissed as merely speculative, but must be given attention in any thought addressed to response. Speculative in some sense this undoubtedly is, as is all thought referred beyond the overt phenomenal world. But it cannot be held to be empty or void of meaning for no better reason than that rationalism is powerless to comprehend it. We cannot be blind, or blind ourselves, to the real nature of response, response that is to reality, which in depth relates to immediate stimulation and so quite certainly differs from what is later recorded in consciousness, as in sense data theory, now shown to be untenable. For that would be as though perception, derived from a process of filtering, were to be aligned with preconscious sensation. Finally, that the external, the extra phenomenal world, is a dynamic, indivisible, interrelative complex is supported – discounting several ancient insights – by the findings of physicists and even more convincingly by those of biochemists, is decisive. Hence, it is difficult now to conceive of tenable alternatives, since that would presume the acceptance of an unchanging structure made up of isolated particulars existing only in the intellect, unless with a reversion to discredited ideas. Thus the way in which reality has to be seen today so differs from ideas with respect to externals latterly held in the West that those must now be discarded, as must the presuppositions on which such ideas have rested.[1] The notion of truth, the most deeply entrenched among them – always to be distinguished from the more modest reliable knowledge – has in this way been so discredited as an end that it has to be abandoned or, if retained, confined to verbal abstractions only. None of the recent findings about the nature of reality are amenable to strict proof. Nor is that really surprising when such absolute proof must have a rationalistic form and refer to what is called 'fact', to what is clearly observable, to "things", as has been said, "certainly known to have occurred and to be true", true in a logical sense. So, thought addressed to "what is out there" is speculative plainly and cannot well be more.

All this, although resisted, is tolerably sustainable, as generally supported by scientific findings or justified inferences on them. Other ideas related to this logical theory may, it must be accepted, be more open to serious questioning. 'Reference', for instance, as understood in this text, or 'ethical sensitivity', cannot pretend to such support; nor can an extended use of phenomenological principles be taken to provide one. Artistic or rhythmic responsiveness, using that expression in its classical sense as referring to nervous response, is a recognized phenomenon. But caution is clearly called for in using any such terms as these, for what is now recognized as presented to us directly is not to be viewed as an object standing in isolation but rather as something to which we respond sequentially, as a phase in a changing manifold. Precisely what 'sensitivity' means, though clearly related to sensorial response, remains uncertain if meaning can only to be precise be intellectual. But it is surely reasonable to proffer the opinion that that is not the only sense it has. For, were we to accede uncritically to that ruling, those forms of it which are general in their bearing and characteristic of normal response would be eliminated from consideration by an exclusive demand for an intellectual meaning. It is then best defined by what it is not or rather by what excludes its real meaning: an attempted detachment from the contingent, a disregard of rhythmic needs and a passage from them into intellectuality, a wholly subjective involvement. “It does not matter if art is impermanent”, said one who should have known better, “provided it makes a statement”,[2] that is to say has meaning in an intellectual sense, however obscure that may be. If anything has conceptual import it refers to ideas entertained by the intellect. It here seems to refer to effects on others confronted by the grotesque or bizarre, who, if they fail to respond appropriately are not to be ranked among the ‘cultured’ or the ‘enlightened’ but, in a strange perversion, the insensitive, the vulgar. Conversely, if response is nervous or spontaneous, as it almost certainly is initially, as revulsion or delight, it is not confined to sophisticates but has, those possibly excepted, a general character. Nor then is it explicable; for, though neurologists may describe some of its physical aspects, its psychical traits are quite beyond the reach of explanation; and so complex is the blending of these two factors in basic response that confining knowledge only to one must present a distorted picture. Again, though common sense supports such a basic finding as this, it cannot be rendered subject to proof making any pretence to strictness, so that sensitivity on this level is in strict sense indefinable. Clearly, however, if can be enhanced and refined by training, in negative form essentially, for that is the means of developing sensitivity. But it yet seems that some persons have a richer genetic heritage, which renders them more susceptible to what is inept or distasteful, which is almost certainly related to the rhythms of nature reflected in bodily dispositions, awkward in immaturity but brought to balance with growth. What sensitivity means, even so, is not simply to be defined, notwithstanding that it is an evident feature of life on a whole range of levels, from simple reflex reaction to the most refined forms of delicacy, both of course related to changes in the environment. Ethical sensitivity has as much a nervous base as any other forms of it, though in that case it refers to a sense of the social whole, just as in artistry it refers to some compositional whole, potential if not actual. And if this has little or no relation to abstract theory, that scarcely denigrates it but rather the reverse, since were it so related it would be contaminated by irrelevant and inept subjective factors and so would lose its basic character.

‘Reference’ could be dismissed as a misappropriation of an

established term with cognitive affinities and derivatives of long standing, referent, referend, referential, transubjective and objective reference. But if it is restricted to meet cognitive requirements, no term is available for direct response to reality, which necessarily differs as dynamic and sequential from what is involved in objectification, both of course presuming relation to presentations. It might then be noted in passing that, as used in the present context, this term is not confined to artistry, since the forms of response it produces are common in social life, where a frown or a smile is understood without need for speech or explanation. Such gestures may not have any rational standing, though even rationalists indulge them when they enter the world of affairs, and even indeed in professional life, as in raising the eyebrows to indicate disagreement. But patently, some such term, however ill-defined, is needed to engage these subtler forms of response, and notably as their bearing on normal life is so great that without attention to them our 'understanding' of that cannot but be impoverished. If anyone can think of a better and less ambiguous term, recognizing the need for it, the author will certainly not object. For he merely makes use of a possible term for which a sufficient alternative with the meaning of projection on to a presentation free from dependence on filtered objectification does not at present exist. If it then relates to a form of response which has been disregarded because it cannot be brought within the range of rational explanation, that is as it may be. Even so, a term with that specific reference yet remains a requirement.

*

So much for debatable terms, let thought be turned to those which are less disputable and may even be decisive. These refer to negation considered as an approach. What is being suggested, then, is that adverse factors influencing life can in certain aspects be discerned with greater acumen and less likelihood of error by the application of negation as an instrument than by attempts to attain to rational explanation with the precision supposed to attach to it when supported by formal logic. The primary reason for saying this is that what is established by such means as that – clearly to be distinguished from experimentation made against external reality – is abstract or ideal and so has no external reference, unless, uncritically and improperly, verbal relations are claimed to extend beyond what words relate to, that is, phenomenal being. It is fondly supposed in answer to this that formal logic has, since the issue of the *Principia* – usually regarded as a fundamental work – and later developments on it, now been rendered infinitely more sensitive and flexible. But that is a questionable claim if it means better adapted to deal with real or vital problems, which it is plainly powerless to do for as long as it holds to its rigour and cultivates formality. Indeed, it cannot even deal with the problem of tensing adequately, but only by recourse to clumsy and unwieldy circumlocutions which no one uses in ordinary speech, since natural logic is infinitely more tractile and susceptible to the nuances of normal communication. Its insistence on rigour, furthermore, has led to many cognitive errors, the products of overconfidence that what is sustained by logic of this abstract character is proven and so correct, when it is proven only in a theoretical sense together with the presumption that reality fits precisely and without occasion for doubt into a rational frame. Natural logic, which not only relates to external events but has been developed to do so, is plainly not so limited, as is evident from the many uses to which it is put, in negative form particularly. Medicine and psychiatry illustrate this sufficiently, since, fallibilism apart, both certainly presuppose the acceptance of contingency, which, unlike falsification applied in formal logic, ultimately rests on a form of holistic ontology. And they do so not because an idea has been expressed improperly, but because their approach is related to the complex of reality, which may not, despite the utmost care, have been engaged correctly. Of course, to apply negation in such disciplines as those supposes long experience and knowledge of effects, empiric in the sense of being frequently observed, positive acquirements which are in part intuitive, so that negation is not alone the means of approach adopted, though always, of course, a needed check. But the point is still that negation is a very powerful instrument for dealing with realities, though one that has scarcely been recognized by formalistic logicians, who have tended to regard it as no more than a means of checking positive truth claims. As a means, then, of detecting signs of the disturbance of balance in some organic or psychical system, as in the disciplines above, it is the essence of diagnosis, which refers to what generates imbalance.

Critical application of implicit principles – for those are not to be defined precisely[3] – is at the very heart of artistic creativity, as of sensuous response to rhythmic presentations, or rather to a failure to sustain the rhythmic sequence. If principles are explicit, clearly expressed and defined as in formal logic, that is because they are tied to words which are strictly defined to render them unambiguous, to eliminate any tincture of suggestiveness from their meanings. But words are largely penumbral and their reference is circumstantial. Fallibilsm is an idea that has to be taken seriously in scientific enquiry, not because it has a character similar to that of falsification in logic, but because sufficient relation to nature has to be established, to mean that one which is seen to be misconceived or inadequate must be abandoned or revised. In the final analysis, then, its principles are those implicit in negative logic, in that they relate to the complex of reality, which cannot be objectified or divided into parts but only engaged in so far as non-fittings can be detected. Ideas with external reference are always in some sense precarious, and findings in respect of what is so engaged then tend to be contingent. They are, to cite a physicist referring to his discipline, "approximate only in the nature of the case".[4] There can be no pretence that they are absolute or definitive, as logical conclusions are, or rather may be, though repeated confirmations may show them to be reliable, justified as working principles. Differences of opinion in pragmatic discourse, directed towards issues which might have other answers, must be based on valid arguments, which are accepted as sound not because they are theoretically immaculate but because their warrant is that with their acceptance a greater, a public interest is served. That is the final criterion, the proper test of worth, when matters of real importance come up for review. It is that by which ideas are ultimately to be judged as justified or *reasonable,* as opposed to rational in a logocentric sense. And that is surely a mode of control which merits more attention than it commonly receives in theoretical discourse. In law the aim is that decisions shall be just, or at least as just as they may be, not absolute or true, which is an ideal and no more. For justice is effectively the establishing of balance between conflicting interests in the complex of social life.

Opinion, which is not to be condemned or despised as second-rate, woolly, biased or tainted, since it is often all that can reasonably be projected, is schooled by taking account of what will not pass or do, which is tolerably definable. For if thought is based on nothing more than what is merely conventional, a measure of subjectivity is plainly introduced, and thus there is no real test for relating its expression to whatever its wider and more far-reaching consequences.

Suggestive statement, finally, without the use of which little of real moment can be said about such highly complex matters as human interrelationships, must also be seen for its worth. This as a point is so obvious that it scarcely needs to be said, though when suggestions are dismissed as beyond the range of rationalistic enquiry, as emotional, subjective, loose, or whatever term is used, it is tolerably evident that no proper attention is being given to certain issues, the most important, it would seem, falling to philosophy. When it is contended that suggestion is merely emotional, as if that placed it outside the domain of responsible, rational thinking, that can only mean, when the last is alone acceptable, that it can never properly be subjected to critique, other than by recourse to summary dismissal. Nor is this a trivial point, since that view in various guises – as that metaphor is suspect though its use is effectively inescapable – dominates rational thinking, with the consequence that many mistakes are made through failure to be sufficiently sensitive in respect of the complexities of volatile conditions. Inasmuch as formal logic cannot find a place for or properly handle suggestion, which cannot be true in a rigorous sense, though it may of course be false, some other means of subjecting it to disciplined critique has to be devised, lest otherwise it is indeed inconsequential and loose. Further, it is not simply the case that the procedures of formal logic are powerless to comprehend such subtle matters as these, the gravamen is rather a reluctance to admit it. It is sometimes presumed that, with its recent refinement, it will be able eventually to effect such comprehension, which is rather a hope than a promise; but that obscures the real requirement: to deal with external relations in the forms that they actually have. Those, however, whatever is thought, cannot have ideal character. What happens in fact, without real thought on what is really at issue, is positively pernicious, since logocentrics claim, and so without further question – though that may not now be entirely the case unless with its devotees – that they are empowered to engage and fully to deal with everything, even oddly with sensuous and emotional response. The result is that both are treated in inept and clumsy ways, as is plain from the attempts of rationalizing aestheticians to expiate on artistry.[5] In belief that pretentiousness of this rationalistic type has the effect of debasing taste and depriving ordinary men of their powers to develop and refine their natural sensitivity – revealed in other cultures if not in our own today – it would seem that a serious issue is raised. For as long, accordingly, as ratiocination reigns effectively unchallenged, an impoverishment of life and of culture generally is likely to be the outcome. The idea that suggestion, of which expression in artistry seems to be a form, is a power to be developed will, of course, be strongly resisted, as an undermining of traditional acceptances: that value be seen in cognitive, that is, in acquisitive terms, related to the cult of the autonomous individual. However, every demonstration of formal logic's limited powers, every suggestion that there could be feasible alternatives to its narrowness and rigour, which need not be undisciplined, helps to bring about a change, to render thought on real problems more flexible and sensitive. And a study of the powers that are latent in negation may well be the key to this.

*

The logic of incongruity may not be an adequate answer to the problem so presented; nor is it pretended that it is the final word. It is, in Leibnitz's expression, simply 'a proposal' – *une hypothèse* precisely – which may or may not prove fruitful, meet the requirement envisaged. However, with the acceptance of a holistic ontology, and with the recognition that there are serious signs of decay in contemporary society and grave flaws in the attitudes that it now adopts, stressing, for example, the primacy of the self, that there is need for another approach is tolerably evident. This, as a possible answer, is advanced for consideration, the warrant for which is the call for a more sensitive procedure, which must itself be disciplined. Discipline presumes the deployment of critical powers, those, that is to say, implicit in negation. To distinguish, then, between the inconsistent and the incongruous constitutes rather more than a mere play with words, when the latter is taken to refer beyond what is at once apparent, subsuming even changes in the external world as it produces effects. For it remains the case, despite all attempts to bridge it, that there is no small difference between falseness in ideal discourse and disturbance in actuality. If these two terms do not engage that difference wholly adequately,[6] inasmuch as disturbance and falseness are questionably contrasted, that does not mean that a difference is devoid of import and has no real significance. It does have meaning here, if only in the sense that disturbance has greater importance, a greater bearing on life, so that as real, and inclusive of various forms of falseness, it is that to which serious thought should be given. Accordingly, let those who recognize the difference between these two related words, the inconsistent and the incongruous, ideal and real respectively, see that their relation to logic as a disciplining instrument implies distinctive approaches.

What takes place in the world external to perception, the world whence stimuli emanate, can only be inferred from the effects that those produce when, through a filtering process, they impinge on clear consciousness, to involve a degree of distortion. The problem is how to avoid that, how to overcome the limitations imposed by reflective objectification. It is evident beyond question that immediate stimulation cannot be known in its actual forms through scientific enquiry, since it is preconscious and accordingly unobservable. The only conscious contact with ultimate reality is that which is made when the intellect is woken to attention by some untoward event in order to effect decisive counteraction. Hence, some idea of the nature of response to external pressures, to impressions as they have an immediate impact, is available only by attending to what impinges instantly on the intellect in this negative manner, as a form of responsive rejection. In order to gather that properly, in the form that it actually has, a clue was drawn from phenomenology, the employment of the *epoché,* to eliminate subjectivity; and this was adopted as a principle. For then the impression is held as it is and can be conveyed to others concerned with its implications, as with reference in artistry, which is related to adequacy in rhythmic presentations. For it is, of course, its general, ultimately social, and not its personal bearing, that is ethically significant.

The process of response, from initial stimulation to its clear recording in the conscious intellect, is not properly covered by physical findings alone, since those relate to no more than its somatic characteristics. It certainly also comprises psychological factors, which cannot at lower levels be caught in any empirical net, a difficulty compounded by the fact, or better the likelihood, that these two aspects of response are inextricably intertwined. Thus, when the word 'sensuous' is employed in the present context, and properly it seems, its reference is to this intricate admixture, this complex combination which characterizes response on other levels than those on which it is clearly recorded, as the outcome of a process involving objectification deliberately undertaken. Though this theory of negation, of which the core is the detection of what is immediately disturbing and has repercussive effects, is not the final answer to the problem of understanding the real nature of response, it is surely an improvement on the attempt to solve it by attending exclusively to its fully conscious forms. For sense data are perceptual and other than involvements with truly external events; and, are with conscious objectification, no more than intellectual constructs of an elementary type. Response in depth and what it involves is not to be aligned with conscious intervention aimed at explanation, tempting though it may be to think of it exclusively as something which is knowable. What is sought, indeed required, if deeper understanding, even if not complete, is to be attained, is a more refined idea of man's relation to nature. And that is very surely the fundamental problem, which is specifically philosophical.

Here again, however, there will be resistance, even to the words employed to express this thesis. 'Understanding', for instance, has, to serve a cognitive end, been given a special meaning, which seriously delimits its wider use in philosophy. Thus "... the way that A knows that *p* is true involves that A understands what *p* means"[7] is in order in as far as it goes but plainly only one meaning. Accepting, then, that that is a legitimate reading, meaning a grasp of relationships, it is yet a narrow one, amounting in effect to a reluctance to allow that 'knowledge' and 'understanding' are distinctive terms and that the last embraces other forms of response which are not dependent on antecedent objectification. As it retains that meaning, then, as that alone which is rational, it is restricted clearly to cognitive enquiry, as if no other had real standing. But thinkers in the past have recognized the need for a word with which to cover certain forms of reception which are other than cognitive when that term is used in strict sense. *Sapientia,* or *sophía,* and *scientia,* for instance, have patently different meanings, as do parallel terms in many other languages.[8] In English, though the difference between 'understanding' and 'knowledge' is not as clear-cut as that, the former evidently does have further meanings: an intuitive grasp, for instance of external relations, which is clearly not explicit. This is not the occasion to enlarge on that definition, even were it possible adequately to do so when definition has to have a lucid rational form. In the present case, in fact, that can only be done by recourse to negation, by discerning that something projected, such as the content of a suggestion, does not constitute strict knowledge, notwithstanding that it may illuminate. Sufficient then at once that those in tune with normal life accept that there is a difference in the meanings of these two terms, even if that cannot be defined precisely, which is not of course a requirement. Obscure though the idea of what understanding comprises may be, it can scarcely be denied that there are limits to the reach of cognitive enquiry, and that that is especially the case when what is truly external comes up for review. If we cannot say precisely what its features are, if only for the reason that they have their being in an indivisible, persistently changing complex, that is not to say that we cannot have ideas, however vague, about them. For we certainly have some power to detect, without pretence to exactitude in whatever our findings, that something is out of order, unfitting or disturbing in the complex we confront, since, as has already been said, whatever has that character objectifies itself, stands out against the harmonic whole and is not a selected particular, torn from its context by an act of prepense objectification. Understanding, like intuition, is a somewhat mysterious power. Even so, there are aspects of it which can conceivably be developed, if not rationally at least by means of reasoning, by the deployment, that is, of an extended negation. For, what is out of order and accordingly disturbing, addresses itself directly, immediately to clear consciousness, which is woken to attention in order to affect appropriate counteraction, to restore a balance which has been upset.

The final point is then this: that, if the problem to which attention has been directed in this book is allowed the status of a meaningful problem, consequences follows. To summarize them briefly, these may be defined in the following manner: 1) that man without question confronts an inescapable reality, which is beyond the world of phenomena or appearances; 2) that this, the external world, is almost certainly, even if that is not proven, a dynamic, indivisible, interrelative complex, both in its basic natural and in its social forms; 3) that a manifold which is harmonious, such that over time all fits into place, cannot justly be split into its components without a measure of falsification and so of misunderstanding: 4) that the implications of this are that a rationalistic approach cannot properly comprehend man's involvement with it, so that, if that is the only approach, it must be misunderstood; 5) that, as that is the case, a further, another approach, which must of course be disciplined, has to be devised. What form this might have is then the point at issue, which, as it is yet without an adequate answer, is still the problem that has to be met. That is the reason why it has now been raised and the warrant for promoting a fuller use of negation, not merely to show that attitudes traditionally adopted leave something to be desired, which is but a preliminary finding, but more importantly to show that that as a latent power could be further developed to deal with what has yet to be dealt with properly: namely, man's relation to the external world, to nature. Let those, then, who can free themselves from a logocentric involvement, to cultivate other interests than an "insatiable desire for knowledge" or explanation, and recognize with Kant that "negation exists essentially to protect us against error", give deeper thought to this problem. For the error in context is to assume that cognitive enquiry linked to formal or positive logic is the only means of dealing with real problems. Propositional logic cannot even begin to engage such problems properly, since in effect it is powerless to pass beyond abstractions, dubiously claimed to refer, without reserve, to phenomena. That is the burden of what has been said; and, if it is unpalatable, that can only be seen as regrettable. For this problem cannot be brushed aside as empty of meaning or pointless, as idle speculation and nothing more decisive, unless the issues considered are held to be insignificant, void of importance or substance, which, with the acceptance of a holistic ontology, will scarcely pass muster today.

APPENDIX I

Defining Limits

It would be improper to claim universality for this doctrine when that is unwarranted. Indeed, to do so in a book which specifically contends that formal logic makes claims beyond its proper reach, so that a further discipline is needed for what it is powerless to engage, would be to fall into the same trap, as refusing to acknowledge limits. Let it be firmly said, then, that the logic in incongruity relates to evaluative discourse only, to interests beyond the reach of rationalistic procedures aspiring to elicit truth or to project explanations in respect of spheres in which neither is applicable. For truth in strict sense can only refer to verbal relations and explanation of what is explicable, namely to what is phenomenally presented. Cognition, on which both depend, can only refer to what is clearly cognizable, that is to say to what can be objectified, which cannot apply to response to interrelative structures.

In recent years philosophy has supposed itself to be a form of cognitive enquiry based on formal logic, largely to the neglect of other concerns traditionally taken to be its responsibility, and so particularly since science, as value-neutral, could not and indeed did not pretend to engage them. Not only, then, has it failed to attend to its proper role, that which is unique to it – unless theology, with presuppositions related to special forms of belief, may be held to share it – but the presuppositions it adopts when its aim is cognitive and suited only to discourse which has that end and no other. The distinction between science *(scientia, epistémé)* and philosophy *(sapientia, sophía)* has accordingly been blurred, with the upshot that the function or involvement of the latter was apparently lost to view. Further, if cognitive enquiry is taken to be philosophy's aim, its contribution is by comparison meagre and it becomes a subsidiary discipline, which cannot pretend to deal with vital problems or to give serious attention to real needs. In view of this confusion, then, the first requirement is to distinguish between these two disciplines and the functions they perform or should perform to be true to their natures, which itself presumes having a clearer idea of the presuppositions, and with them the methodologies, that either adopts or should adopt to serve its proper end.

Science, very properly, seeks dependable, positive answers or effective explanations in respect of what is observable, and ideally measurable. And whether its findings refer to the external world, tapped through experimentation, or to the world of phenomena is at once beside the point, as is the question whether they are nominal (*als ob* to one view) or real. For that some are highly reliable, usable that is, cannot sensibly be doubted, although that all have that character and are free from speculation is surely to be questioned. Sufficient that its proper aim is always the attainment of reliable positive knowledge, on the road to which falsification is evoked as a means to that end. In other words, science proceeds by means of trial-and-error in order to achieve acceptable or cogent, not necessarily absolute or conclusive, answers. Whether, then, the knowledge so attained is beneficial to humanity or brings disturbance in its train, even to upset the balance of society, is not a question now to be engaged, except to say that judgment on a question such as that has to be external, since it is evaluative and so falls to another discipline, presumably philosophy. Negation for science is then no more than a means to a further end, a way on the path to what is sought, findings that are positive. It is not in itself or in principle a means of sustaining value, unless that is advisory. Its adoption as a procedure, other than in this ancillary sense, would in science amount to a betrayal of all that it aims to do, since negation itself explains nothing and so would empty it of content. It is, in fact, a critical instrument and no more.

What is to the point, however, is that in order to proceed, science, employing objectification, can only assume that the world is compounded of objects, though that as a reading of its form is now subject to serious questioning. For in recent times, science itself has discovered that the world it ultimately confronts is an interrelative complex, a holistic structure which is in principle indivisible. With that it has now to come to terms, a consequence of which is that its traditional presuppositions – that the world is compounded of objects, complies with knowable laws which are characteristically regular – and its inherited methodologies do not correctly apply to what is now presented, at least as penetration goes deeper. That is not to suggest that the logic of incongruity should be seen as an answer to the methodological problem that such discoveries raise; but only that it is a problem that has to be confronted if holism renders induction untenable, at least for the exploration of certain aspects of nature as that is now understood. However, as has been said, this problem falls to science, accepting the implications of its own discoveries, as it endeavours to meet a world which is infinitely more complex than that which it engaged in the past.

Meanwhile, there is a sense in which this logic seems to apply in other fields of enquiry, to discourse which does not aspire to verifiable knowledge or explanation, in recognition that those are not in such fields as these attainable. Ethics, as enquiry into general relationships, wherein it is to be distinguished from personalized moral philosophy, does not aim to establish value, since that, as general in form, accrues from successful rapport with the complex of reality, with nature or society. It rather concerns itself, initially at least, with the detection of *dis*value, as that which militates against its acquisition and is alone to be distinguished as a standing out against an underlying harmony. There is a sense in which prescriptions are essentially negative, imposed to ensure that something inapt shall not be done because it will almost certainly have disturbing effects. And in that form negation, the logic of incongruity, refers to action as distinct from cognitive enquiry. It is applied not merely to protect us against cognitive error or falsity, but to ensure that action which tends to be disturbing shall be subjected to check, to critical comment or censure in the greater or public interest. For though prescriptive rulings bear on the individual, bearing responsibility which cannot be passed to others, since it is that in which his dignity resides, they bear on him effectively as a social being, a member of society, in the interests of which they are projected and applied. If they differ in aspects in various parts of the world, that does not allow him to flout them whatever his private beliefs. For the social interest is paramount and indeed affords the criterion for imposing prescriptions at all, which cannot in that sense be applied, with proper justification, by the whim of a tyrant or some group of ideologists, taking it upon themselves to determine what is required. When action is under review, it must always be seen in terms of its greater effects, which, unlike observable facts, seen in isolation, cannot be gathered at once since they may have distant consequences, so that to regard them as having empirical form, as factual in an immediate sense, is effectively to revert to an improper approach. For example, abusing the confidence of an inexperienced child may not have repercussions until much later in life, playing a part as it does in the formation of character. And if this is a simple example, it is enough to illustrate how actions leave their mark; and it is that in long terms which is of concern to society. By contrast cognitive findings, always presuming a witness, are generally specific, unless they too are likely to have repercussive effects, as with some scientific discoveries, when the same principle applies. The need to judge from what has occurred as to whether it is likely to have similar consequences in the future, is a form of speculation, unfitting for the most part in cognitive enquiry, but plainly needed in other fields, where it has, of course, to be used with care and discretion. And so it will be seen that evaluative enquiry differs from the other, since the aim is not explanation but a better social balance. It must therefore have a different form from that of which the end is the projection of firm findings.

To conclude, though science, under obligation to accede to a holistic ontology, may find something suggestive in the logic of incongruity, a negativistic approach, there can be no pretence that that meets the methodological problem with which it is confronted when its aim is positive. Meanwhile, it can scarcely be doubted that a negative approach is apt when the interest is evaluative. For with that it is not value, which might be considered positive, as successful attunement to the complex of reality. It is by contrast disvalue to which attention has to be turned, as that which can be detected in that it stands out against and objectifies itself. Incongruity refers to action undertaken in the form of responsive rejection to what occurs in reality, to events which are transient and in that sense impressional, in no sense verifiable. Falsification, conversely, in scientific enquiry, although it in some sense refers to what appears to be incongruous in experimentation, is really rather a failure to take all factors into account, so that further investigation (scepticism in pristine meaning) is plainly a requirement when what is studied remains unchanged. All serious enquiry refers to ultimate reality, in effect in two different forms: to physical conditions as relations between them can be detected correctly *and* to the effects of changes on the human psyche, together with their further effects on society at large. Nor is this a division between the physical and the psychical, since on a subconscious plane they are indivisibly intermixed. It is one between the explicable, or at least potentially so, and that which does not admit of adequate explanation. Procedures are accordingly necessarily different, and to think that one can simply embrace the other constitutes a failure to understand the problem with which either has to deal. Just, then, as we contend that approach through objectification cannot properly be applied to what cannot be objectified by means of prepense selection, so we presume that a means which can only be negative cannot be claimed to apply in any fuller sense to positive enquiry. It is not for us, however, with a wholly different interest, to speak conclusively on this point, since the methodological problem now confronted by science may in the course of time be resolved by means not yet envisaged. Science in its early days developed induction as a procedure to serve its emerging needs. And although that had some precedent, it was then applied empirically to further a great advance. It is not clear at once how a holistic complex may be engaged through objectification, unless the idea that what objectifies itself provides a clue on which a further system might be devised. If so, this theory has meaning beyond the task that it was projected to meet. But that is not a claim to be made in respect of another interest.

Appendix II

Human Potentiality

There are several passages in the later pages of this book which a reader, bred to modern acceptances, may find some difficulty in understanding, namely those that refer to the notion of 'lifting the masses' to what is held to be a higher culture. It is perhaps necessary, then, to look more closely in to what that highly regarded idea implies when it means something more than economic advance which, as material, seems to be its opposite, an aid perhaps to the end in view but not that end itself. For other ideas of what 'lifting the masses' involves differ even profoundly from what that expression is usually taken to mean: to raise them to the status of liberal intellectuals, to urge them to adopt the value sets that they do, to which, it would seem, many neither aspire nor have the desire to emulate. Further in this aim, worthy though it is, there is a feature which certainly complicates the issue: namely that, if intellectuals, specialists and experts consider themselves a superior class, exceptionally gifted, then that all should enjoy a like status, privilege and prestige would mean that that as a distinction would cease to be meaningful – a reason perhaps for the cult of specialization in the academic as opposed to the professional world, where no one can sensibly question its social value. Perhaps, then, to eliminate this difficulty and to relieve the specialists of the quandary it imposes, another idea might be projected, which may even prove to be more valid and more liberal. Thus, when we give thought to the nature of human potentiality, our thoughts about it are other than those outlined above, which are always a little equivocal, quite apart from the fact that they are effectively unattainable; and, since they cannot be all-inclusive, produce a measure of resentment on the part of those who do not have access to higher education and so are condemned to lower status, however intelligent they may be. For the examination system is by no means perfect as a means of selection, in that it may exclude slow starters or those who, not wholly without reason, are reluctant to accede to what is currently fashionable. Let us then consider a not unreasonable alternative.

This might be put in the form of a question: What is meant by the expression 'human potentiality'? One of its forms, undoubtedly, is intellectual capacity, apparently unique to the human species and, incidentally, not unallied to mnemonic powers. But there are clearly others which are no less human, such as sensitivity and spirituality, which, when uncorrupted by subjective sentimentality, are closer to each other than is sometimes supposed. For, though the second is an ambiguous term, commonly associated with transcendent states, it is as justly considered in less exalted forms, as referring to simple secular modes – sympathy, affection, courage, sense of others, generous impulse and so on – all of which are other than materialistic postures. Yet they are as much a feature of life, and even perhaps the most significant aspect of it. Since sensitivity is nervous at base, a state in some sense shared with animals, it would seem improper to link it with spirituality. But that would be a mistaken or at least a limited view, allied to the Western idea that spiritual states are essentially involvements with the supernal, the numinous or the divine, and so transcendent of nature or normal relations to it. That is not how the Chinese view it, holding rather to the idea that it is immanent in nature or, more directly, in vitality. That vitality is other than physical might again be questioned, since there is a tendency in the culture to which we are heirs to see everything which is not to be considered sublime in physical terms exclusively, in those that are cognizable, as though that were the only way of viewing nature, a term which surely subsumes everything there is, the psychical no less than the physical. This tends to blind us to a deeper understanding of the nature of man himself, by reason of the projection of a dubious dichotomy, inherited from various sources in the past, and hanging around despite persistent resistance to it. However, it is now recognized that the psychical and the physical are inextricably intermixed in response below the level of consciousness, and, though that is not so readily seen, on conscious planes as well, so that that dichotomy is effectively discredited, notwithstanding that it still haunts rationalist thinking today. It can scarcely be doubted, to confirm this point, that affection is a spiritual state and that attempts to define it in physical terms exclusively, albeit there is an affinity, presumes a grave misunderstanding of its character, even on the level of its higher forms, love, *ai, karunā.*

Nor, despite these prejudices, are we so far removed from this Chinese reading of spirituality as immanent in vitality, for it is implicit in common Western acceptances in all sorts of contexts. We speak, to give an extra-human example, of 'a spirited horse' or, in social terms, of "the spirit of an age", then meaning rather more than its economic or political characteristics. But there are other usages readily discoverable in accessible dictionaries, which show that we employ such telling expressions as "the spirit in which it is done", "show a little spirit" and again "the spirit and not the letter of the law", all of which refer to the manner in which action is or should be undertaken in the normal course of life. Again, we commonly associate this vivid word with courage, which very plainly has links with the nervous system, with verve, panache, *élan,* especially in children, "bursting with energy" as is said. Hence, the idea of the spirit as intimately related to vital human response, to *vis viva,* to animation, is certainly not far-fetched. To suggest that sensitivity, which is one of the forms that it takes, is linked to the process of living, living in its most vital form, and so a human potentiality, is then even a requirement if we are to understand, in more or less concrete terms, the real nature of human response to continually changing conditions at other levels than those of intellectuality. That, no doubt, is spiritual if only in the sense that it is predominantly psychical; though oddly, as oriented cognitively, it is referred to the material world, as that alone that it can comprehend, in which sense its spirituality – it is remarkably insensitive – is not as full as are several other forms of it.

Sensitivity is nervous at base, and so discovered to a degree in other sentient beings. But in humans it is much more acutely and finely developed and is present, since it seldom involves direct or actual contact – unless as response to external pressures

– in such forms as grace, elegance and delicacy. As always this is most clearly seen in response to rhythmic structures, since the effects of that have phenomenal features, which in other forms are generally more obscure. The dance is, for instance, a feature of all social groups, from the most apparently primitive to the most refined, as is the music that accompanies it. As such it is fairly said to be a universal or general human characteristic, which opens the door to thought of others. For the interest is to discover deeper potentialities which are common to humanity on other levels than those that are intellectual, which have been unduly stressed. That man is 'a rational animal' is a well-known generalization, which on the surface seems to sustain a rather restricted view. For there has been a tendency, in part the product of the ambiguity of the adjective 'rational', to interpret this sentence as though he were an intellectual. Rather should it be taken to mean that men in the main are 'reasonable', act and speak in a sensible manner, taking circumstances into account or, as might be said, using 'natural logic' when they communicate with each other. And if they sometimes act irrationally, with failure to control their more disruptive passions, that is fairly said to be an occasional occurrence; and well that it is so, for otherwise there would be social chaos and co-operation would in effect be impossible. To be reasonable, then, is a common characteristic, which is open to abuse and to misinterpretation when it is taken to mean something far from common and thus confined in effect to a class. Reasonableness in thought, in speech and action so describes an aspect of the human make-up, which is indeed the very basis of practical life, since that could scarcely be conducted without it. And if, as has been said, its meaning in that sense is sometimes overlooked, as when it is purloined by those who believe that it should refer to something more sublime, that does not remove the need for its basic meaning as referring to relations between persons in society. It is requisite, however, to go a little deeper when searching for a human potentiality, which is not only utilitarian but also has spiritual features and in that sense engages a further human power, the power behind human creativity, man's poetry, his music, his plastic arts and the higher forms of practical achievement, which call for inventiveness, insight and imagination.

In sum, if intellectuality is stressed as the highest state to which man can aspire, as that uniquely which raises him far above brute beasts, the effect, if paradoxically, is actually to coarsen his attitudes to life and to weaken his relation to nature as one of its modes. Such brashness may even be a form of reaction against rationalistic pretensions, with their tacit implications that those who cannot attain to what they represent are to be considered inferior, the 'lumpen masses' so said. By disregarding or pushing into the background of consciousness capacities that are shared potentially by everyone – and it might be remarked in passing that in his own field the gardener is as knowledgeable as the physicist, and what is philosophy after all but thoughtful common sense, for otherwise it is non-sense – a vicious situation is undoubtedly produced, as becomes increasingly evident. 'Potential' is the term which has been used in this context, for it would be absurd to pretend the characteristics considered were at present universal, or anything resembling it. The reason for this is then worth consideration: that, though these powers are latent, they have been repressed, inhibited, overridden, or at least discouraged, because they are alien to the cult of the knowing self, the idea that the only pursuit is personal aggrandizement or material acquisition in its crudest form. It is then a point that a culture, as distinguished from civilization, which is the product of reason, has its roots in sensuousness, a sense of what is graceful, decorous and shapely. In its most modest form this is seen when a woman arranges the table, pats the cushions, brushes the carpet prior to receiving her guests for a reception. In its more elaborate forms, it is readily detected in all sorts of actions that people undertake. It is scarcely to be denied, then, that this is a universal tendency, found in all human cultures in different parts of the world. Just, then, as there is no really primitive language, since all have subtleties and nuances, which it would be prejudicial to deny, so no peoples are without a sense of fitness and propriety, harmonizing tendencies and responsiveness to form, disguised to a superficial view since contingencies always have to be met. If vulgarity is found in advanced societies, we may fairly ask why this is so, when, for the first time in history, the cultures brought to being by the privileged classes could, with freedom from unremitting toil and with increasing prosperity, be developed generally, shared by everyone, the criminal class presumably excepted.

The suggestion is that attempts should be made to release the ordinary man from rationalistic domination, and to further the powers that are latent in everyone, to become more refined in their attitudes to life and to each other. This is not to imply that intellectuality as an interest should be abandoned, for scholarship, its product, has plainly enriched our understanding of many phases of life and its involvements. But it is to contend that, if it is regarded as the *summum bonum,* as compared with which all else is inferior, a price has to be paid: a divisiveness, which is socially undesirable, and a coarsening of attitudes, which is to be deplored. Both of these conduce to degeneration, regrettable especially when, with increasing wealth and its wider distribution, the fruits of inherited cultures might be gathered and extended, in time to produce a yet finer development. This may seem unduly visionary, and doubtless account must be taken of passion which in some forms rides against it. That may render it little more than a 'nice idea' pitted against what are no less human characteristics, frailty, perverseness, prejudice, obduracy, and yet more vicious proclivities than those. Even so, a movement towards it, a grasp of the potential latent in humanity, that is in all people whatsoever, cannot be wholly misplaced. The present system, its value set, surely leaves something to be desired: a divisiveness which impoverishes and a degrading of the interests of those below the line which at present marks it. They may well have intellectual powers, sufficient for dealing with the contingencies of living; but buried, so to say, beneath them are others, which are certainly no less valuable. The point, at last then, is simply to recognize that in this the general or universal has priority over the specialized, more or less unique to the individual. That recognition itself would carry matters part of the way, for what obstructs an understanding is the cult of the autonomous self, which is relatively recent origin.

Appendix III

The General in Actuality

The general in actuality is an expression designed to allow us to refer to real events, relations in actuality, in a way, as has long been recognized, that cannot be done when the only available approach for dealing with the general is to project the logical universal. But that is and cannot be other than ideal, and so does not in strictness refer to real events at all. The need for an all-embracing principle, behind which lies the idea that there is something in common in what is presented to us, has been felt in all philosophical cultures, since it is the basis of laws, those of science for example, and of principles, such as those required in ethics. Indeed, the attempt to discover universal principles has been at the heart of metaphysics, searching for what are designated 'essences', for something which is definitive, constant and unchanging in any substance or thing, so that particular instances of it may be recognized as having common characteristics. As a general finding it then affords a law or rule which will serve as a basis for explanation. That there are limits to the establishment of any such principles is well-known; and the difficulty in so doing becomes the more acute as what is presented is seen to be more complex and more volatile, as in human behaviour and very much else with recent scientific discoveries.

Although it is somewhat improper, since all is interrelated and man is himself conditioned by nature, of which he is a mode,it is not only convenient but allows of the making of a telling point, to deal with aspects of what is involved in this connection separately. That is, to consider what is actually general in two of its aspects: the universal in nature *and* what in depth is common in the human make-up. For the last allows of an answer which is more or less decisive, whereas the first has features which are not amenable to any wholly convincing answers, despite the many attempts to find them. They may then be considered in the order set out above, giving thought first to the complex called 'nature', which of course includes ourselves, and then to the form of it designated 'man', since that is an arrangement which will allow of a fuller consideration of the latter than it normally receives. For the point is to develop a better understanding of what is common to the human species, which has largely been overlooked because a prejudice has tended to falsify thought about its character.

If then we turn to the world, regarded as external, as in some sense it is, nature may be said to act without our intervention, or, if we now have power to modify its effects, that is partial as an influence and may prove rather perilous with reactive consequences which could be destructive. Turning to a time before such powers as these were developed, the characteristic of nature has always been of interest to those who have given thought to it, seen as a power with which men had to come to terms. The classic example of this is the old and perennial problem of the One and the Many, the idea that something binds the many together, however varied they are, since there is, it is presumed, some principle that all obey and comply with which brings them into harmony to form the intricate complex of nature and, as an aspect of it, society. That the latter sometimes breaks down, later to reform itself into relative equipoise, is a historic phenomenon which is readily observed, since it has happened time and again. But why precisely it does so, either with new or with old components or an amalgamation of them, we do not clearly know, although it is apparent that there is something in the human make-up which allows it to happen, to produce societies able to sustain themselves over quite long periods in tolerable balance. However, the point at once is to consider what constitutes the dynamic balance of nature itself and how that is persistently sustained, despite irregularities. This from the earliest times has been the subject of thought, of theories, insights and speculative projections, both secular and religious. The last are more familiar and have been so in the main since post-classical times. But the first, at least in philosophy, have a clearly recorded history. Thus, the doctrines of the *apeiron,* number theory, the Heraclitan *lógos,* panpsychism, cyclic action, condensation and rarefication, love and hate, atomism, and so on, are all ideas referring to the unity of nature, as in another sense was the doctrine of the Forms, blueprints of the Demiurge. Of these projections *lógos,* strangely echoing *tao,* though differing from it with respect to the animating forces, *eris* and *yin-yang* – corresponding in some sense to Western and Eastern attitudes – is of particular interest as the most convincing. But, as it was impersonal, dynamic and holistic, there was nothing to which the intellect could cling, as stable and definable in positivistic terms.

So, turning from philosophical to religious ideas, we find a more rationalistic approach bound to subjectivity, that is to say to a reason, no less mystical in character, with which those seeking certitude could feel a little more comfortable. Accordingly we discover in various parts of the world, in Palestine and Persia, with a dualistic system of Ormazd opposed to Ahriman, echoed by God and Satan, with complications in Egypt, the idea of a personalized supernatural power, external to and transcendent of an otherwise all-embracing nature. The Hebrews were the first to develop absolute monotheism with belief in Jehovah, a tribal god initially, whilst others, with, for instance, Zeus, Baal, Ishvara, Ptah and later Ra-Atum, saw them as chiefs among a constellation of gods, reflecting aspects of nature, were rather pantheistic. As ideas became more refined, especially in India, there arose the conception of *ātman,* the belief that spirit *(purusha)* was enshrined in the self. With *anatta,* Buddhism opposed this, without however projecting an external power or influence, so that ideas were then subjective and lacked a universal reference. This was the earliest instance of man pivoting on himself, which, with an external God was not similarly developed in later Western religions, albeit that those adopted an analogous idea of personal salvation, of turning one's back on nature, to which no serious thought was given. As will later be said, a consequence of this was that man regarded himself, as endowed with intellectual powers, as riding above nature, exceptional, self-sufficient, even semi-divine.

Before that can be dealt with in greater depth, however,

modern scientific discoveries must be given consideration, since those comprise a serious and determined attempt to explain the characteristics of external nature. With the aid of elaborate instruments, a world has been revealed beyond the reach of naked perception to which enquirers had hitherto been restricted. This, the subatomic world, is apparently compounded, put rather simply here, of electronic charges, stable and instable, in play against each other. Ultimate reality, in other words is shown to be constituted physically, as material and no more. How far knowledge has been achieved and how far it is firm is not for a nescient outsider to say, since he has no access to the instruments with which such findings have been made and, more significantly, lacks the training which would allow him to interpret what has in this way been elicited. But if these findings are firm and if the world is compounded exclusively of electronic charges produced by nuclear activity, that is a remarkable scientific discovery which certainly seems to relate to the general in actuality. And there the matter might be left, met by a purely physical answer, when it would seem impertinent to raise a further question: Is that all that should be said? Is ultimate reality simply and solely physical or does something else inform it? It is worth remarking in passing that in Chinese *ch'i,* one meaning of which is 'energy' – something seen at work of which the source is not fully understood – is held to be the manifestation of *tao,* taken itself to lie behind as a vitalizing power, accepted as spiritual in character. This may, of course, be regarded an archaic conception, but it cannot simply be dismissed and may well have meaning in context. For otherwise how do we account for psychical traits in man and other sentient beings, which have always been supposed to be other than strictly physical? To argue that the brain is an organ stimulated electrically surely involves a failure to account for non-physical elements – desire, anxiety, sympathy, sense of others, and so on – which, by no stretch of imagination can be regarded as merely hylic. But without elaborating on this, which goes against current acceptances, the issue does arise and no answer is available, even on something as basic as the origin of consciousness, which yet remains a mystery. And so with other spiritual powers, insight, creativity, even intellection, which show that something is still cryptic, unexplained, and cannot be defined in purely physical terms.

Let us then turn to what the general in actuality might mean in human terms. For, though man is conditioned by nature, its effects are not simply physical, but plainly inclusive of all that occurs, for nothing exists outside it, unless it should be the supernal. Man *(homo* not *vir,* of course) is but one of its modes, as the *jên-hsing* doctrine evinces. He is a spiritual being; and spirit, as has been said, is closely aligned with sensuousness, that is with sensitivity, which, as a form of vitality, is psychosomatic at base. It is not necessary now to elaborate on this matter, as that has already been done above where thought has been addressed to human potentiality. Enough to remark that in various forms human beings have clearly many features in common, that all have limbs and organs similarly disposed and that all, with rare exceptions, have the power of speech and behave in general reasonably, and must do so for survival, whereas relatively few and on occasion only adopt rationalistic procedures. Unhappily a prejudice, peculiarly Western, urges the idea that those ought to be adopted as the only proper approach, to limit understanding of how people really respond to pressures bearing on them. It is not by means of logic, then, that we understand man's nature, since that is powerless to engage his sensuous, spiritual powers, unless in one aspect of them, which has a very limited range. What is general in his make-up, is only to be discerned by referring to his nature as a sentient being, which is misunderstood if the only approach permitted is rationalistic or cognitive, since that excludes a deeper, more sensitive comprehension of his extra-physical life. Indeed, it effectively distorts proper ideas about it by rendering them rigid and lacking in flexibility, as is seen in logicians' thoughts on language. And in as far as passion is strengthened by the intellect, it becomes more vicious and centred on the self. For, though nervous at base, it is infused with subjective self-consciousness and so ceases to be spontaneous. As the Christians wisely say 'sin is in the mind' or, more precisely, the intellect. It is not in subjectivity that common features are found, since that is very clearly a variant between persons. It is in something more basic, which, if it does not reflect man's glory as an intellectual, neither does it, as extra-subjective, reflect his more vicious propensities.

What emerges from this is that to understand what generality means in depth it is requisite to abandon an approach through objectification, and to adopt more subtle procedures. As for the world itself, it has now to be seen as a holistic complex in which there are no objects, since those are necessarily engendered in the intellect and so are simply ideal constructs. And as for man himself, if we search for what is basically common in the human make-up, we must see, the obvious apart, that that is discoverable only on preconscious levels, which are inclusive of the psychical with the mnenomic and the intentional intervening on that plane. Sensitivity, furthermore, has a nervous base, as is seen in rhythmic response, which is itself, of course, holistic in its character, as dynamic, indivisible, sequential or interrelative. If this constitutes a challenge to rationalistic approaches, that is as it may be. For, in as far as they impose limits on deeper penetration and cannot but involve a measure of distortion, since the object is something torn from its context, they cannot engage the general unless in elementary terms. It is clear that that is an obstacle that has to be overcome and that deeper thought, through another approach, is needed if we are properly to engage the general in actuality, the real world in which man is enmeshed as a responsive being who must learn to attune himself to the pressures it brings to bear. Failure to do so is at the root of many modern problems, of an *hybris* which is bound to bring *némesis* in its train. Nature is the determinant, and that should never be forgotten.

Notes

The primary purpose of these notes, which might otherwise appear unduly extensive, is to demonstrate that there are good precedents for certain somewhat unorthodox ideas I project. Selective reading seems to permit some failure to pay attention to what has been thought by philosophers in the past in our own tradition, not to mention almost total disregard of that of thinkers outside it. It is as though sceptics, wherever active, of the reach of rationalism are not worthy of consideration, but merely frivolous and void of a proper sense of discipline. The neglect, indeed, of some penetrating thinkers of modern times, Whyte and Harris for example, speaking only of those writing in English, is even to be deplored as a vicious restriction of philosophy's potential to deal with serious current issues. The consequence is that it has largely lost the readership of the educated public for whom it once had some significance. These notes then serve to bring to attention contributions with philosophical bearing of thinkers who have been interested in other forms of thought than rationalism and of those in other traditions who have been neglected since logocentrism became the dominant and almost exclusive concern of philosophy. They also serve to give support to ideas projected in the text, which might otherwise be regarded as unworthy of serious consideration.

Introduction

1. Since *scientia* means 'knowledge', this claim is rather tenuous, not to say presumptuous when formal logic assumes for itself the prestige that now attaches to science. For the knowledge it provides with respect to real events is far to seek, limited as its interest is to abstract verbal relationships.
2. It is arguable that Aristotle devised his *analytiké* for classificatory purposes in his empiric or scientific studies. But whether that is the case or not, it is the demand for rigour that really restricts the reach of formal logic and confines it to symbolic relations, when nothing in reality has that simple character.
3. Science is obliged to use technical terms as it probes into ever more complex relations for which ordinary language has no suitable terms, as also to avoid unwieldy circumlocutions. If then, aping science, formal logic indulges technicalities, it does not have the same justifications. It would be invidious to cite authors, but anyone who cares to glance at typical texts or even at no more than their titles *(An Axiomatization of One Modal Theory of the Veiled Recession Frame, Distributive Lattice with a Dual Homomorphic Operation* or *Interpolation Properties of Superintuitionist Logic* – to cite but a few) will find himself in a world apart.
4. It must be evident to a little thought that influence bears upon us in many ways, most of which are not detectable even to recollection, so subtle and evasive are they. Whyte, a sadly neglected thinker, *The Unconscious* (London, 1958). 70f. speaks, for example, of unconscious assumptions, which are meaningful in the sense that they undoubtedly exert an influence.

Chapter One

1. That man has the power to reason, which animals seem to lack, has been seen as an almost divine characteristic, which raises him to a godlike state. That he has a capacity for sensitivity, as in a sense of the needs of others, in a more refined form than animals, which distinguishes him no less,

is scarcely taken into account in philosophy, albeit that Scheler gave attention to it, *The Nature of Sympathy* (1923, tr. London, 1954). That it involves direct relation to nature, and so in some sense has animalic character, as nervous responsiveness, suggests that it is a more lowly state, though it is surely involved with the soul rather than the self. But such is our "disinterested, detached, unrestricted desire to know" – Lonergran, *Insight* (New Haven, 1957), 630 – that all else is secondary; and hence our failure to deal with the general, as contrasted with the logical universal, which is nothing more than an intellectual construct.

2. Whereas *tao* was never associated with language, *vāc,* originally related to thunder, the Wind God or Spirit, a creative power thus communicating with men, came to mean speech, later in Nyāya with a logical sense.
3. Cusanus, *De Docta Ignorantia,* Book III, where he writes: "...the endless variety of species and genera in the universe, each of which has its limits, though all exist together linked by some indivisible force", to which he adds: "God makes the bond among them all".
4. Fishler, in Runes *Dictionary of Philosophy* (New York, ND), 125, citing Diels, *Frag. d. vor,* I, ch 12.
5. Habermas, *Knowledge and Human Interest* (Frankfurt, 1968, tr. London, 1972), 161.
6. *Tao* may be said to have two related meanings, the ontic, as the underlying flow or pulse of nature *(tao te),* and the ethical, concerned with how to act in relation to it *(tao hsien).* That attunement to *tao* gives personal power, Wing, *The Tao of Power.* (New York, 1986), is a gross misreading of *tao te,* interpreting it in a subjective Western manner, which is wholly alien to its real meaning and so confuses ideas about it.
7. There has been dispute as to whether the *Nichomachean Ethics,* should be understood as an ethical or moral doctrine, as addressed to the person as an individual or to those involved in society. Hampshire, *Innocence and Experience* (London, 1989), 155f, seems to be inclined to the latter, which is unorthodox in terms of the individualistic tendencies of today.
8. Kahn, *The Art and Thought of Heraclitus* (Cambridge, 1979),

45, is surely mistaken in translating *lógou* in Fr. XXXVI by a later meaning of *lógos,* related to speech and not to a creative power. For "listening to me" and "to the (my) report" can only have the same meaning.

9. Heraclitus urges strife *(eris),* whereas Taoism commends adaptation or attunement to nature, an idea with roots in the interplay of *yin* and *yang,* which is an early insight long predating commitment to writing, either of Chuang Chou or of the quasi-mythical Lao Tzu. These attitudes represent a fundamental difference between Western and Eastern approaches to nature.
10. It is normal practice to divide the *Dialogues* into three periods in Plato's life, early, middle and late. Of these the first were almost certainly written with the memory of Socrates in mind and so tend to reflect his approach. For it is doubtful whether Socrates would have approved of some of the later, even dogmatic doctrines, projected in his name.
11. Russell, *Wisdom of the West* (London, 1959) tends to regard that, particularly with respect to classical antiquity, as a rationalistic advance, though in fairness he deals with other attitudes justly. In his earlier work, *History of Western Philosophy* (London, 1946) he is scarcely fair to Bergson, dismissed as 'an irrationalist' and treated with biased misunderstanding.
12. Little is known of others than the schools that stemmed from Plato, notwithstanding that it is recognized that two of these, the Cynics and the Cyranaics, were by no means rationalistic. For Antisthenes regarded himself as the spiritual heir of Socrates and Aristippus was sceptical of rationalistic procedures. Nor were the last alone among the sceptics of antiquity, as with the later Sceptics. Moreover, this posture is found both in Patristic and Scholastic times (with Sextus and Autrecourt for instance) and is actively present today, with Adorno, *Negative Dialectics* (1966, tr. London, 1973) and other members of the Frankfurt School. In short, scepticism arises whenever rationalism becomes too assertive.
13. That the influence of Heraclitus persisted is shown in Sextus's comment (Hyp. I, 240), that Aenesidemus intended his scepticism only as a preparation for the Heraclitan philosophy. Zeller, *Outline of the History of Greek Philosophy*

(1844 - 1855, tr. New York,1957), 298.

14. After the bringing together of the two meanings of *lógos* by Philo, one (speech) became dominant in two forms, as *Lógos,* Divine Reason, which had some links with creativity, but ceased to be of much importance after the condemnation of 451 AD, and as *logica,* which was strictly linked to verbal concerns, so that its Heraclitan meaning was lost to view. Nonetheless, it continued to be evoked in other terms, *natura naturans,* for instance, as by the Pantheists, using such expressions as *colligatio divina.* Now with the emergence of holism, ideas have undergone some change, to produce a reversion to ancient insights, in some sense confirmed by science, thus to end the long reign of Parmenides. But the implications of this for philosophy have yet to be properly grasped.
15. As the poet Spender in an early poem, withdrawn for no known reason, said: "The Great Wheel turns". Or if, with Plato, poets must be dismissed, let Lovejoy, *The Great Chain of Being* (Cambridge, Mass. 1936), 327, be cited as one among many thinkers for whom the correlation of *ratio* in thought (intellectual conceptualization) and *ratio* in nature (apparent causal ordering) is altogether too simple.
16. Urban, *Beyond Realism and Idealism* (London, 1949), 97.
17. This, the expression of a starry-eyed scientist, was used in a lecture many years ago, to evoke a sceptical reaction in the author, then but a student.
18. When *epistémé* came to mean 'knowing that', as opposed to 'knowing how', is not readily determined, though it had certainly acquired that later meaning in classical times. But meanings change. *Gnósis,* for instance, seems to have meant justified knowledge for Socrates, though it later came to mean revealed knowledge. Just so, *nous,* though it yet retains its original meaning, was later taken to mean intellectual reasoning, although careful thinkers understood it as the ground on which *noésis* rested.
19. This requires some modification, for Alexander (of Aphrodisias) and others of the Peripetetic School, and even Porphyry, the Neo-Platonist, concerned themselves with Aristotelian logic, while Sextus thought it pertinent to oppose it. Finally Martianus incorporated it in the *trivium,* to

show that interest in it persisted, if only for its value as a pedagogic instrument. But, of course, the desire for truth, irrefutable truth, was a felt need in religion.

20. There has been a tendency in the West, linked to the idea of man's uniqueness as rational, to equate truth in a logical sense with Divine Reason; or so until, as secularity became prevalent, to hold that there is nothing greater than man, in his highest state a rationalist, a logician, a mathematician, a metaphysician or a cosmologist, tended to replace it. But it is worthy of note that Clemens (Alexandria) elected for *lógos endiáthetos,* contending for the world as an organic whole, thus showing that a form of the Heraclitan *lógos* survived into early Christian times (II' Century AD).
21. For he (Leibniz) began by saying *calculemus* but later developed the doctrine of *vraisemblance (New Essays on the Human Understanding* (1701, 1765, tr. London, 1961), 457, which had very different implications. As for Pascal, his scepticism is sometimes very marked, notably in *Pensées* (1666) 931.
22. Gomperz, *Greek Culture* (1893, tr. London, 1901), IV, 54.
23. The 'tacit knowledge' of Polanyi, *Tacit Dimensions,* (London, 1967), affords an instance, since that projection cannot be proved in any strict sense, nor can it, as beyond observation, be faulted.
24. It would be absurd to contend that intuition involved no thought process, albeit that it is subconscious. Quinton, *The Nature of Things* (London, 1975), 120f, effectively confirms this with his interesting suggestion that intuition is 'hidden inference', contending that that may well be justified, as Peirce held that it should be, although it is not necessarily true, as has sometimes been supposed.
25. That some 90% of all response is subconscious was first brought to the author's attention by McCullough at a seminar (MIT, 1954). Subsequent study has shown that this finding is widely confirmed by neurophysiolgists and psychologists (eg. Gregory). This matter, the importance of which for philosophy cannot be overrated, will be further considered in Chapter V.
26. This was specifically confirmed in a letter to the author by the eminent Hellenist, Professor Dodds, stating that *aisthésis* in

classical Greek meant what we now call 'perception', that is clearly conscious response. In fairness to Baumgarten, who reintroduced the term (*Aesthetica,* 1750), he defined it as 'sensuous perception', a state presumably in which we become conscious of response which is basically nervous or sensuous. The introduction of the word 'perception' has had unfortunate effects, for conscious perception of a rhythmic sequence is, properly speaking, a second stage. If it is regarded as basic itself that permits of the entry of all sorts of irrelevances of intellectual type, provenance, what the artist meant, 'his message', and so on, commonly called 'appreciation'. That that approach is divisive and effectively deprives the ordinary man of a natural form of enhancement in life is a matter that will be considered in depth in a further book, *Artistic Issues,* as the fourth in this series.

Chapter Two

1. Haack, *Philosophy of Logics* (Cambridge, 1978).
2. In view of the arguments in Haack, *Deviant Logics* (Cambridge, 1974) and in conformity with the views of Frege, it is just to stress that findings in formal logic are verbal and no more. In strictness they do not refer, unless in simple even obvious instances, to external events, so that deviant logics, such as that of Łucasiewicz, have some justification. No doubt, within its limits, formal logic serves some purpose, but that is not the purpose present in normal discourse when that is referred to human interrelationships, as in ethics. The point as to whether (113) formal logic can 'tidy up' ordinary discourse is doubtful, if, as formal, it cannot refer to externals at all. At best, it is confined to criticizing false statements.
3. Notwithstanding scepticism with respect to the reach of formal logic, no sceptic appears to have given thought to an alternative procedure. However, Abelard, Locke and Bergson all used the expression 'natural logic' to refer to the procedure used in normal discourse. 'Irrational logic' is rather the term to which rationalists are given though 'non-rational' would be less prejudiced.
4. Jaynes, *The Origins of Consciousness and the Breakdown of the*

Bicameral Mind (Boston, 1976) though his reference is rather to self-consciousness, since consciousness has plainly a much earlier origin.

5. Whorf, *Language, Thought and Reality: Selected Writings* (ed. Carroll, Boston, 1956), referring to differently structured forms of language.
6. This is the definition given in private conversation by Dr. John Rose. But many others, Dewey, Maratain, Cohen, Weinberg, Quine and Dummett have essayed to do so in various ways, sometimes as if there were need for justification.
7. Kepler, influenced by Brahe, showed clearly that deduction alone, as used by Copernicus, was insufficient as a means and that experimentation was the key to advance. Bacon sought to refine on this approach through inductive procedures.
8. It is well known that *analytiké* was not used as a term in philosophy until Aristotle employed it for his 'logic'. By contrast, *dialektiké* meaning 'conferring' in Homer, had been used from early times, probably by Zeno (of Elea), plainly deploying negation.
9. Harris, *The Foundations of Metaphysics in Science* (London, 1965), 17, 22, is scathing in his dismissal of the logocentrics; the Logical Positivists and the Logical Atomists' approaches to science.
10. Though the term was originally used by Smuts, *Holism and Evolution* (London, 1926) in a relatively narrow cognitive sense, its wider meaning 'emerged' so to say a little later. Exemplication of it is to be found in Böhm, *Wholeness and the Implicate Order* (London, 1980), or even more convincingly, as grounded in well-established evidence, in Lovelock, *Gaia* (Oxford, 1979).
11. Whereas consciously objectified percepts are not. This is the implication of Warnock's remark in *Modern British Philosophy* (Oxford 1955), 167.
12. Lichthaim, *Lucács* (London, 1970), 60, expresses this admirably. But the idea has a long history and is implicit in the Sanskrit doctrine of *māyā*.
13. Spengler, *The Decline of the West* (Munich, 1918 - 1922, tr. London (Abridged Edition), 1932, 1961, Introduction), very properly makes a distinction between Culture and Civilization, implying that the second is the product of

intellectuality and the first of sensuousness or sensitivity as his use of the term 'becoming' confirms. As sensuous the first is universal whereas the second tends to be subjective and divisive, though that is not stressed as fully as it might have been to bring out the full significance of this distinction.

14. It was once thought that this comment was in Kneale & Kneale, *The Development of Logic* (Oxford, 1962), ch. 1; but, though it is suggested, it must be some other source. Later, however (313), Locke is cited as making a somewhat similar comment.
15. This system originated with Gotama (III BC) and influenced Indian thinking until its decline some 2,000 years later. *Mo che* in China, emerging about the same time, fell into desuetude and failed to exert an influence prior to the Han, as was the case with the *Ming chia pien che* (the debaters) - Hu Shih, *The Development of the Logical Method in Ancient China* (Shanghai, 1922). Buddhist Logic was a later development, active at the end of the first millennium AD - Keith, *Buddhist Philosophy* (Oxford, 1923), Part IV. It is noteworthy that three of these developments were linked to religious interests, as was the case in the Scholastic period.
16. Sartre, *Being and Nothingness* (Paris, 1913, tr. New York, 1957) agonizes over the choices he must make, admittedly in exceptional circumstances, as though to suggest that that was the normal practice. This echoes the typically Western idea that knowledge is the key to moral excellence, a legacy of the Attic School, stressing knowledge, rather than sensitivity, as the supreme requirement.
17. Strawson, *An Introduction to Logical Theory* (London, 1952) 174, illustrates this superbly with 'his common sense syllogism". Incidentally, *sýllogos* carried the meaning of 'reassembling' well before Aristotle used it in a technical sense.
18. Fisher, "Re-engaging with Real Arguments", a paper read at the R.I.P. in November 1991, in which he contended that Aristotle, apart from *analytiké,* to which we are so attached in our passion to elicit absolute answers, also devised two other logics, *dialektiké* and *rhetoriké* (for lawyers). Paradoxically, it is the second of these, deploying negation on equal terms, which is used in normal philosophical discourse when that is

directed towards real problems, rather than the first, though that is supposed to be the procedure used.

19. Beveridge, *The Art of Scientific Investigation* (London, 1950), quoting (45) Trotter, *Collected Papers* (1946) and paraphrazing (46) Bacon, with further citations from Planck, *Where is Science going?* (1933), in confirmation of his contentions.
20. Schiller, *Studies in the History and Methods of Science* (ed. Singer, Oxford, 1917), 82.
21. Cohen, *Preface to Logic* (London, 1946), 1, for a definition which has the merit of being free from pretentious or questionable aims.

CHAPTER THREE

1. According to Bambrough in his Introduction to Lindsay's *Republic* (1976), *aporía* is to be interpreted as Socrates' failure "to produce the desired definitions", as though he were a modern rationalist. There is some precedent for this in Aristotle, as cited by the Kneales (op. cit. 113) but even with that authority that reading may be questioned.
2. What Aristotle sought, it seems (Schiller, *Logic for Use* (London, 1929),7), were trustworthy answers in his scientific enquiries. As *syllogíein* in one of its senses meant 'to weigh', syllogism could refer to the classification of species, certainly one of his interests. A reliable answer need not be absolute; for, as modern science shows, it may be contingent, standing for as long as it cannot be bettered. A comment of Arendt, *The Human Condition* (Chicago, 1978), 291, has some bearing on this.
3. These are the titles of works by O'Hear (London, 1985) and Lindley, Fellows & Macdonald (1978), of which there are many others, aiming, it seems, to justify its activity, as if that were in some doubt,
4. Stebbing, *Thinking to some Purpose* (London, 1936) made a gallant effort to apply philosophy to practical, specifically political problems, when, it is to be noted, her findings are framed in negative terms.
5. *Sophía* had many meanings in antiquity, ranging from 'good

sense' (Herodotus) to theoretical thinking (Aristotle). He opposed it to *phronēsis* (practical reasoning). Allied to experience, that might be taken to mean 'understanding' in contrast to 'knowledge'; and that is apparently what it meant for Pythagoras.

6. That knowledge cannot refer beyond phenomena or what is observable is tolerably obvious, even if experimentation addresses reality, interpreting phenomenally if it is to constitute knowledge. But that is not always clearly recognized because of some ambiguity attaching to the word 'real'.
7. It is found, for instance, in the work of Manegold of Lautenbach, Al-Ghazali, Judah ha-levi, Siger of Brabant, Nicholas d'Autrecourt, William of Ockham, John Gerson, Raimond de Sabunde, Nicholas von Krebs (Cusanus), not to mention such mystics as Hugh and Richard of the Abbey of St. Victor.
8. Lichthaim has already been cited, but another thinker Penrose, in a paper read at KCL (25.11.1987) entitled "Why is mathematics so unreasonably effective in physics?" might be said to have raised the stakes, for effectiveness does mean that some relation is established between the ideal and the real, however remarkably.
9. Truth has at least three meanings, in formal logic, in life and law, and in religion, which are certainly not the same, though formal logicians sometimes assume that their reading of it has universal bearing. But the others are not opposed to falseness, but to lying in the one case and to disbelief or failure to assent to some credo, itself a variant, in the other. Some logicians, very properly, repudiate this assumption: Dummett, *Truth and Other Enigmas* (London, 1978), xliv, 456 et passim, following Frege, holds that the concern of formal logic is restricted to the study of 'essential structures,' and Tarski, *The Concept of Truth in Formal Languages* (1933, tr. London, 1956), 266, also contends that truth should be restricted to a specific meaning in this connection.
10. Church, under 'Truth', in Runes, *Dictionary of Philosophy* (New York, ND) takes proposition to mean "a statement claiming to be true".
11. That an event has a single cause is a characteristic intellectual

acceptance, since it permits of definitive explanation. In fact every event is the consequence of many causes, notably as referred to human action. This relates to Hume's "succession of impressions succeeding each other with inconceivable rapidity" in which of course he is speaking of perceptions which are selected out of the complex. If, then, impressions are fleeting and inextricably linked and are singular only when perceived, many escape awareness, so that some of their causes are not detected. When, with a Gestalt, they culminate in a single event, that gives a limited picture. Behind much human action, for instance, lies an accumulation of causes built up through past experiences, only a fraction of which are present to consciousness. To generate a single cause in experimental enquiry is an artificial device and gives no true index of what happens in reality, judged from insights into human reaction.

12. Brentano, *Psychology from an Empirical Standpoint* (1874, tr. London 1973) 103, observes, citing earlier thinkers, that intention and memory both operate on subconscious levels. Gestalt psychologists have since confirmed this. The idea that all response is conscious then no longer holds. Furthermore, the mind-matter dichotomy is refuted once it is accepted that psychical factors are intermixed with physical factors below the level of consciousness, with obvious ontic implications: that what is ultimately confronted is the complex of reality and not simply the phenomenal world, which is amenable to cognitive enquiry, but the world of becoming, which is not.
13. Discounting the idea that metaphysics refers to what is extra-physical, since it might refer to the sequence of Aristotle's writings, its ontic aspect is without doubt important as referring to the assumptions made about reality. As that is beyond perception, all such assumptions are necessarily speculative, as the term 'assumption' implies. It is therefore a question of which projection it is wisest to accept. This might be determinism in science, but it must certainly be something else in ethics, holism presumably, since society is a holistic complex.
14. Bradley, *Appearance and Reality* (London, 1893), 363 ff.
15. Polanyi, *Personal Knowledge* (London, 1958), 312, indicates that this is so. Strawson, *Individuals* (London, 1959), 184 f,

demonstrates the difficulties in assuming that particularized perceptions are indeed claims that can be justly generalised, even when of material bodies.

16. Although Bradley, *Principles of Logic* (Oxford, 1883), devotes a chapter to negation (I. iii), he shows no sign of grasping its potential as a disciplining instrument referred to externals, since he confines himself to its propositional applications.
17. The ambiguity of the adjective 'rational' has permitted rationalists to claim that their approach embraces every form of enquiry. Among others, Popper, *The Open Society and its Enemies* (London, 1945), II, 352, shows the necessity of making a distinction between rationalism and reasoning, projecting reasonable answers.
18. Philosophy's relation to a confident science is now a little ambiguous, since recognising the last's prestige, it aspires to be like it. At the same time, however, it clings to the idea that it is in some sense superior, affecting to believe that that sprang from its loins, so to say, and is still its protégé. But in its present form that claim will not stand up to inspection, since, with cognition as its aim, it is, by comparison, sterile and has little of value to contribute.
19. It is assumed, by Lewis, *Mind and the World Order* (Cambridge, Mass. 1929) that 'material' as opposed to 'strict' implication renders formal logic referential. His was a brave attempt to overcome the limitations of formal logic. Those will, however, remain, for as long as it insists on rigour, which confines it to abstractions or, at very best, to 'glimpses of the obvious'.
20. Free translation of Bergson, *L'évolution créatrice* (Paris, 1907), 60.
21. Kant, *Critique of Pure Reason* (1787, tr. London, 1953), 574.
22. Supporting citation is scarcely required to sustain this finding, since it must be obvious to simple common sense and was recognized by historians and sociologists well before holism was projected. There are no closed societies, unless in monasteries, and even they have interrelative features.
23. The core doctrine of Confuciamism – that you are first and foremost a social being enmeshed in a network of responsibility such that your personal freedom is limited – cannot readily be ascribed to a single thinker. For it runs through Chinese thought from K'ung fu-tzu, or more

precisely those of his disciples who stressed the social aspects of his thinking, onwards. It is exemplied in the doctrine of *kang,* linked to that of *wu lun,* the elements of which are found in *Chung Yung (The Doctrine of the Mean),* once attributed to Tzu-ssu.

24. Though these aims are sometimes regarded as coincident, what they achieve is not the same. For the first amounts to an involvement with abstractions whereas the second relates to projected ideas, so that it serves a more concrete function, to give it greater justification.

Chapter Four

1. For that is a mere truism and is meaningful only when the interest is cognitive and when what is reviewed is presumed to be constant. Popper, *Unending Quest* (London, 1992), 184, still seems to regard the phenomenal (stilled for inspection) as the real world. It is rather the case that everything is in process of change, though that may be so slow as to be undetectable.
2. Haack, op. cit (1974), 2, considers two types of deviant logics, "proposed as rivals or as supplementary", with particular reference to the justification of the first. This is confirmed in a telling sentence (123): "It could be admitted that classical logic embodies some existential assumptions, but denied, nevertheless that any modification is called for". For, if referential claims are questioned as improper, there is surely need for a discipline (?rivalling or supplementary) which can refer to externals without the need for such dubious assumptions – as that the ideal reflects the real, for example.
3. Leibniz, *Monodology* (1714, tr. London, 1898), mocked as Dr. Pangloss by Voltaire, who assumed that he referred it to human action, influenced by passion strengthened by intellectual powers, rather than to nature, formed for him by God, to whom such attributes do not apply. That nature and humanity have distinguishable characteristics has long been recognized by philosophers, Dilthey, for a late example, demanding that different approaches be applied to each.
4. Leibniz, op. cit (1701, 1961), 459 ff, on *vraisemblance,* of

which the implication is that, though a finding can be shown to be erroneous, it cannot be shown to be true (of reality), but only likely.

5. Van Vloten & Land, *Benedicti de Spinoza Opera* (The Hague, 1914), III, 173.
6. Carnap, *The Logical Structure of the World* (1928, tr. London, 1967), 290.
7. Subjective generalization has long been adopted as a procedure in moral philosophy. Singer, *Generalization in Ethics* (London, 1963), 271 f), attempts to defend Sidgwick's advocacy of this principle *(Methods of Ethics,* 1875). But both are idealistic thinkers failing to see that this is prejudicial and involves the dubious assumption that personal or class preferences are those of everyone. Nor does this, with its rational bias, touch natural sensitivity, which alone appears to be general.
8. Heidegger, *An Introduction to Metaphysics* (1953, tr. New York, 1961). 21.
9. It is of the utmost importance to stress that everybody is potentially sensuous, formed to respond to rhythmic presentations, whereas, though all are 'rational animals', they are not contemplative intellectuals analysing what is before them. The decay of culture that distinguishes modern life is the consequence of stressing intellectualism and of propagating the idea the 'appreciation', of the artist's intention and so on, as the mark of a cultivated person and as the attitude to which everyone ought to aspire. Scott, *The Architecture of Humanism* (London 1924) 143f, shows that sensitivity is a capacity generally present. Vulgarity, paradoxically, is the product of overrefinement, preciosity.
10. That intellect and mind have different meanings and serve different functions is contended by Roe, *Semantic Issues* (London, 1995), ch III, to show that mind, unlike intellect, is not 'independent of' but directly involved with the external world.
11. Projected by Heraclitus and resisted by Parmenides, 'becoming' has had a chequered history, as though it were a disturbing idea, even a threat to entrenched beliefs. 'Being', meanwhile, as potentially knowable, invariably carries a capital, as though to give it the requisite sublimity,

presumably for that reason, and to contrast it with 'beings', its parts.

12. This doctrine was promulgated by Hui Shih, a near contemporary of Aristotle, who contended that there was no power by means of which *ming* (concept/conception) could engage *shih* (actuality, as contrasted with phenomenal being).
13. Nietzsche, *The Birth of Tragedy* (1872, tr. New York 1956), xii, xv, though Nietzsche himself, far from an analyst, was even a rhetorician, whose attitude, when not 'yea-saying', was critical or negativist.
14. It has been suggested (source not recovered) that the ancient sceptics argued as they did in defence of ethical interests, which could not be dealt with rationally. A passage in *Magna Moralia* (1.6.1186a) seems to confirm this, which is more clearly expressed by Bury, *The History of Greece* (London, 1959), II, 148, when he says: "In ancient Greece there was no morality *(éthos)* but only a sense of propriety *(ĕthos)*". In other words, as attempts were made to rationalize ethical involvement, something was lost, sensitivity gave way to intellectuality, spontaneity was replaced by self-conscious subjectivity. This change took place as early perhaps as the V' century BC (if Gorgias' scepticism was so projected), to reach its apogee with the Patristics. Ethical understanding, as the sceptics seem to have recognized, involves a negativistic approach. Habermas, as cited, confirms this.
15. Beveridge, op. cit., (1950) and Medawar, *Intuition and Induction* (Philadelphia, 1969), deal with this matter.
16. Bradley, op. cit, (1983), 173 et passim.
17. Elaborating on Note II. 10, Lovelock, op. cit (1979), renders holism more convincing, since his findings are based on well-established scientific evidence, related to the proportion of gases in the atmosphere, of which philosophers must surely take account, notwithstanding its influence on the presupposition they traditionally adopt.
18. Thought at the turn of the century, of which the thinkers named are but a representative selection, was remarkably creative. For reasons that are not easy to discern, the promise of this development was, in the English speaking world, not so much dismissed as overridden in favour of an upsurge of

logocentrism and linguistic analysis, which has been dominant for almost a century and is the cause, no doubt, of a separation from richer developments on the Continent.

19. Brown, *Laws of Form* (London, 1969), 105, expresses this admirably and with considerable wit.
20. Hampshire, *Morality and Conflict* (Oxford, 1983), 115, speaks well on this matter, and Gadamer, *Reason in the Age of Science* (Philadelphia, 1969), gives consideration in depth to the causes that have brought this state of affairs about.
21. Aristotle, *Problemata,* Book IV, ch. 26, 879 b 35-36, a citation for which the author is indebted to Dr. Jeffrey Carr.
22. Of course, there is a distinction properly to be made between the recipient and that to which he responds. But that he is necessarily a conscious subject as opposed to an agent who responds at all levels and that what he responds to is an *object* is another matter. For objects are creations of the subject (taken in a Kantian sense) and only have existence as intellectuals constructs. For fuller discussion of this matter see Roe, op. cit, (1995), ch.IV.
23. Popper's doctrine of falsification (*The Logic of Scientific Discovery* (1934, tr. London, 1959), 41ff) refers to cognitive or scientific enquiry. To a degree it does so with respect to ethics, though 'understanding' should not be equated with verifiable phenomenal 'knowledge', which is what interests positive science.
24. Since all statements of truth are in Wittgenstein's phrase 'tautologies' tied to the conventional use of words ("If the earth turns it moves" - Maritain, *Formal Logic* (1923, tr. New York, 1946), 101, and if further they must be strictly defined, their reference is restricted since even relations in the phenomenal world are complex, fluid and diffuse.
25. It is not a requirement to accept that scientific findings are true in a logical sense ("... they are sometimes fruitful without being true" – Einstein; and holism cannot in strict sense be verified), but of grasping their implications – those of holism especially – in order the better to understand man's relation to what impinges on him. If that, as is claimed, can only be done in rationalistic terms, that constitutes a failure to look at what actually occurs with sufficient sensitivity.

CHAPTER FIVE

1. 'Subjective' now has two meanings, which are effectively antithetical. Its original meaning was 'thrown under' *(subjectus),* that is, subjected to natural and social pressures (Roman *subjectivi,* British subjects – subjected to the law). Its modern meaning derives from Kant's identification of the subject with the I, the knowing self, which *hypokeimenon* did not mean (*Critique of Pure Reason,* Transcendental Dialectic, Book II, ch. 1), thus to give it a meaning diametrically opposed to its basic, social meaning. For it now meant looking down on and attempting to manipulate or control what was presented to consciousness in place of being involuntarily under external pressures. Roe, op. cit. (1995), deals with effects of this change in some depth, ch. IV.
2. For the word 'form', from the Latin *forma,* has acquired two distinctive meanings, which are sometimes confused: 'shapeliness', which it refers to in artistry *and,* particularly in adjectival use, to 'procedures by means of established rules' (The Rules of the Game). Vitruvius used it in the first sense, as do artists in the classical tradition to this day.
3. Gurney, *The Power of Sound* (London, 1880), 881, writing at the height of the Romantic movement, expresses this admirably with a comment worth quoting: "People often think that they are yearning for the ineffable when all that they are really sighing for is the next note".
4. Following Brentano (Note III, 12), Merleau-Ponty, *Phenomenology of Perception* (1945, tr. London, 1962), frequently speaks of the intermixture of physical and psychical influences (eg. 10, 77, 174 et passim), as of the inability of rationalism to engage perception in the form that it actually has (eg. 25f, 57, 142 et passim).
5. When self-consciousness does not intervene we are normally in attunement with our environment, as when walking in the street or doing quite elaborate things, indulging in sporting activities, dancing and even writing books; and nature so arranges things to ensure that this is so.
6. It is idle to deny that those with the means to do so, whatever their backgrounds, have been perpetrators of wars. But they were not entirely without a sense of responsibility, as in the

attempt, after the atrocities of the Thirty Years War, to civilize conflict. Ferrero, *The Napoleonic Campaigns in Northern Italy* (1936, tr. London, 1939), ch. III, citing Vattel's Six Rules of War (1758), merits attention in this context, particularly with respect to the consequences of flouting them.

7. Curiously, it is less terrorism, which is localized in space and time, than attitudes to life (eg. stress on rights as opposed to duties) which carry the greater threat to social stability today. The decay of discipline does more to undermine norms than the violence which is its product. Heinz, *Xenokrates* (Leipzig, 1892), 160, Fr. 4, cites that thinker as saying: "The reason for discovering philosophy is to ally what disturbs in life". It still seems to be the reason.
8. Stankiewicz, *Aspects of Political Theory* (London, 1976), may be interpreted thus: If we distinguish three forms of democracy, political, economic and socio-cultural, we must see that they do not have the same character, to be treated as though they were equally rationalizable. For the last depends on ensuring that the norms absorbed in childhood are not confused with rationally determined law, though that rests on them, but cultivated for themselves as the key to social cohesion. 'Norms' for Stankiewicz are implicit principles of behaviour, such as courtesy and decency, which are prior to and deeper than explicit law *(nomos)* – cf *fa-li* doctrine.
9. Hartmann, *New Ways in Ontology* (1949, tr. Chicago, 1953), 80.
10. Commenting on this passage, a critic, Dr. Lund, contends, very justly, that "commercial greed, systematic mendacity and gratuitous cruelty" have more damaging social effects than the factors named. But the point is that those, as major crimes, are controllable by law. Law is not so readily applied to what are rather social offences, which certainly have repercussive effects. If those are to be rendered less disturbing, then it is the value sets that society adopts which must be promoted in extra-legal form. And that is a philosophical not a legal concern. No doubt, time is needed for a modification of attitudes; but unless thought is given to this matter the weakening of a social sense is likely to continue with unfortunate consequences. Philosophy has its own role and should not, in belief that it has universal

bearing, attempt to intervene in spheres in which others, with specific experience, are better equipped to deal. 'The Philosophy of Law', if that, once called 'Jurisprudence', is a justified expression, is a matter for lawyers, facing problems with which they are familiar and have been trained to meet. Plainly, no fine line can be drawn between the social and the legal; but enough that what cannot readily be controlled by the threat of force has to be so in some way which will be effective. All that is then suggested is that thought be given to what that may entail.

11. Russell, *Mysticism and Logic* (London, 1918, 1954), 80, who, as a logical atomist, limited to engaging the phenomenal world, was surely a naïve realist himself.
12. This figure echoes that given in Note I, 23. Although, then, no figure, in any case approximate, can be applied to this process by science, common sense nevertheless informs us that some such process must take place below the level of consciousness to protect us against the showers of stimuli to which we are continually subjected. Unhappily, cognitivists are reluctant to acknowledge this, since what takes place below the level of consciousness is beyond the reach of strict cognition.
13. 'Sensation' derived from the late Latin *sensatio,* for *sensus* was used in classical times, is taken to cover both perceptual response and the action of the sense organs, which leads to some confusion. Hirst, *The Problems of Perception* (London, 1959) 56, stresses the distinction between perception and sensation in rather scathing terms, noting that the last has two meanings, "one philosophical or popular and the other scientific (caused sensory reaction)".
14. James, *The Principles of Psychology* (Cambridge, Mass. 1890), I, 468, in which he was surely referring to conscious reception. For the underlying world is undoubtedly ordered, though so in such a subtle and complex way that we cannot grasp it with our conscious minds. But see Appendix III, where this matter is discussed.
15. Köhler, *Gestalt Psychology* (London, 1930), ch. V, is the chief proponent of this finding, the importance of which for philosophy, as that seeks to deal with real problems – man's relation to the world which he confronts directly – cannot be

overstated. The distinction between dim and clear perception (a few lines below) is a theme developed by the author, *Semantic Issues,* ch. II, as one supported by common sense.

16. If direct response is inhibited or misrepresented by such an attitude, for the ordinary man is drilled to believe that he, to be cultured, must imitate intellectual's attitudes, he is effectively denied easy access to what naturally enhances life. Hence the descent into vulgarity that characterizes modern life. Santayana, *The Sense of Beauty* (New York, 1896), 200, had a better understanding of the value accorded by artistic response, when he wrote: "This critical incapacity has always been a cause of failure and a just ground for ridicule; but it has remained for some thinkers of our time – a time of little art and much undisciplined production – to erect this abuse into a principle and to declare that the essence of beauty is to express the artist and not to delight the world". This comment is still meaningful a century later.
17. This expression was first used in the author's *Ethical Issues* (London, 1990), 228ff, to refer to a form of reaction which takes place on all levels of response, subconscious, quasi-conscious and fully conscious, from instinctive avoidance, such as flinching, to the repudiation of truth claims. Its relation to negation is obvious.
18. War generates acute disturbance, but societies can recover from its effects relatively rapidly. Disturbance produced by flouting the norms, as with undue stress on individual autonomy, has repercussive effects which work more slowly, gradually to undermine social cohesion and to produce social and cultural decay, as has been the case with certain ancient cultures. Rome, for instance, though it finally fell to barbarian invasions, did so primarily because of a failure to sustain morale. Lecky, *The History of European Morals* (London, 1869), discusses some of the reasons for this, which are not without some bearing today.
19. Horkheimer, *Eclipse of Reason* (New York, 1947), 133, speaks astutely on this matter, primarily with respect to the responsibility of philosophy.
20. Husserl, *Ideas* (1913, tr. London, 1931), 107ff, was by no means the first to use this expression, since it had already

been employed by Lambert, Kant, Hegel, Hamilton and Lazarius, roughly to distinguish philosophical from psychological studies of mental action.

21. Merleau-Ponty, op. cit. (1945, 1962), Part II, ch. 1 to 3 particularly, in which he refers to response to reality, 'our reality', the phenomenal world that is. This is the response I have called 'dim perception', treating it by comparison superficially. This may be M-P's 'marginal perception', though that is but an aspect of what he considers in this penetrating work. However, that perception, dim or clear, is influenced from below, by pregestalten, preconscious response to stimuli immediately received, is surely operative as a factor on the phenomenal conditions that he discusses.
22. It is a Western contention, largely of Christian origin, that the difference between humans and animals is absolute, though that is now undergoing some modification today when, in some quarters, the tendency is to see it in terms of intellectual power rather than of those of the immortal soul. As an alternative the Chinese doctrine of *hsing* is of interest. *Hsing* means 'nature' in both its sense: nature as all that there is and nature as referring to the characteristics of the various species it comprises. Thus *jên-hsing* (human nature), is distinguished *ma-hsing* (horsiness). Given this, one of the features that differentiates man is his power to reason, which is itself dualistic, as the seat both of his glory and his viciousness. Hsün Ch'ing, *Hsün Tzu, Basic Writings* (tr. New York, 1963), ch. 23, expresses this astutely: "Left to himself man works for evil, not because he desires evil, but because his passions (strengthened by his intellect) are greater than his powers of controlling them". There is an echo of this in the Christian doctrine that sin is in the mind, in subjective involvement, surely a more subtle dualism than that of Descartes.
23. When Read divides the arts into the static and dynamic he makes a typical rationalistic dichotomy. For, properly, all the arts are rhythmic and evoke empathic response (Lipps). Some arts, architecture and music, for instance, carry this rhythmic evocation over extended space or time. Response is initially always nervous or spontaneous and cannot, as rhythmic, well have any other form, unless at a later stage we

still and study a presentation.

24. Reflecting does not mean imitating, since the arts have their own vitality related to human responsive nervous needs. Literally, *ch'i-yün-shêng-tung,* the first principle of Chinese painting, means 'spirit-harmony-life-movement', variously translated (by Waley, Soper and Sullivan) but never wholly satisfactorily. Its meaning, however, is readily sensed in confirmation of what is said above.
25. It almost amounts to a heresy to place 'the spiritual' on such a lowly plane. But that is what the mystics have down throughout the ages – admittedly with the implicit suggestion that they refer to the supernal – as it is that which ordinary people accept, as apart from that association, without question. For sympathy, affection, feeling for others and so on are spontaneous or nervous forms of response, such that to intellectualize them renders them artificial, even false.
26. Although 'norm' is a term derived from *norma,* a carpenter's tool, and later acquired the meaning of 'rule' or 'precept', it would be a mistake to align it with *nomos.* For though that also meant 'custom' (having the force of law), its primary meaning was (written) 'law', itself a word of Saxon origin, meaning 'that which is laid down' 'Normative' is fairly taken to mean 'what ought to be done' without implying that the law imposes it. In other words 'norms' refer (as Stankiewicz held) to something more subtle and deeper which, if not innate, are engrained in the socializing process. A rationalistic bias blinds us to this deeper meaning.
27. It is difficult to illustrate this precisely, but all artists proceed by means of trial-and-error, that is, by standing back from and criticizing their initial thrusts, as do philosophical writers revising their texts. Any original manuscript will be marked by corrections, of which a text of Mill (BM Add. MSS. 41624 - 41627) affords a sufficient example.
28. It is of interest that the Pūrva Mīmāmsā System, represented by Prabhākara and Kumārila (VII AD), projected the doctrine of *apūrva* as an "unseen force referring to the future effects of actions" a doctrine which has ethical no less than religious, salvational bearing.
29. Wittgenstein, *Philosophical Investigations* (New York, 1953), 124, paraphrased. By contrast Marx, however disastrously his

followers behaved, endeavoured to contribute to life in place of shrinking into an intellectual shell and confining himself to mere verbal problems.

30. Berlin, *Against the Current* (Oxford, 1979), 351 paraphrased.
31. It is difficult to attribute this doctrine to any one thinker, since it runs through Chinese thinking. Han Fei and Tung Chung-shu might perhaps be cited, the first as demanding that law *(fa)* be applied firmly, to specific and clearly defined offences, and the second because of his insistence that *li* (broadly, ethical principles) should take priority as the criterion, such that law should be applied only when there was failure to comply with them. From this sprang the doctrine of *fa-li,* applied in effect at Tiananmen Square, after *fa-li* had five times been evoked. But the idea has deeper roots both in Taoist and Confucian thinking. There is wisdom in it, since too much bureaucratic interference in private lives (not to mention misplaced sentimentality) brings the law into contempt and blurs the distinction between what is certainly anti-social and what are rather human foibles, which in China were disciplined by family and neighbourly disapproval. 'That is not done" is a Western form of the last, which is unhappily losing its force as self-interest becomes dominant over a social sense. Dworkin, *The Theory and Practice of Autonomy* (Cambridge, 1988), 6, glorifies precisely the opposite view, with total failure to grasp the manner in which it is corroding Western society and oblivious to the destructive powers of passion.

Conclusion

1. This is of the utmost importance and is indeed the justification for the thesis here projected. For all enquiry whatsoever must take its start from presuppositions, that is from assumptions which, in respect of reality at least, cannot be proven but only assumed. If, then, the world is indeed a holistic complex, any idea that it is made up of particulars cannot be sustained, since those are brought to being by the intellect and have no true external existence. No doubt, their generation is essential for acquiring scientific knowledge. But

that is not the end of philosophy, which is rather a deeper 'understanding' (*sapientia* as opposed to *scientia).* There is no escape from this finding unless it is simply disregarded. Hence the problem is to come to terms with it, whatever the consequences for formal logic. If he and other sceptics were speaking in ethical or even ontic terms, Gorgias is certainly vindicated.

2. Serota, who as Curator of the Tate Gallery shows himself to be both insensitive and irresponsible, a characteristic product of an intellectual training. He may know a great deal about painting and sculpture but he lacks any real 'feel' or 'understanding'. For him 'expression' means the expression of ideas, not expression in an artistic sense, as Croce understood that term.
3. Rationalists are given to supposing that artistic principles are definable, but no real artist would agree with them, since that as an idea is crude and insensitive. The Golden Section has been projected as one (Le Corbusier, for instance); but what fits in composition is sensuously developed, as is any judgment made upon it. Crude clashing of colours, inept proportion or scale are readily seen as out of order, but those solecisms are initially felt by the nerves, not by the intellect, which later records them essentially because they have a jarring effect on the nerves. Such principles are indeed implicit but they cannot be expressly asserted. Focillon, *Vie des Formes* (Paris, 1955), 19, says that they have *une logique interne;* he also uses the term *la touche* as characterizing creative action.
4. Capra, *The Tao of Physics* (London, 1951), 317f, paraphrased.
5. Von Mises, *Positivism* (New York, 1951), 301f, is positively elephantine, a bull in a china shop, when he essays to enter this area.
6. Disturbance is primarily a physical event or response, falseness or falsification are intellectual readings or acts. The first could, of course, be considered as a form of physical disturbance, to blur this distinction. But to use a well-known expression, these terms refer to "two different realms of discourse".
7. Gallie, *Peirce and Pragmatism* (London, 1952), 59.
8. The meanings of most terms are to be gathered from their

etymons, which tell us what they initially signified as meeting some human need. In the case of 'understanding', a peculiarly English word, that scarcely affords a clue. That is only given by the fact that the word was evidently developed to mean something other than firm 'knowledge' – "grasping instantly" is one dictionary definition. In as far as it allows of rational definition, the matter is discussed, essentially in negative terms, in the author's *Semantic Issues* (1995), ch. VI (Understanding and Knowledge).

Index rerum

This index Rerum refers essentially to matters in the text and not to the Notes, which elaborate on given passages, to which their numbers are given in the text itself, which would merely mean that entries were repeated.

Index Nominum

Works of the Author

Letter to a Patron (1961)

Letters from Afar (1975)

Unacceptable Essays (1984)

Modern Censorship (1994)

The Issues Series

Ethical Issues (1991)

Semantic Issues (1995)

Logical Issues (1996)

Artistic Issues (in preparation)

In addition, there are a number of works, which have never been published, of which the following might be noted, in some cases as showing the development of the thought that culminated in the Res Architectonicae, The Philosophy of the Person (translation of Romero's little-known but important work *La Filosofía de Ia Persona*), Comparative Thinking, (Chinese, Indian and Western – studied in terms of the presuppositions each adopted), together with a number of essays, which again, with certain exceptions, were not published.